The Burro

THE BURRO

by Frank Brookshier

UNIVERSITY OF OKLAHOMA PRESS
NORMAN

Library of Congress Cataloging in Publication Data

Brookshier, Frank, 1903–
    The burro.
    Includes bibliographical references.
    1. Donkeys—History. I. Title.
SF361.B76   636.1'8   72–860

Preface

The purpose of this book is to tell the story of the burro. It is about the ass of the Bible, the donkey of the English, and the burro of the Mexican.

My interest in the burro began many years ago—more years than I care to record! It started during my first year at the two-room elementary school in Kenna, New Mexico, about three miles north of our little ranch home. My father had purchased two burros, a dark brown one and a gray one, for the pleasure of my sister, my two brothers, and me. Perhaps the greatest, and no doubt the most lasting, educational achievement of my first school year was the knowledge I gained from Ted, the brown burro, while my sister and I tried to ride him to school. While gentle and kind, Ted seemed to have doubts about the importance of the educational process, for too often he would make us late for school. This introduction to the burro, while at times exasperating, gave me a hint of the animal's insistence upon his right to determine the proper rate of speed for his travels.

My experiences with Ted and with other burros that have crossed my path both here and abroad have, I believe, qualified me to tell something about them. I have long since come to respect their loyalty, sturdiness, and patience and to enjoy and even admire their idiosyncrasies. To support my own observations, I have spent many years in research on the history of the little animal. I have tried to indicate his historical importance in helping men on the road to what we call civilization.

My main purpose has been to upgrade the burro in the minds of men. More often than not he has been the underdog among domesticated animals. I have tried to demonstrate that he is not stupid or stubborn, or even odd-looking, as many unknowing persons have claimed. It is my hope that the reader will come to understand that the burro possesses many sterling qualities, among them an intelligence too often overlooked.

I encountered many difficulties in uncovering the history of the burro. Records are scanty, and, though he has been around for a long time, he has often been taken for granted or ignored. Therefore, figuratively speaking, a spade (a prospector's implement, by the way) was essential in digging for the fragments. Those bits and pieces of information were uncovered in various sources at many different times and in many places.

I extend thanks to the personnel of a number of public and institutional libraries for their efforts in behalf of my research, as well as to persons who were kind enough to allow me access to their private collections. Acquaintances have graciously assisted me, and individuals whom I have never met personally but only through correspondence have contributed greatly to this book. A goodly portion of my information has come to me through personal letters, whose writers are acknowledged in the text.

Illustrations have been provided by individuals, museums, art galleries, personnel of the United States Foreign Service, and information services of many foreign governments. Former colleagues of mine who were engaged with me in work abroad have also provided illustrative material.

Special appreciation goes to the editors of the University of Oklahoma Press, who were patient with me in my efforts and provided constructive criticism.

My warmest thanks and gratitude go to my wife, Florence, who courageously and patiently read my longhand script of the first draft, offered suggestions, and then typed the final manuscript.

FRANK BROOKSHIER

Maxwell, New Mexico
July 15, 1972

Contents

Illustrations

The Burro

1. The Burro

According to my dictionary, the subject of this book has three common names: ass, donkey, and burro. As one may guess from the title of this book, I favor burro. It has been the dominant term in the Western Hemisphere since the arrival of the conquistadors. The influence of Spanish culture persists in a very large portion of the New World. The burro is a part of this heritage, and his Spanish name is a part of the vocabulary of the people who inhabit the region.

In the United States the mechanization of industry, transportation, mining, and agriculture has almost completely replaced domesticated work animals. As a result they have greatly dwindled in numbers. A similar condition prevails in a few other industrialized countries. Yet in spite of the machine the burro persists and is increasing in world population. In 1971 the Food and Agriculture Organization estimated, on the basis of a five-year average established, using the years 1947–48 and 1951–52, a world total of 36.4 million burros, whereas the census of 1969–70 revealed a figure of 42.7 million burros, an increase of 6.3 million in about nineteen years. In the same years the population of mules also increased, but the horse population dropped.[1] The burro, tough, resilient, and economical to purchase and to keep, hangs on and even increases his kind—especially in Asia, Africa, and Latin America.

My dictionary also states that the burro, *Equus asinus*, "is patient, slow, and sure-footed, and has become the type of obstinacy and stupidity." The dictionary continues with analogies: "A dull, stupid person; a dolt, especially one who is stubborn or stolid." These writers of dictionaries terminate their definition by quoting Shakespeare, a playwright well known for his allusions to the animal:

O that he were here to write me down an ass![2]

At this point I am tempted to write in the margin of *my* dictionary, as did the Nobel Prize winner Juan Ramón Jiménez, author of the literary classic *Platero and I* (1916), a series of essays addressed to his donkey, Platero. Upon reading the definition of *assography*, Jiménez wrote:

> I read in a dictionary: *Assography: n.: used, ironically, of the description of an ass.*
> Poor donkey! So good, so noble and knowing as you are! Ironically. . . . Why? Don't you even deserve a serious description, you whose real description would be as a story of springtime? Why, a man who is kind should be called an ass. And a bad donkey should be called a man. Ironically. . . . Of you, so intellectual, friend of old men and children, of brook and butterfly, of the sun, of the dog, of the flower and the moon; patient, thoughtful, melancholy, and loving, Marcus Aurelius of the meadows.
> Platero, who no doubt understands, looks at me out of his great shining eyes of a soft hardness in which the sun is gleaming small and sparkling in a brief convex sky of blackish green. Oh, if his huge, hairy, idyllic head could know that I do him justice, that I know better than those men who write dictionaries, that I am almost as good as he!
> And I have written in the margin of the book: *Assography: n.: should be used, ironically, of course, of the description of the imbecile who writes dictionaries.*[3]

Both Jiménez and Miguel de Cervantes, two of Spain's literary giants, made important places in their masterpieces for burros. One carried Sancho Panza, the servant and practical-minded companion of Don Quixote, the elderly and overimaginative knight (who rode a horse). And, of course, Platero, the lovable donkey of Jiménez, was the star listener to the author's charming monologues.

To return to my dictionary, the first part of the definition, "patient, slow, and sure-footed," is correct, but the remainder is an injustice. It indicates a common practice of writers and others to turn to the burro when in need of something to deride. His long ears and his bray have made him easy prey of those who would ridicule.

Man has chosen many ways to try to relieve himself of his burdens, both physical and spiritual. One means was to select an

Jiménez and Platero. From Juan Ramón Jiménez, *Platero and I* (tr. by Eloïse Roach, drawing by Jo Alys Downs, Austin, University of Texas Press, 1957, *i*). Reproduced by permission.

animal to carry the burdens. The ancient Egyptians considered the burro unclean and impure. They despised him because of his supposed association with Set (Typhon), an evil god who had escaped from battle riding a rust-colored burro. To the Copts, the early Egyptian Christians, the burro was symbolic of all that was bad. They selected him to bear their troubles. Sometimes the people of a whole village would figuratively load all their ailments—epidemics, bad luck, wrongdoing, drought—on the back of the burro. They would then lead him from the village and destroy him, usually by pushing him over a steep precipice. By his death the burro rid the village of its troubles.[4]

The goat was also a participant in this symbolic ritual (probably antedating the burro, for the goat was almost surely one of the first animals to be domesticated). He was loaded with mankind's woes, including insults, led to a precipice, and pushed to his death. These were the "scape-animals." The practice among the Copts had its origins in ancient Jewish rituals. On Yom Kipper, the Day of Atonement, the high priest loaded a goat with the sins of the people, led him to the barren desert, and turned him loose, an easy prey for wolves and other natural enemies. As the burden of sins became heavier, a larger animal had to be selected—hence the use of the burro.

One reason for the scorn and derision that has been heaped upon the burro lies in his refusal to pace his speed to that of man. Perhaps in exasperation, S. Omar Barker penned these lines in a 1945 issue of *Country Gentleman*:

> The burro is a languid gent
> Who simply does not choose to went
> To whip him is a waste of muscle—
> Nobody ever made one hustle!

The burro's distaste for speed is legendary among those persons who are acquainted with his nature. He is a consistent foe of hurry. He has his own reason for holding back and insists on his rights in this basic matter. Just because he refuses to comply to an order or does so in leisurely fashion is no indication that he is short on intelligence or fails to understand what is wanted of him. He does know. But he is not ready.

Now what is this animal called a burro? What size is he? What are his colors? What are his characteristics? What makes him tick, even though slowly?

Many people, especially Americans, have no personal acquaintance with him. But to the people of the Orient, the Middle East, North and East Africa, the Mediterranean countries, South America, and Mexico he is invaluable. To the peasant family a burro's death is a serious loss, often signifying bankruptcy.

For those readers who are unfamiliar with the burro but acquainted with another member of the equine family, the horse, some nontechnical comparisons between the two animals may be helpful. I own what I believe to be a horse typical of those ridden for pleasure on western ranches or used for work with cattle where the truck has not replaced them. I also own a burro, also representative of the common, average-sized animal. Both Pal, the horse, and Catrino, the burro, are geldings. Pal is ten years old, and Catrino is almost seven. Pal weighs 1,245 pounds; the burro, 600. Their weights are fairly typical of the two species in the southwestern United States. Pal is a rather uncommon white blending into cream. Catrino is gray, a common color among burros, with off-white belly and upper legs. This underside color is virtually universal among all breeds of burros. The wild onager and the kiang, the two prominent breeds of Asia, and the gray donkey of northeastern Africa, from which the domesticated burro was very likely derived (see Chapter 2), have the same white or oyster coloring in common, regardless of variations in upper-body color, size, bray, length of ears, and other traits.

In common with most other burros Catrino's muzzle and the area encircling his eyes are also of this near-white color. He has a transverse stripe across his withers that extends down each shoulder

Pal and Catrino. Photographed by Steve Pompeo.

about twelve inches. The stripe is two inches wide at the top and tapers to a fraction of an inch at the lower end. The hairs of the stripe are brown in winter and much darker in summer. This stripe is also characteristic of a very large number of domesticated burros and, together with the bray, serves to identify them as descendants of the wild species that inhabited Nubia and adjacent regions. The markings and especially the stripes that occur quite frequently on the rear legs indicate an ancestral kinship with the zebra, also a native of Africa.

Catrino is forty-five inches tall, measured from top of the withers to the ground, whereas Pal is sixty inches, or, to use the horseman's terminology, fifteen hands high (a hand equals four inches). Ca-

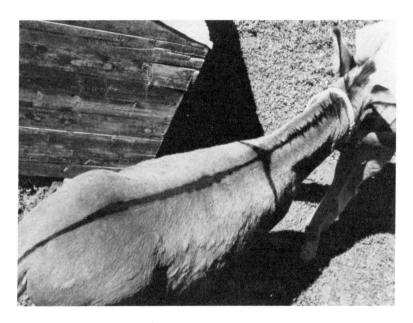

The characteristic transverse stripe over the burro's withers. Photograph by author.

trino's total body length, from the poll, or top of the head, to the rump, is sixty-one inches; Pal is seventy-one inches long. The head of a burro looks out of proportion to the rest of his body; Catrino's head is twenty-two inches long, only one inch shorter than Pal's.

Pal's flowing tail measures forty-eight inches, while Catrino's measures only twenty-two inches; however, the bony part of Catrino's tail is fifteen inches long, only one inch shorter than Pal's. There is a noticeable difference in the hair coverings of the two animals' tails. The hairs on the burro's tail is merely an extension of both the body covering and the dorsal stripe that extends from in front of the transverse stripe and along the backbone to the end of the tailbone. The texture and color of the dorsal stripe are the same as those of the cross over the shoulder. This dorsal band, while common, does not appear on all burros. Pal's tail hairs are of a different texture and color from his body hair.

Since Catrino's tail is shorter than Pal's, he cannot flit flies from his anatomy as effectively as Pal can. However, flies and other insects do not seem to molest Catrino as much, for his hide is tougher than Pal's and therefore more insect-repellant. Of course Catrino and others of his kind rejoice in rolling in sand, dry soil, or even ashes, and this indulgence helps discourage vermin.

Catrino's mane is shorter than Pal's, and he does not have a forelock as Pal does. But Catrino's ears, probably his most distinguishing characteristic, leave Pal's way behind: they are ten inches long, whereas Pal's are five and a half inches long. The ears of the burro, though the object of jokes and funmaking because of their size, nevertheless serve him well. His hearing is better than that of many other animals. In the rough and hilly terrain of his native habitats of Africa and Asia the big ears can better detect the approach of natural enemies. On the level and broad expanse of gravelly plains in the Orient and Africa animals such as the wild ass and the gazelle depended upon their speed to elude their natural enemies.

The burro also possesses keen eyesight. Rarely, if ever, is a burro bitten by a rattlesnake, for he is quick to discern the presence of this enemy, even before the snake gives its warning rattle. The burro reacts quickly to danger, and in this instance at least moves on the double.

The burro's good eyesight, hearing, and speed made him difficult for man to hunt with success until the advent of fast-moving vehicles and improved death-dealing guns. Today man's mechanical ingenuity and desire for the trophy have driven the wild ancestor of the burro into virtual extinction, along with the graceful gazelle and the oryx.

There are other differences in the two animals. Pal has four chestnuts, or collosities, one on the inside of each leg, whereas Catrino has only two, one on the inside of each front leg. Catrino's chestnuts are larger than Pal's, however. The original function of the chestnuts is not known for certain. Cecil G. Trew offered the theory that they may be vestiges of scent glands, similar to those on members of the deer family. He observed that when a chestnut is cut it gives off an odor that attracts horses in the near vicinity.[5]

Perhaps the fact that the burro has only two chestnuts indicates that he is farther along the evolutionary trail than the horse. However, the male burro has vestigial teats on its sheath, whereas the horse does not.

Catrino can perform a little trick that Pal cannot: he can scratch his ear with his hind hoof. Young horses can also do this but lose the ability as they grow into maturity. The feet of the burro, like those of the horse and the zebra, are distinctive. No other animals walk on four toes, one on the end of each leg. The other toes, several in number, were lost somewhere along the misty trail of the equine's evolution. The hoof of the burro is small but hard. Catrino's hoof, two and a half inches wide, is only half as wide as Pal's, and its circumference is ten and one half inches, compared with eighteen inches for the horse's hoof. The two animals have the same number of teeth, forty each. But the burro's teeth will last longer, and so he will outlive Pal.

The weight and size of the burro vary, depending upon his food, the care he receives, and the kind of work he does. Burros owned by persons living on or below the poverty line are usually small and underfed. They are commonly put to work long before they reach maturity, which retards their growth.

Some burros, by virtue of selective breeding, are small in stature. Sicilian and Sardinian burros are representative of the miniature animal native to the Mediterranean region. They average less than thirty-six inches in height, and many weigh less than a man. These little animals have become popular in the United States, chiefly for riding or pulling carts for children, and they are especially appropriate for the handicapped. They make excellent pets; some owners even allow them the privilege of coming into the house.

The large jacks and jennets that are used in mule breeding—raising jacks to cross on mares—are at the other extreme of the breed, though they are derived from the same ancestral stock as the burro. They are large animals. Selective breeding over hundreds of years in Italy, Malta, France, and Spain developed the large breeds that attained perfection in Tennessee, Kentucky, and Missouri, outstanding mule-breeding states. Crossing the jack with the mare produces the hybrid mule, an excellent pack and work animal. Breeding the other way around—crossing the stallion with the female of the donkey family—yields the hinny. The hinny has never been as numerous as the mule. Both the mule and the hinny are usually sterile. Prominent bloodlines of these mule-breeding jacks and jennets include the Maltese, the Poitou, the Majorca, the Andalusian, and the Catalonian, named for the European locales in which they were developed.

The big mule-breeding sires entered the United States along the Atlantic Seaboard, whereas the smaller member of the breed, the burro, entered from Mexico. It may well be that George Washington was the first person to give impetus to improved mule breeding in the United States. In 1785, King Charles III of Spain made an exception to a strict law prohibiting the exportation of registered breeding jacks and sent Washington two of the fine animals. One died on the journey; the other, whom Washington named Royal Gift, arrived at Mount Vernon in December, 1785. The Marquis de Lafayette sent Washington a jack and two jennies from Malta. They arrived in November, 1786, and Washington named the male Knight of Malta.[6]

The colors of burros are varied: gray, black, brown, white, and "polka dot"—pinto, or piebald—a relatively recent addition. There are shades and hues of the two basic colors, gray and brown, and of the other colors. White burros have long had a special significance. From ancient times white was a symbol of all that was good— cleanliness, purity, sacredness, and godliness. The white burro was held in high esteem and was considered appropriate for the sacrificial altar. The nobility and the clergy chose white burros to ride and to pull their carriages. The Egyptians preferred white burros to all others for use in their pageants. Today in certain areas of the Middle East the white burro is predominant, and some villages or towns appear to own no other color. In Hofuf, a town in eastern Saudi Arabia, all the burros are white. The burros of Hofuf are also generally larger than those found in other centers of Saudi Arabia.

The burro has a normal body temperature of ninety-nine degrees. Man is closer to the burro temperature-wise than to any of the other domesticated animals. The burro jack, like the stallion, is historically a symbol of sexual vigor. Referring to the breeding qualities of the jack, J. W. Thomas wrote: "The exceptional physical development of the male . . . and the unusual potency of the species in the mythology of the reproduction of life, are known to have been held as of special significance by ancient oriental people."[7]

The jenny (or jennet) begins her reproduction cycle at about three years of age and continues to produce young for as long as thirty years. The gestation period of the jenny—rather long, in keeping with the pace of burro life—is about 374 days, compared with that of a mare, which is about 340 days. Seldom does a jenny produce twins; in fact, no such births appear to have been recorded. Seven days after foaling, the jenny is ready to entertain the male.

The age of any given burro is not easily determined. The condition of the teeth is the best indicator. After the burro is twelve to fifteen years old, the determination of age becomes even more difficult. Only in the registry of elite animals is there a written record of age. Among the commoner burros legend seems to have it that "he never dies" and that "no one has ever seen a dead burro." The Hawaiians have an expression about the burro's longevity: "Ola mau loa!" ("He lives forever!"). Fairly authentic records indicate that some burros have lived to the age of forty or fifty years. In general it can be said that the burro lives much longer than the horse and that the jenny lives longer than the jack, probably because she receives better care.

Burros have distinctive "personality," as well as physical, traits. A burro in a pasture with other grazing animals—cattle, horses, or sheep—will almost invariably be the first to detect the approach of a stranger or invader. Therefore, burros make good sentinels or guards. The burro is also courageous; he is not afraid when a dog or wolf enters the pasture but, on the contrary, often chases the invader away. This is especially true of a mother burro with a foal to protect. She is fearless in her duty.

Female burros make good mothers, are very proud of their babies, and will fight a mountain lion to protect them. The gelding, with his calm disposition, is a stabilizing factor and is sometimes placed in a corral or paddock with high-strung race or show horses to quiet them. A small male burro is sometimes placed in a paddock with fillies and show mares to detect the oestrum. The females are then mated with stallions (the burro jack, because of his short-leggedness, cannot reap the rewards of his discovery).

In burro societies individual personalities vary, just as they do among people (this statement also holds true for other breeds of animals, including sheep). Each burro has his own attitudes about and responses to matters that concern him. A burro also has his own idiosyncracies. These sometimes present a formidable problem to the person trying to deal with the animal. It often takes both patience and time to persuade a burro to modify his behavior.

While burros are universally known to be peaceable and friendly, in at least one instance they demonstrated that they are capable of retaliating when punished severely and without cause. One day in July, 1882, one Juan Madilla, who lived several miles south of Albuquerque, New Mexico, returned to his home after a few days of wood gathering with his burros loaded with firewood. Later Juan went out to his woodshed, picked up a club, and proceeded to beat the burros for no reason. The usually docile and obedient animals turned on him, biting his shoulders, arms, and legs and inflicting severe wounds. Blood flowed; he yelled for help. His wife and son came to his aid, pulled the burros away from him, picked him up, and carried him into the house. The news item hinted that, should he survive, in the future perhaps Madilla would be more considerate of his burros.[8] The burros of the world must have a stock of good qualities; otherwise their clan would have been eliminated long ago, for they have often been treated harshly.

The burro is curious and, despite the dictionary definition, intelligent. The common expression "horse sense" implies that his cousin the horse has a high degree of intelligence. But Robin Borwick, operator of a donkey-breeding farm at Maidenhead, England, has written: "It is my opinion, and I am quite prepared to argue the hind leg off any horse about this, that a donkey's intelligence is greatly superior to that of the horse."[9] I will take the other hind leg and continue the argument.

Unlike the horse, the burro never cuts himself on barbed wire by running into it as a horse will do. Even when he is frightened, he does not lose his head to the extent that he dashes into such a "barbarous" obstacle. If by some quirk of events beyond his control one of his legs becomes entangled in wire, he will not fight or attempt to extricate himself. He will use his innate intelligence and characteristic patience and wait for his master to come to his rescue. Smart burro.

Burros thrive on attention and affection, and, as mentioned previously, they make good pets. Obviously, however, the larger ones present some problems, especially when they are permitted in the house. Borwick is enthusiastic about donkeys as pets and the fun of allowing them in his home, but warns: "Do not allow your donkey on sofas and chairs. The springs will suffer."[10]

The burro dislikes being led. Photo by Ian Bentley. Courtesy of Public Relations Service, Philmont Scout Ranch, Cimarron, New Mexico.

One of the idiosyncrasies of the burro is his distaste for being led. It does not come naturally to him. However, unlike the horse, he does not have to be broken to ride or to carry a pack. These chores do come naturally to him. Another little idiosyncrasy of the burro is his objection to backing. Normally he does not like to throw himself into reverse gear (perhaps, it has been suggested, because the effort he had to make to get started makes him reluctant to lose ground). More likely he is opposed to backing because he cannot see where he is going—another indication of his intelligence. Nor is the burro enthusiastic about crossing a stream. He wants to know how deep the stream is and whether or not enemies are lurking in its waters. Perhaps he instinctively reacts with the caution bred into the genes of his ancestors in remote times, when crocodiles and other cold-blooded reptiles relished burro flesh (the few remaining feral burros still occasionally fall victim to these age-old enemies).

A modern tall tale illustrates the burro's preference for warmth and his aversion to water. A traveler was surprised to note a swim-suited burro reclining on a sand dune in the Sahara Desert. Upon being asked why the beachwear, the burro replied that he might go swimming.

"Swimming!" echoed the traveler. "You're three hundred miles from the sea!"

"I know," said the burro. "Beautiful beach, isn't it?"

As mentioned earlier, the burro is quick to perceive danger. On the trail he refuses to continue if he senses that trouble lies ahead. His surefootedness on mountain trails is legendary, but he knows his limitations and protects himself—and his rider.

Seldom, if ever, will a burro voluntarily walk on ice. If forced to do so, he proceeds with the utmost caution. He will not lift his hoof to take a step unless it is perfectly safe to do so. The rider may feel secure in riding him across a sheet of ice, provided the burro is permitted to proceed in his own manner.

The burro is native to warm climates. Taken to cold regions, he is forced to make the best of the problems of an alien environment, including snow and ice. His small feet sink readily in deep snow, and snowdrifts present agonizing frustrations for him. Catrino depends upon Pal to open the way through drifts and across snow-filled ditches. When drinking water is covered with ice too thick for the burro to break by thrusting his muzzle against it or striking his hoofs on the edges of the ice, then man must help him. Horses can paw the ice to break it or use their front feet to crush the thinner ice at the edge. I have watched Catrino stand safely on the bank until Pal has broken the ice. Then, after Pal has drunk—often muddy water resulting from its disturbance close to the soil—Catrino will carefully approach and drink, provided the water has cleared and is fit for a burro.

The Prospector. Etching by Edward Borein. From *The Etchings of Edward Borein.* Courtesy of John Howell—Books, San Francisco.

The burro has a sense of humor. Prospectors, mountain men, wood haulers, and others knew of his bent for pranks and his ability to hide. Lonely prospectors, with only their burros as companions and listeners to their monologues, were sure that their animals came to understand what they said. A recorded conversation between two prospectors serves to illustrate. One day, in a small, temporary camp, one prospector asked another if he was going to the new strike in the Skull Mountains, in what is now southern Nevada. The burros that belonged to the man addressed were standing nearby.

"No," he answered, "I don't reckon I'll go."

Later, however, after his burros had strayed a little distance away, he drew the prospector aside, saying: "Sure, I'll jine ye. I was figuring on getting an early start in the morning, and didn't want them damn burros to know."[11] The prospector believed that the burros would hide if they learned of his intentions for an early start.

The burro is often criticized for his stubbornness, his recalcitrance in regard to the wishes of his rider or driver. But is "stubbornness" the right word? Perhaps "independence" is more appropriate. His unwillingness to take part in some projects is, to my mind, thoroughly justified. Such projects may be entertaining—entertaining for human beings, not for burros. In some areas of the country touring basketball teams ride burros in the games. The official (usually the manager of the team) carries a battery-charged prod, which he uses to induce the burros to move about the court. Understandably, the burros are less interested in the score than in the location of the official with the prod.

There are other "sports" in which the burro is sometimes required to take part—baseball, golf, polo, tennis, and pack races. Pack races come closest to fitting the burro's taste, ability, tradition, and sense of purpose, and in a later chapter we shall attend two of these annual races, one from Leadville to Fairplay, Colorado, and one at Beatty, Nevada.

Were he able to communicate in human tongue, the burro would doubtless be the first to admit that he has no desire to compete in races or to have his rate of speed recorded. The following estimates have been given of the speed of various animals, in miles per hour:

In the air:
  duck hawk, 175
  golden eagle, 120
  canvasback duck, 70
  hummingbird, 60
  house fly, 5

In the water:
  sailfish, 30
  barracuda, 30
  whale, 20
  trout, 5
  man, 5

On land:
  cheetah, 65
  ostrich, 50 +
  gazelle, 50
  jackrabbit, 45
  race horse, 45
  greyhound, 40

  house cat, 30
  elephant, 25
  man, 20
  snake, 2
  turtle, $1/10^{12}$

The burro? He wasn't ready.

Because burros have always had to scrounge for a living, they have often been accused of stealing. Perhaps a better term is one used in the Virgin Islands, "progging." When a Virgin Island boy steals bananas or other fruit and eats them, he is progging, and the charge against him is of no great consequence. However, if he sells the fruit, then the act is considered stealing. The burro takes something for only one purpose—to eat it. He is a progger, not a thief.

A woman from New York once had a frustrating experience with a nondiscriminating Virgin Islands burro. She purchased some land in a beautiful location on St. John Island but was defeated in her efforts to build houses on the tract when a hungry burro walked up to the construction site, picked up the blueprints, and ate them.[13]

In his personal habits the burro is clean and tidy. He eats and drinks daintily, making little if any noise. When he drinks, his lips barely touch the surface of the water (incidentally, he can go longer without water than any other burden-bearing animal except the camel). He never thrusts his muzzle deep into the drinking trough as a horse will do at times. Nor does he wade into shallow water in a pond or lake and lie down, as a horse may. He looks upon water as a necessity for life, for drinking purposes only—nothing more. A horse will occasionally make himself sick by consuming an excessive quantity of water at one drinking. Regardless of the arduous task he has performed or the length of time that he has gone without water, the burro does not overindulge. In his eating habits, he is almost never guilty of foundering—perhaps because he seldom experiences a surplus of food. He has been characterized as willing to eat anything, and perhaps that is so; out of necessity he has been forced to eat indiscriminately to survive. He has even been accused of eating tin cans. Obviously this is not true, but he has been observed trying to eat labels off dis-

Burro parade, Flagstaff, Arizona, 1967. From *Arizona Sun*, Flagstaff, Arizona.

Yemen burros, 1971. Courtesy of U.S. Foreign Service.

carded cans—perhaps those with tantalizing pictures of corn, carrots, and the like. For some burros that may be as close as they get to such delicacies. Grain, alfalfa, a good-quality grazing pasture are his delights, though weeds, thistles, and straw have more often been his lot. Hungry though he may often be, seldom does this cautious animal eat poisonous plants, such as the white-flowering locoweed of the western ranch country.

It is believed by some researchers that animals, like human beings, dream. Dogs often interrupt the calm of sleeping with subdued yips occasionally accompanied by muscular jerks. Pliny, the early Roman writer, claimed that burros dream and cautioned owners about this trait, suggesting that corrals or barns should have ample room for the burro to kick in his dreams.[14] All this may be true. Yet in my years with Catrino I have never found him asleep, much less dreaming. Of course, I readily admit that sometimes it is difficult to tell whether he is asleep or awake.

2. His Bray

Perhaps the burro's most distinctive characteristic is his bray. It has inspired man to ridicule and to proverb: "If a burro brays at you, don't bray at him," and, "Every ass loves to hear himself bray." Upon a clay tablet in cuneiform writing, a Sumerian who lived four thousand years ago left a message: "My burro was not destined to run quickly. He was destined to bray." Thus in ancient Ur at the head of the Persian Gulf the burro had become noted for his slow speed and his bray.

Hundreds of desert miles southwest of Ur, in the land of the Egyptian pharaohs, burros were apparently rebuked when they brayed. On an inner wall of a tomb an ancient Egyptian artist depicted a scene showing a peasant walking along the banks of the Nile River with a herd of burros. One of the burros is trying to express himself. His head is raised, his nostrils are distended, and his mouth is open, revealing his large teeth. The artist even provided symbols of the sound of the bray. The peasant has turned and in apparent disgust thrown his arms in front of the braying animal in a clear gesture of restraint. Many Egyptians so detested the burro's bray that they objected to use of the trumpet because it produced a sound similar to that of the burro.[1]

Comparisons between the burro's bray and the trumpet can be found in literature. In *The Tragedy of King Richard II*, Shakespeare, never one to give the burro a break, alluded to the "harsh-resounding trumpets' dreadful bray."[2]

But the Egyptian farmer wisely recognized the role of the bray in the burro's mating customs. During the tame jenny's oestrus the farmer would lead her to the edge of the desert and tether her there. In the darkness her braying attracted the wild jack of the desert, and mating occurred. The foal resulting from the union had, in addition to the tameness of his dam, the hardiness of the wild ass. This practice of blood renewal was not confined to the Egyptians; the Berbers on the west did the same thing.

The bray has had historical significance. Herodotus tells of a battle whose outcome was decided by the brays of burros and mules. During a battle between Persian cavalry and Scythians, whose homeland was the Russian steppes, the loud bray of the Persians' pack animals frightened the Scythians' horses. In the ensuing confusion the Persians won the battle.[3]

The burro has toiled long and hard in the Orient, and apparently his bray has not offended these farmers of forty centuries. In fact, a Chinese historian recorded that it was once common for persons to set their timepieces by a burro's dependable periodic bray. (I can bear witness to the regularity of some burros' vocalizing. In the village where I live, an acquaintance of mine had a male burro that brayed at seven o'clock every morning, including Sundays.)

At least one prominent personage in ancient China, one Wang Chuang Suan not only tolerated but even enjoyed the bray of the burro. When he died, Emperor Wen of the Wei Dynasty, a good friend of Wang's, attended his funeral. When the services ended, the emperor arose and reminded those in attendance of Wang's pleasure in hearing the voice of the burro. He suggested that, as a parting eulogy to Wang, all present imitate the bray. The people complied with the emperor's suggestion.[4]

Like the Chinese, early Greek and Roman writers thought the burro's bray a dependable timepiece and even calendar. A fifth-century Latin translation of a Greek work, *Physiologus*, explained the practical use of the bray of the wild ass. According to this work, when twenty-five days of March have passed, the ass brays twelve times during the night and twelve times during the day, signaling the arrival of the equinox, and persons can tell the time of day or night by counting the brays. But apparently the twelfth-century writers of *The Bestiary*, who based their work on *Physiologus*, did not concur, claiming that the ass brays only when he is hungry and quoting the Bible for support: "Doth the wild ass bray when he hath grass?" (Job 6:5).[5]

Probably because Jesus rode a burro into Jerusalem, many religious ceremonies involving the burro developed in various parts of the Near East and Europe. No doubt these ceremonies were at first of a quiet, sacred, and dignified nature. As the centuries rolled along, however, they degenerated into a kind of burlesque, perhaps designed to improve church attendance. One such ceremony, held in northern France during the Middle Ages, was the Feast of the Burro. During the feast a burro was led to a table, on which a lavish meal had been placed for him. An attendant of the priest opened the services by chanting a doggerel. Vespers followed, and then prose and verse of both sacred and profane content were recited. Finally the clergy and members of the congregation joined hands, dancing around the feasting and bemused animal, giving loud imitations of its bray. The ceremony lasted until midnight, at which time the priest concluded the affair by braying three times.[6]

Perhaps it is because of his bray that the burro was once associated with whooping cough. The spasms of the sufferer were said to be soothed by plucking hairs from the distinctive cross on top of the burro's shoulder, placing them in a bag, and hanging it around the whooper's neck. A child could supposedly be immunized from the disease by being passed three times over the back and under the belly of the burro in the name of the Trinity.

There is an old legend among the Moslems which accuses the burro of introducing the devil into Noah's ark. As a penalty for this deed, it is said, descendants of the two burros that Noah took aboard the ark are compelled to bray whenever they see the Father of Evil approaching, a warning which has supposedly saved souls.

The people of Thailand (Siam) also have their legends about the burro's bray. An early-day king of Siam credited his rescue from death to the timely braying of a burro. As he lay sleeping, a knife-wielding assassin crept near. Suddenly a donkey stabled nearby uttered a loud bray and put the would-be murderer to flight.[7]

There is a proverb that says, "The unexpected braying of a burro is a sign of a visit from an unpleasant acquaintance." Apparently, however, the people of India did not subscribe to this proverb. The little burro, so common a feature in rural India, has been an important factor in the economy of that country from time immemorial. Rudyard Kipling's father, John Lockwood Kipling, who lived in India for many years, recorded his observations of the animals and people of the country. He described how many a farmer, irritated by his burro's bray, slit the animal's nostrils to lessen the noise.[8] (It should be observed that the burro has not always been treated in such fashion in India. One of the principal castes of India, the Carvararadonques, claimed to be descended from the burro species. They treated the burro with kindness and respect, protected him, and prosecuted those who abused or overloaded him.[9])

In folklore the burro's bray has been considered an omen: "If a burro's bray is the first thing you hear in the morning, make a wish and it will come true." The burro has been credited with the ability to predict the weather: the Belgian farmer knows that "it is time to shock the hay when the old burro blows his horn." Early-day American harvest hands were sure that "when a burro brays the weather will change." The Iranian truck farmer believes that "when a burro brays the onions are sprouting."

The Germans have less confidence in the occult powers of the burro. They say, "Burros that bray must eat least." In early times the English believed that the burro's large ears and his bray were related: the long ears took in all the gossip, and the burro passed it along through his bray. Shorter and smaller ears would presumably hear less, and so it became a common practice to prune back a portion of the animal's ears.

The Zuñi Indians of present-day New Mexico, who were introduced to the burro by the Spaniards, were amused by the bray. They were not amused, however, by the burro's habit of straying

Burro aiding the coffee harvest, Hawaii, ca. 1940. Courtesy of Paradise Publishing Company.

A "Kona nightingale" being fed passion-fruit vines. Courtesy of Paradise Publishing Company.

into their cornfields for some nibbling. In punishment the Zuñis cut off a bit of ear for each offense. After several seasons a tough old burro presented a ludicrous appearance. The Zuñis did not invent the punishment; centuries earlier, Egyptian farmers slit the ears of burros that too frequently strayed into grainfields or vegetable plots.

Jonathan Swift, famed for his satiric writings, especially *Gulliver's Travels,* referred to the lowly burro as the "nightingale of beasts." The people of Hawaii call him the "Kona nightingale." In North and South Kona, two districts on Hawaii Island, burros were used on the coffee plantations. Until the mechanical age caught up with him, the burro was ideally suited to the task of transporting heavy bags of coffee beans. The short-statured burro was able to move around under the low-growing branches of the coffee plant and yet was sturdy enough to carry the heavy loads.

Along the coast of Hawaii Island a story is told about a Kona nightingale who, by virtue of his dependable clear voice, helped his master return safely from a voyage to another island. As his master approached home port, the burro sent forth his nightingale call to guide his owner to the dock.

In Colorado, where the burro became the prospector's faithful and loyal companion, he is known as the "Rocky Mountain canary," while on the desert of Arizona he became known as the "desert canary" or the "desert contralto"—further evidence that, regardless of his geographical whereabouts, the burro's voice is his most characteristic feature.

In 1871 a Denver, Colorado, newspaper reported the commotion caused one Sunday by a Clear Creek County burro. A herd of burros was grazing in a pasture near a rural church. The preacher was exhorting his congregation. As he reached the climax of his sermon, he quoted from the Bible, "Hark, I hear an angel sing!" At just that moment one of the burros issued a clarion bray. As might be imagined, the preacher had difficulty restoring calm among his greatly amused flock.[10]

In 1889 the Reverend George M. Darley, a circuit preacher in the San Juan area of Colorado, wrote of his experiences in his work. One Sunday his sermon was regularly interrupted by a group of burros near his church. He named as the chief culprit a jenny named Maud, who originated the choral blast—and who, incidentally, belonged to the preacher's son. Darley described the racket as "a kind of duet, the outgoing breath making one sort of noise, the incoming another. This was followed by a quartet composed of the most hideous noises."[11]

Not only preachers but members of the laity resented the burro's bray, sometimes with reason. An Idaho wagonmaster's story is a case in point:

> In 1877 a train of twelve-horse wagons was struggling through heavy sand near Camas Creek in southern Idaho when it met a drunken prospector with two burros. The prospector stopped and offered a drink to the wagonmaster. One of the burros shook itself with a great clatter of pots and pans, and the other let out a resounding bray. One wagon string stampeded for half a mile and stopped only when the wagon was hub-deep in sand, and then the horses squealed and bucked until exhausted. It took forty-eight hours and all hands with shovels to get the lead wagon free.[12]

Pioneer Judge Moses Hallet was introduced to the bray on his first visit to Silverton, Colorado, in 1875. He and his companion, Wilbur F. Stone, who later also became a judge, stopped for the night at the Silverton Hotel. Stone described their efforts to sleep:

> Adjoining the kitchen was a corral full of pack mules and burros . . . and these raucous songsters started a braying concert at two and closed at four A.M., an interlude of foghorn snoring fifteen minutes, and then the hyena cooks in the kitchen began to pound the India-rubber beefsteaks with clubs on a pile of loose boards.[13]

The burro's bray has even on occasion taken him to court. In 1919 a case arose in Sierra Madre, California, about the location of a burro corral. The corral owner hired out animals for riding and work. Local citizens with sensitive ears filed a complaint about the noise the animals produced. The lower court ruled in favor of the owner and the burros, but on appeal the decision was reversed. The tongue-in-cheek opinion issued by the appellate judge borders on the classic:

> . . . we know of no heaven-sent maxim to invent a silencer for the brute, . . . a sound so fine there's nothing lives twixt it and silence. We fear that until nature evolves a whispering burro . . . we shall oft in the dead vast and middle of the night . . . hear the loud discordant bray of this sociable but shrill-toned friend of man, filling the air with barbarous dissonance.[14]

With the passage of years the burro's bray has generally failed to meet wider acceptance. Recently the administrator of a nursing home in Ohio was ordered to remove from the premises an old donkey named Hambones. The donkey was a pet and a mascot of the home, and the elderly people would steer their wheelchairs to his pen to watch him. It was Hambones' braying at 5:30 A.M. that got him into trouble, causing one or two sleepy neighbors to complain. Presumably Hambones went to greener pastures. The sorrow of the residents at the nursing home has not been recorded.[15]

The burro's bray has not always been the object of derision or the cause of trouble, however. One sympathetic friend, who extolled the burro as the "philosopher of the desert," asked whether the bray was "a cry against the pain of existence; or does he smell some change in the weather, such as rain or snow, both of which he objects to, and therefore brays his feeling?" But, the writer added, the bray is not always plaintive: "A burro stands, he considers, he attains Nirvana, meets the riddle, solves it, comes back to earth and gives us the laugh."[16]

Philosopher Theodor Lessing thought of the burro as a mirror of the soul of the people. To him the animal represented the patient nature of the common people, and he suggested that the sum of all the miseries of mankind became articulate in the bray of the burro.[17]

The bray has had other interpretations. In his poem "Burro," Henry Knibbs offered a hint of the meaning of the burro's utterance:

> Beloved burro of the ample ear,
> Philosopher, gray hobo of the dunes,
> Delight of children, thistle chewing seer,
>
> . . . .
>
> Your melody means something deep, unseen;
> Desert contralto you are called; perchance
> An ear attuned to mysteries might glean
> More from your song than simple assonance. . . .[18]

Man has put the bray of the burro to his own sometimes cruel purpose. Trappers experienced in the ways of predators know that the flesh of the burro is relished by wolves. William McLeod Raine and Will C. Barnes recorded how one cattleman used burros to trap wolves. The man owned two thousand head of cattle. Two yearlings had been lost from the herd, killed by mother wolves for food for their whelps. Two of the rancher's hands were sent out to trap and kill the wolves:

> Long before daylight the next morning the two men were on their way to the spot where the yearlings had been killed. One led a mother burro at whose side trotted a little one about a month old. Of all animal food the wolf prefers burro meat. . . . Arriving near the place where the second yearling had been killed, one of the men leaned from the saddle and knocked the mother burro on the head with an ax brought for that purpose. . . . He cut from the dead burro's leg several pieces of flesh. . . . To these pieces of flesh the man attached [a] small package of strychnine.
>
> After setting the traps the men mounted and rode away. The baby burro followed the men for a short distance, braying at the top of his small voice, then suddenly turned and raced back to the spot where his mother lay.

Throughout the long night the orphaned burro raised his voice on the clear night air, crying for attention from his dead mother. That was exactly what the rancher had hoped for. The crying of the burrito would attract the wolves to the poisoned flesh and the steel traps. Somehow the motherless baby survived the night and the next day was taken to the ranch house, where it was raised on a bottle.[19]

The voice of the jenny sounds more moderate than that of the jack, and the bray of the gelding is even lower. All burros possess a repertoire of vocal emanations. One sound expresses happiness; another, sadness; and still another, hunger. At the approach of danger the burro sounds a warning note to other burros in the area. The burro mother has a special bray when calling her young for a meal or warning it of danger. The burrito has its own infant cries signifying hunger and fear. During the mating season the braying of the jack is loud and vigorous. The jack, a jealous male, has a bray of challenge to other males and uses it when the occasion demands. Though more moderate in tone, the voice of the gelding is not easily ignored. Persons who have pet burros cannot resist their soft half-crying or sniffling plea for a tidbit. Indeed, only the man with a heart of stone could ignore it. Surely such a little burro followed the English poet Samuel Taylor Coleridge, who wrote:

> Poor foal of an oppressed race,
> I love the patience of thy face;
> And oft with gentle hand I give
>   thee bread,
> And clap thy rugged coat, and
>   pat thy head.[20]

3. Over the Horizon

At some time, somewhere, human beings began the slow process of domesticating wild animals. Among those animals was the ancestor of the burro, the fleet and freedom-loving wild ass, whose origin is hidden behind the curtain of time. The search for the remote beginnings of one of nature's creatures is frustrating; the trail has a way of growing dim and then vanishing from view. Pierre Teilhard de Chardin indicated the inescapable problem: "Nothing is so delicate and fugitive by its very nature as a beginning."[1] The burro's origin bears out that observation. The burro evolved along with the other Equidae, the horse and the zebra.

Where and when man first met the wild ass is unknown. The two may have met in Asia and Africa. But the ass did not confine himself to those continents; members of his kind—the onager (or koulan) and the kiang of Asia and the ass of Africa—grazed in Europe during the ice age, and the meat of the wild horse and the ass became man's chief diet. One writer believes that the wild ass was tamed within ten to fifteen thousand years after the warm intervals of the last ice age.

The Nubians domesticated the African ass, and the Sumerians of the Tigris-Euphrates Valley tamed the onager.[2] Apparently, however, the wild ass the late Paleolithic hunters knew, whose carved likeness appears on rocks in both Spain and Switzerland,[3] disappeared from Europe, not to reappear until after its domestication in Africa and Asia.

Geologic eras, periods, and epochs passed, accompanied by slow climatic changes. At the beginning of the Eocene epoch, eighty million years ago, grass was beginning to grow in some areas; the earth was a little drier than it had been during the previous epoch, when birds and a few mammals had appeared. Millions more years passed, and the Oligocene epoch came into full bloom, thirty million years ago. The little horse was moving faster—and was compelled to, for the saber-toothed tiger was on the prowl. He managed to elude this awesome cat, for he continued to survive after the dreaded enemy had become extinct. It was probably during the Miocene epoch, fifteen to twenty million years ago, that the mammals reached the evolutionary stage at which we know them today.[4]

Ten million years ago the Pliocene epoch arrived. Mountains had formed, the climate was cooler, and the mammals were larger. Then the climate became cold, and during the Pleistocene epoch, beginning about one million years ago, the glacial ice started southward. Plant and animal life had to adjust to living in interglacial regions, perish, or go south. They did all three.

Something else happened during the earlier part of the Pleistocene epoch: a primate arrived on the scene in South and East Africa. Scientists who discovered his bones called him *Australopithecus africanus*. He had gained an advantage over his contemporaries, thanks to his thumb and to his larger brain. According to Robert Ardrey, this hunter picked up the humerus (the upper foreleg) of an antelope and adopted it as a weapon to protect himself from enemies to secure fresh meat.[5] Fossilized bones of animals, taken from the caves where Australopithecus gnawed at the meat and then broke the bones to suck the marrow, attest to the variety of his meat diet. Among the bones were those of the baboon, the horse, and possibly the zebra and the ass as well.

At about the same time man stumbled over the horizon. Thanks largely to his larger brain, he widened the gap between his kind and the other primates.

Fossilized bones of *Equus*, the first true horse, also date from the early part of the Pleistocene epoch. His bones are found on all the continents except Australia. Though most of the evolutionary development of the ancestors of the equines took place in North

America, none of the Pleistocene species left any descendants here.[6] But his progeny had traveled other continents.

When and where the equine stem divided and brought into existence the present members of the horse family is buried in the rocks of ages past. The structural differences of the horse, the zebra, and the burro are slight but important. In their wild stage they do not mix, and it seems doubtful that any extensive crossbreeding took place. Under domestication and supervision crossbreeding does occur between the horse and the burro, less often between the horse and the zebra, whose offspring is generally considered inferior. The coloration, personalities, traits, voices, habits, and even instincts vary considerably among these animals, and man has designed different stations for them in the scheme of things. The zebra is a

Onagers. Courtesy of Los Angeles Zoo.

Nubian wild asses. Courtesy of Los Angeles Zoo.

recalcitrant animal and in the Western world generally is of value merely as a zoo animal. The burro has traditionally occupied the lowest position.

The members of the horse family started out upon the evolutionary trail fifty million years ago. During the Eocene epoch a small, four-legged, many-toed animal browsed on the lush plants of the once spongy swampland that is now Montana and other western states. Fossilized bones of this scampering, dog-sized animal indicate that he was no more than a foot tall. Scientists call him *Eohippus*, from the Greek *eos* ("dawn") and *hippos* ("horse")— the Dawn Horse. He had four toes on each hind foot and three on each front foot—fourteen toes in all. During the Eocene epoch a land bridge connected North America and Asia, where the Bering Strait now separates the two continents, and the little equine-to-be migrated to Asia. There on that expansive land mass he remained. Eventually, some of his descendants, larger and changed in form, made their way to Europe and Africa.

Eohippus browsed in the swamps and grew, doubling his height over the next ten million years—and losing a toe from each hind foot. *Mesohippus*, as the larger equine has been termed, ran faster than his ancestor—out of necessity, because the enemies that stalked him in the new Oligocene epoch were picking up speed. Ten million more years rolled by with many changes in climate and environment, in plant and animal life. Drier pastures prevailed. With an improved tooth structure, he grazed more and browsed less and was found on low, rolling hills. His speed continued to increase, and his name was now *Merychippus*. He still had three toes on each foot, but something was happening to the middle toe: it was longer and stronger, assuming more of the responsibility of carrying him. The side toes had become superfluous. His height, too, had increased fifteen inches. He and the other members of his herd were traveling and grazing on harder, drier ground, and they no longer needed as many toes. The Miocene epoch lasted twelve million years, giving way to the Pliocene. A one-toed animal had evolved; his other toes were now concealed, and his height at the withers was four feet. He was *Pliohippus*, the first one-toed horse, but not yet the horse or the burro or the zebra of today.

Evolution kept on its endless course. Sometime during the Pliocene epoch the herds may have split into several bands, into groups of individuals. Some of these new herds grew, while others withered and died out, no doubt as others had done along the way. The survivors adapted themselves to new environments and became the ancestors of the horse, the zebra, and the burro, with their identifying characteristics, the neigh, the stripes, and the bray.

Two Spanish veterinarians, Luis Salvano and Mateo Torrent, believe that the ancestor of the domestic ass is the kiang (or hemionus) of Asia. They also believe that the primitive animals developed in northeast Africa and Asia. Others believe that the Nubian ass was the ancestor of the burro, pointing out that he has qualities superior to other breeds—more strength, a better temperament, and a more stable nervous system.[7]

A million years ago the Pleistocene epoch got under way, and the age of man dawned. Members of *Equus* finally appeared silhouetted against the landscape—three strong, fleet, quick-witted quadrupeds, each with his individual traits and characteristic markings. Each of the three, the burro, the zebra, and the horse, carried all his weight on four toes, one on the end of each leg. The other toes had evolved into "splint bones."

Wastelands, harsh and rocky terrain, isolated and uninviting to most other forms of life, became the favorite habitat of the ass. His hoofs, hard like steel, enabled him to climb and scamper over the rocky surfaces of his domain. His durable hoofs also served as lethal weapons. Kicking with his hind hoofs and pawing with his front, snapping his strong jaws and teeth, he displayed formidable weapons in combat.

Man, the unique mammal, came with his kin, changing and adapting, both physically and mentally. He was emerging as a dominant creature upon the world stage. He and his family sought refuge in caves, contesting with bears for possession. These were hunters, for meat was important in their diet. From the mouth of the caves and projecting ledges they could watch for wild game, especially the woolly mammoth, and lay plans for capture. In time the woolly mammoth was reduced in numbers, faded to the north, and disappeared. Man increased in numbers, traveling more, spreading his kind. The hunter followed the wild horse and the wild ass in Europe and in Asia and added the zebra to his diet in Africa. The methods used to snare game were varied and ingenious. But the wild animal was no easy prey, and the hunter and his family sometimes went hungry.

During the latter part of this long cultural age Paleolithic men learned to carve, draw lines, mold, sculpture, and paint. The walls and ceilings of caves in Spain, France, and elsewhere bear witness to the handiwork of these artists. They carved, sculptured, and painted to express their feelings and needs—their dependence upon the wild animals—bison, deer, bear, horse, and ass. The wild game

Onager and koulan crosses. Courtesy of Munich Zoo.

also led to spiritual consciousness, as did other aspects of the natural world. The animals were revered because men's survival depended upon them.

As man continued to adapt to his environment, so did the wild ass. He learned to thrive in the dry, rugged areas of south, central, and southwestern Asia and northeastern Africa. In a region of arid lands with sparse vegetation and little water, he developed hardiness, tenacity, and fleetness. He was at his best in the hot, dry areas that later comprised Mongolia, parts of Tibet, Afghanistan, northwest India, Persia, Mesopotamia, Syria, Arabia, Palestine, Egypt, Nubia, Ethiopia, and Somalia.

Several species and subspecies of the wild ass are native to Asia and Africa. The Zoological Society of London reports the following known species, some of which are now extinct:

Mongolian wild ass (*Equus hemionus hemionus*). It is still fairly common in one area in central Mongolia, but is considered very rare in China.

Persian wild ass or Onager (*Equus hemionus onager*). It is extremely rare in Persia, but fairly common in the Badkhyz Reserve in the U.S.S.R.

Indian wild ass (*Equus hemionus khur*). It is only found in the Little Rann of Kutch on the Indo-Pakistan border. In 1962 it was estimated to number 870. Its numbers have certainly decreased since then.

Tibetan wild ass or kiang (*Equus hemionus kiang*). Found on the Tibetan plateau and in parts of Nepal, Sikkim, Ladak and Chinghai. Rare but not endangered according to the Chinese.

Syrian wild ass (*Equus hemonius hemippus*). Thought to be extinct.

Nubian wild ass (*Equus asinus africanus*). Red Sea Hills south of Suakin and Eritrean Border as far south as Atbera River. Very rare if not extinct.

Somali wild ass (*Equus asinus somalicus*). There are several hundred in Ethiopia and may be a few scattered herds in Somalia and Sudan.[8]

Not all scholars are in agreement on the classification of the Asiatic asses. Frederick E. Zeuner believes that, because they resemble in appearance both *Equus caballus* and *Equus asinus africanus*, the Asiatic asses should be referred to as half-asses. "They are an Asiatic group of horses with a certain number of ass-like characters," he claims, and "must be regarded as a separate species or better still as a subspecies, intermediate between the true horse and the true ass."[9]

The wild asses referred to in both the Old and the New Testament were very likely the fast-running onagers. It is probable that Abraham used tamed onagers for transportation when he saddled up and led his family up the banks of the Euphrates and out of Mesopotamia looking for the Promised Land. In recent years the Russians have taken an interest in the preservation of onagers (and perhaps of other species), affording them protection on the Badkhy Reserve.

Persian wild ass. From *Wild Life in Danger* (Viking Press, 1969).

As mentioned earlier, the characteristics of the present-day burro point toward the Nubian wild ass, *Equus asinus africanus,* as its chief progenitor. The ancient Mongolians and Tibetans apparently never domesticated the asses within their domains. The farmers of China, long dependent upon burros, probably first obtained them from merchants who traveled the long trade routes from the Middle East and Egypt. The millions of burros laboring in China possess characteristics that tie their ancestral origin with the asses of northeastern Africa and adjacent parts of the Middle East, not with those of Mongolia or Tibet.

It is curious that the kiang of central Asia was never tamed. The kiang is dark in color, with a narrow black stripe along the mane and backbone, and is, like virtually all of his other kin, white or pale underneath. He differs from the domesticated ass in some respects and may form a "missing link" in the evolution of the species. This wild, fleet animal possesses similarities both to the horse and to his relatives in the Middle East and Africa. The kiang is larger than the onager but smaller than the horse; his mane is longer than that of the Persian or Nubian ass but shorter than the mane of the horse. His voice is different from either the neigh of the horse or the bray —an "in-between" sound. Like the ass, the kiang has no forelock.

The kiang's ears are longer than the ears of the horse but shorter than those of the burro. The horse and the kiang are compatible and tolerate each other in the wild state. This fact pulls the two species closer together, for such social harmony does not prevail between the wild horse and the other species of wild asses.

Perhaps the most startling difference between the kiang and the domesticated burro is the former's fondness for entering water, even icy-cold water, for a lively swim. The domesticated burro will have no part of such nonsense. Water, to a burro, is for drinking.

The burro has five lumbar vertebrae, one less than most horses have. Some Arabian horses are reported to have only five. If a tale from the Sudan Desert is accurate, this exception may stem from the amorous activity of a wild male ass in the western portion of that territory who "crossed over the line." The story concerns the alleged origin of the fine Barbary horse, the Haymour breed of Arabians. It seems that an Arab chieftain left an injured mare at an isolated oasis in the desert, believing that the mare would not recover. A year later, however, while the chieftain and some companions were hunting in the area, they saw his mare. Noting that she was about to foal, they brought her to their camp. When the foal was born, it was named Haymour, an Arabic word that means, loosely, "foal of a wild ass." The Arabs were positive that no other horses had been in the area during the year. This foal thus became the founder of the Haymour breed.[10]

Somali wild ass. From *Wild Life in Danger* (Viking Press, 1969).

Pair of asses. Bronze plaque, Scytho-Mongolian, ca. 200 B.C. Courtesy of Montreal Museum of Fine Arts.

The fact that crossing a burro and a horse in domestic breeding usually produces a sterile foal may indicate a considerable gap in heritage between the two species. It may be hazardous to do so, but I venture the opinion that the burro has changed less than the horse, perhaps because he is tougher physically, mentally, and psychologically. He is endowed with more emotional stability and is better able to survive under adverse conditions than *Equus caballus.*

In some ways the burro and the zebra appear to be closer kin than either is to the horse. The quagga of South Africa, an extinct species related to the ass and the zebra, has provided an opportunity for interesting conjecture about its relationship to the burro. The quagga's front portion was striped, but the rear half of his body had the appearance of the burro. The transverse stripe on top of the withers, characteristic of many domestic burros, together with the visible markings on the neck and front legs of the newborn foal, hint of a not-too-ancient common ancestry with the zebra.

The burro's ancestor, the wild ass, came over the horizon a long time ago. Lines from a poem called "The Donkey," by G. K. Chesterton, offer poetic insight into the remote origin of the burro:

> When fishes flew and forests walked
>   And figs grew upon thorns,
> Some moment when the moon was blood
>   Then surely I was born———.[11]

The evolutionary trail taken by his earliest progenitor is faintly discernible over a period of fifty million years. But insofar as the three identifiable animals of the horse family are concerned, they arrived with the progenitor of true man at the beginning of his age, a million years ago.

Zebras. Courtesy of Los Angeles Zoo.

4. Woman Corrals Him

The human male early enslaved woman, and she in turn enslaved the wild animals. The taming of animals was not a rapid process. It is unlikely that animals were domesticated before about 8000 B.C. Woman packed the burdens for thousands of years before she transferred them to the backs of animals. Eventually and gradually she converted the wild to the tame, probably first for milk and then for work. One by one, she enlarged her animal herd.

There is no certainty about which animals were first domesticated. Some authorities believe that the goat was the first animal to be tamed, even before the dog in the Near East.[1] Prehistoric woman early recognized the benefit of goat's milk for her children. The reindeer is also counted among the first animals to be tamed, milked, and worked, and some historians believe that it may have been the very first animal domesticated.[2] If the reindeer was indeed the first animal brought under subjugation, man probably accomplished the feat in one of the interglacial regions of Asia before the last ice age receded to its present line.

Wherever and however it was accomplished, domestication of animals was a momentous achievement that changed the course of human events and signaled the dawn of civilization.

The study of primitive culture emphasizes the dominant part that woman played in it. Woman was the first farmer—and she founded animal husbandry. Looking for help with her burdens and tiresome tasks, she turned to the animals around her, perhaps ones that she had raised from babyhood. She and her children, while gathering roots, honey, berries, frogs, snails, and birds' eggs, may have discovered a whelp near the mouth of its den—a dog, a lamb, a kid— or a burro (dwarfed animals were probably the first to be domesticated because they were easy to handle). Now and then a hunter, after killing a mother animal, would bring to the cave an orphaned baby to be fondled by the human mother and her children and raised as a pet. Milk was often provided to the baby animal by the human mother, who allowed the orphan to suckle at her breast with her own baby or in place of a baby who had died. The suckling of baby animals by human mothers was not uncommon in early societies. Puppies, kittens, pigs, lambs, and very likely baby burros too have nursed at women's breasts. In many line drawings, paintings, and sculptured likenesses of the adult female portrayed by early artists, women's breasts are large enough to suckle a whole corral of burritos.[3] Animals so reared until they were mature enough to eat forage grew up tame.

There were, of course, other avenues through which the burro was tamed. An injured burro, pregnant or with young, might be captured and fed and raised her young in the presence of human beings. In some such fashion the first steps in domestication were taken.

Portuguese burro, 1926. Courtesy of Grolier Society.

The association of burro and humankind had a biological basis. Burro milk and human milk are very similar. Burro milk is easily digested. It possesses large amounts of sugar and protein and does not readily curdle. From early times it has been recognized as beneficial for infants, invalids, and those with delicate stomachs.

The domestication of the burros relieved the human mother from prolonged periods of nursing, freeing her for other duties. She began transferring burdens from her head and back to the now-willing animals; she and her children also began riding them. The burros and their passengers, especially the children, became friends. Animals and young children seem to have a natural affinity; animals are generally tolerant of children and their sometimes clumsy and even rough handling.

And so the burro became a pet and eventually a companion and burden bearer. Men tamed the horse for war and the hunt. Women tamed the burro for peaceful pursuits. Loading a burro was easy for a woman, and because of his convenient height she and her children could mount him readily. He soon developed a serene dis-

Portuguese burros, Lisbon. Courtesy of U.S. Information Service, Lisbon.

Haitian burro, 1970. Courtesy of U.S. Information Service.

position that led him to stand quietly while he was loaded or mounted. He had such an easy gait that women could nurse their babies while riding along. Even today Oriental and African women card wool, spin yarn, and even knit as they ride. The women of the desert, preferring burros to camels for much of their work, use them to haul water and wood and camel dung for fires, load them with handicrafts for market, and bring them home laden with necessities. Desert burros share with camels the ability to survive on little food and water.

Burro, Dominican Republic, 1970. Courtesy of U.S. Information Service, Santo Domingo.

Down through history, patient, conservative, and hard working, woman and burro have complemented each other in work and have shared companionship. During the gold rush in the beautiful but forbidding Colorado Rockies in the 1860's, a burro helped assuage the loneliness of young Augusta Tabor, the wife of prospector H. A. W. Tabor (later famed as businessman and politician). Augusta shared the rigors of Tabor's search for riches. While they struggled to drive an ox team over the Mosquito Range, they found it almost impossible to cross the high mountains of South Park that blocked their route to reported gold diggings beyond. Augusta recorded in her diary:

> The fourth day in the park we came late at night to Salt Creek. Tried the water and found that we could not let the cattle drink it, neither could we drink it. We tied the oxen to the wagon and went supperless to bed. The night was very cold and a jack came to our tent and stood in the hot embers until he burned his fetlocks off.[4]

Ladies of Colorado Springs riding burros, ca. 1900. Photo by H. S. Poley. Courtesy of Denver Public Library Western Collection.

The Kiva at Taos. Etching by Edward Borein. From *The Etchings of Edward Borein.* Courtesy of John Howell–Books, San Francisco.

On the following day, while Augusta guarded camp, Tabor and other men in the party continued the search for a pass through the range. It was a cold, windy day. The oxen were restless and thirsty. Augusta's baby fretted. No one passed by, the valley was empty, and the mountains looked cold and silent. Night came, and the darkness closed in on Augusta, but Tabor had not arrived. She wrote, "I felt desolate indeed." Then the little burro who had come into camp the night before entered her tent, perhaps looking for warmth and company. Augusta wrote, "I bowed my head upon him and wept in loneliness of soul."[5]

5. Egyptian Bondage

More than five thousand years ago the first domesticated Egyptian burro, after a hard day's work, walked over to the Nile and took a drink. Thanks to the ancient artists of this river-dominated country, much visible evidence remains of the burro's early work with man. There is little doubt that the burro was the first domesticated animal in Egypt.

Before the first of the long line of Egyptian dynasties, which began about 3200 B.C., the Libyans living west of the Nile Delta kept large herds of burros. They were first utilized as dairy animals and then as work stock and as meat for food.[1] The jenny, who has a long milk-producing period, made a good dairy animal. Burro milk was used not only as food but also as a cosmetic by the women of ancient times, and the Libyan women were perhaps the first to discover the benefits to the complexion of the protein-rich liquid.

The wild ancestors of the Egyptian burro, ranging from the Delta at the lower reach of the Nile to the First Cataract and even beyond, drank from its waters, coming cautiously to the river's edge, drinking quietly and with eye and ear alert to danger—particularly from the crocodile. The wild burros spread westward from Libya across northern Africa, as their descendants were to do after domestication. The broad expanse of the Sahara Desert contained little water, though in places sufficient rainfall at the proper time produced a wild melon similar to the watermelon, which provided liquid for the gazelle, the ostrich, and the wild ass.

Like other early peoples, the Egyptians respected the animal kingdom, and some animals, such as the cat, became sacred to them. The burro was also respected. In the Book of the Dead, which has been described as the Egyptian Bible, the burro was accorded a

Relief from the tomb of Ptah-hotep, Egyptian Middle Kingdom, Saqqara. Reproduced from Frank J. Roos, Jr., *An Illustrated Handbook* (New York, Macmillan Company), 1954.

special position: "Heart which is Righteous and Sinless say . . . come in peace; come in peace . . . for I have heard the word which was spoken by the Ass with the Cat."[2]

During predynastic times the Egyptians took care to prevent the spirits of the dead from returning to plague them. After death human bodies were burned or cut into pieces and wrapped in hides of gazelles and other animals.[3] Very likely burro hides were used, since they were tough enough to hold the unwanted spirits.

At one time the burro was so deeply revered by the Egyptians that he was considered worthy of being sacrificed to the god of learning. Later, however, the Egyptians lost their high regard for him. Artists represented an ignorant person by drawing him with the head and ears of the ass.[4] They also traced his form on the cakes they offered to Set, the god of evil.[5]

Wars, invasions, plunder, and rapine prevailed in ancient times as now, but somehow the work of the farmer, the merchant, the trader, and the craftsman continued and even prospered. The burro was an important part of business activities. He was led on trade routes connecting the Nile Valley with the Sudan, Nubia, and Ethiopia in Africa, and across the Sinai Desert to the trading centers of the Middle East. Early paintings and bas-reliefs portray the burro contributing to trade and communication. The articles of trade were not so much necessities as luxuries. Most caravan leaders bound for far-distant lands sought unusual, scarce, exotic items, for they were generally more easily transported and more profitable. Necessities were usually available, but luxury items—jewelry, perfumes, spices, gems, and metals—were harder to come by. Burros first carried these precious items; only later did the horse, camel, and mule assist. The ox was not a desert traveler, and the horse did not arrive until about 1700 B.C., when the Hyksos, or Shepherd kings, rode out of Syria and other parts of the Middle East, across the Sinai Desert, and into the Nile Valley. The domesticated camel came even later. (Because he was the product of crossbreeding, the mule was never popular in lands influenced by Mosaic law.)

Under the Ptolemies, who ruled Egypt from 332 to 30 B.C., the peasant—and his burro—worked ten days before they had a day of rest. The Jews and Christians, citing the authority of the Bible, said that both man and beast were to rest on the seventh day. The Moslems failed to give the burro any days off. Friday was the Mos-

lem's holy day, but also his chief market day, and so he said an
additional prayer on Friday and loaded his burro with wood, handicrafts, and other items and led him to the market centers. The burro
returned bearing the day's purchases and, if the purchases were few,
the owner, his wife, and a child or two. In such fashion the burro
celebrated the Sabbath, after six days of laboring on the farm,
hauling wood, building materials, and water.

The prospector and the burro, partners from time immemorial in
the search for precious metals and gems, worked together in the
desert hills of eastern Egypt and the Sinai Desert. In ancient times
slaves sank shafts in the mica schist near the Red Sea to mine
emeralds.[6] The Egyptian burro complemented his counterpart, the
human slave. In the hills of the Sinai Desert the ancient Egyptians
and their burros mined blue and green turquoise. These gems were
eagerly sought by the rulers of the Nile, who maintained a monopoly on more important natural resources, a precedent that was
established in ancient times in Egypt and throughout the Middle
East and is continued in the present day.

For two thousand years the pharaohs sent burros to the copper
mines in the Sinai to carry the ore to the smelter. Later, when tin
was added, they carried the refined metal to the royal warehouses.
After Nubia had been conquered by Egypt, the Egyptian burro
transported gold from Nubian mines. These pack animals brought
to the pharaohs amethysts, beryl, silver, and, after 1300 B.C., iron
from greater distances. The burro also carried back to Egypt white
quartz sand, which was used in the manufacture of glass, an industry that flourished in 1000 B.C.

Burros carried myrrh, a spice made from a spiny shrub of the
southern Arabian Peninsula, and other forms of incense and exotic
spirits. They transported stibnite, used by the women of Egypt to
groom their brows and darken their lashes, and ferric oxide, which
provided rouge for the women's lips and cheeks. Adopting the practice of the Libyan women, Egyptians used burro milk as a skin lo-
tion. Cleopatra, queen of Egypt, bathed in burro milk.

Ancient Egyptian harvest scene. Courtesy of Ministry of Tourism, Cairo.

The burro, traditionally associated with sheep and goat herding, went with the Egyptian herders (often women and children) into the desert and its wadis to seek grazing or browsing regions for the animals. The burros carried herders and their water, food, and bedding. The burro was a part of the herding culture, and also, along the canals, ditches, and in the marshes of the Delta he helped care for other livestock—sheep, goats, cattle, water buffalo, hogs, and after they were introduced into the Nile Valley, horses and camels.

The burro played an important part in the architecture of the ancient Egyptians. The engineers found burros necessary in the construction of a canal that linked the Nile Delta and the Red Sea. The burro, and his human counterpart, removed thousands of tons of earth to construct this ancient water passage. Engineers also depended upon burros, along with conscripted laborers and slaves, to erect the massive pyramids and the Sphinx.

The burro, carrying water, food, and tools, labored in the hot desert sun alongside the thousands of slaves who set into place the large blocks of stone cut in a distant quarry. The pharaoh, half god and half mortal, must have an appropriate place for his royal bones to rest. Each pharaoh wished to surpass his predecessors in grandeur. More blocks of stone, more slaves, more burros were employed to construct the pyramids. Perhaps we should think of the pyramids as monuments not only to the kings entombed in them but also to the human and animal slaves who worked and died to make these grandiose structures a reality.

To the Egyptians death was an important step toward immortality. Therefore, preparations for the death journey were elaborate

Egyptian breeding jack, 1970. Courtesy of Ministry of Tourism, Cairo.

Working farm burro in the Nile Valley, 1970. Courtesy of Ministry of Tourism, Cairo.

and meticulous, especially for the pharaohs, their wives, and other members of royalty. Costly perfumes, incense, and embalming chemicals were carried from distant lands on the packsaddles of burros.

In the towns of the Nile Valley the burro carried materials for construction, crafts, commerce, and trade. He went from door to door with his hawker-master, carrying milk, water, vegetables, carpets, and other items. He was at the dock to meet riverboats carrying metals, hides, dates, stones, and grain from up the Nile, from Nubia, and from the Sudan, to be transported to market centers.

When the chariot and the cart were introduced into Egypt, probably about 1700 B.C., the burro was hitched to them and was thus able to haul larger loads than he could carry on his back. Farm produce—vegetables, grain, dates, melons, and fodder—were piled in the carts (as they still are today), to be hauled from fields to places of storage, threshing floors, and markets. (Today in Egypt the burro's lot has not changed with the coming of the engine, automobile, tractor, and pump: the burro carries tins of gasoline, diesel fuel, and kerosene strapped to his sides or pulls them in a two-wheeled cart. He has carried every conceivable item on his back or has pulled it in a cart.)

Trade and commerce were not confined within the boundaries of Egypt, of course. Art of the periods shows that friendly trade relations existed between Egypt and the Middle East. Pack trains of burros were moving between Arabia and Egypt by 3000 B.C. and very likely earlier.

The burro carried human as well as trade burdens. People of all social and economic classes rode burros. It was a common practice to ease the load by placing a board between two burros, on which the rider sat. As mentioned earlier, members of the royalty and priests favored white burros for their mounts; the Ptolemies selected white burros to pull their chariots in the royal pageants in Alexandria.

The burro was an integral part of the inventive culture of the Egyptians. Hieroglyphics, one of the earliest systems of writing (dating back at least five thousand years and continuing in use into the fourth century A.D.) were incised upon sheets of papyrus, the tall, reedlike aquatic plant of the Nile Valley. The Egyptians cut the plants along the riverbanks and in the marshes and packed them on burros, who transported the loads to processing centers. There thin strips of the pith of the plant were placed together, soaked in water, and then pressed and allowed to dry. After the Egyptian scribe had written his messages, the burro carried both the messenger and the documents to their destination.

In later centuries the Jews were an important segment of Egyptian culture. The work of an artist who lived during Abraham's time preserved for history proof of the burro's contribution to Jewish trade, social, and entertainment relations with Egypt. The painting

appears on the wall of one of the tombs constructed about 1900
B.C. for the nobles of the Beni-Hasan area on the bank of the Nile.
It portrays a party of Jews on their way from Palestine for a visit
to Egypt. Men, women, and children are shown. Two burros are
a part of the group. One of the animals is pictured carrying the
young children on one side of its packsaddle and provisions on
the opposite side. The second burro carries an anvil and a spear
used in hunting game. The women are barefooted and wearing
ankle rings. They have black hair, and their tunics are so fashioned
to leave their right shoulders bare, the characteristic dress of the
women of Palestine. One man is carrying a harp, an indication that
the group may contain minstrels, as well as tinkers, coppersmiths,
and craftsmen. The mission is obviously a peaceful one.[7]

One of the pharaohs, Rameses II, who ruled from 1300 to 1280
B.C. conquered Jerusalem and other cities of the Middle East and
also gained dominion over Ethiopia and part of Arabia. Rameses II
ordered the construction of a long defensive wall in eastern Egypt
and began a canal that was to connect the Mediterranean with the
Red Sea. For both of these projects the pharaoh conscripted the
services of thousands of burros. The burro, strong for its size, low
in stature, durable, and surefooted, was ideal for such work—for
carrying stones, mud bricks, and baskets of earth dug from the canal
trench.

Directly and indirectly, Egyptian burros became servants of the
many armies that invaded Egypt over the centuries. The decaying
power of the pharaohs and the squabbling political parties within
the country invited foreign interference. About 900 B.C. the Libyans
moved in from their western stronghold, penetrating the Nile
Delta and holding sway for three centuries. Later the ironclad
Assyrians arrived and relieved the Libyans of their control. Beginning in 525 B.C. the armies of the ever-expanding Persian Empire
pushed into the Nile area and exerted their influence, which lasted
until a young Macedonian general named Alexander, leading his
countrymen and Greeks, destroyed the decaying Persian forces in

the Middle East. The armies of Alexander the Great ate the meat of wild onager as they pushed their campaign to the edge of the Punjab in India. There, exhausted, the soldiers proclaimed that they would go no farther. Later, in Babylon, perhaps frustrated because there was little more territory to conquer, Alexander died, in 323 B.C. According to Plutarch, he died as a result of drinking a liquid so cold and heavy that only the hard hoof of the wild onager could contain it.

The burro had witnessed centuries of political upheavals. But he, like the peasant, continued to perform his endless tasks, including supplying food for the invading armies and the conquered populations. He did his share of construction work, too. He helped build Alexandria, founded in 332 B.C. and destined to become the intellectual and commercial center of the Mediterranean world. He watched the Romans take over the fertile Nile region and saw the advent of the Christian era. His duties and his way of life changed but little after his long ears first heard the call to prayer by the mullah when the Moslems took over in A.D. 842. Nor was his burden lessened in succeeding centuries, when the Turks, the French, and finally the British invaded the country. His work remained essential, his status fixed.

Nonetheless, the Egyptian burro traveled to foreign climes. By 1000 B.C. the early slave-driven Egyptian galleys traveling from the mouth of the Nile to other Mediterranean ports had burros as passengers. The islands of Cyprus on the north and Crete on the northwest received the burro, as did some of the islets of the Aegean Sea and the ports of Turkey, Greece, Sicily, and northern Africa. The sea-roving Phoenicians, the first navigators, who sailed among and colonized islands of the Aegean Sea and established permanent settlements in Malta, Sicily, and Sardinia, undoubtedly included burros as part of their cargoes from their own ports in Phoenicia and from Egypt. The burros so transported and distributed three thousand years ago were probably the ancestors of today's miniature Mediterranean donkeys.

Ethiopian burros, 1970. Courtesy of U.S. Information Service, Asmara.

Though records of the burro's history are more plentiful in Egypt, there is no doubt that the burro has played an important role in other areas of Africa—in Nubia, in the Sudan, in Ethiopia, in Eritrea, in Somalia. Today Ethiopia leads all other countries on the continent of Africa in burro population; in fact, it is second only to China in numbers of burros.[8] In all probability Ethiopia also possesses the largest population of wild burros.[9]

The burro was doubtless ferried back and forth in Arab dhows and Ethiopian craft across the narrow strait separating what is now Eritrea and Yemen or Aden, during prehistoric times and assuredly later. At various times in their history the Ethiopians have been subject to other peoples. The Ethiopians became powerful themselves at intervals between the second and sixth centuries A.D. They crossed the strait connecting the Red Sea and the Gulf of Aden and in A.D. 525 conquered the Hamyarites. With elephants and burros loaded with military equipment and supplies they marched northward along the coast of the Red Sea to the outskirts of Mecca, where they were forced to withdraw. By A.D. 570, the Ethiopians had recrossed the Red Sea and had faded back into the highlands of biblical Cush.

As with all peoples who have domesticated the burro, the Ethiopians have their legends about him. More than a century ago an English traveler named Henry Dufton wrote of his travels in Ethiopia. He related a story he heard about a blacksmith who had occult powers. Women and children were afraid of the man. One day a mother who lived near his shop disappeared. Her sons looked every place for her, to no avail. One of her sons had noticed a female burro, who, whenever she was tied at the blacksmith's shop, would look longingly toward the woman's home and bray. The sons went to the blacksmith and accused him of witchcraft, sorcery, and other powers of the devil. Finally the blacksmith confessed that he had transformed their mother into a burro. When the sons threatened to kill him, he began undoing the spell. He had completed the transformation except for one foot when the sons became so incensed that they murdered him. The mother, restored to human form except for that one foot, was afterward known as the "mother with the burro's foot."[10]

Today in Egypt, as in Ethiopia, the burro remains an acknowledged part of the social and economic fabric of life. But times are changing, however slowly. One day some Egyptian girls watched travelers in a Mercedes-Benz passing through the streets of Siwa. The girls composed a ditty:

> We won't marry the boy with a camel
> Nor even one with two donkeys,
> We are going to marry the boy
> Who takes us away in a Mercedes.[11]

Nevertheless, in the valley of the historic Nile, the burro still provides his services. Throughout the autumn week of 1970 that witnessed the death and funeral of Egypt's President Gamal Abdel Nasser, "the short and simple animal of the poor" was seen carrying the lower-class fellahin into Cairo to pay last respect to their nation's leader.[12]

6. Middle Eastern Heritage

For the purposes of this book, the Middle East is the region adjacent to or near the eastern end of the Mediterranean Sea, more particularly present-day Jordan, Israel, the United Arab Republic (the Syria portion), Lebanon, Iraq, and part of Turkey. Ever since antiquity varied names have been periodically applied to these areas, depending on the fortunes of war.

The wild ass roamed the Middle Eastern countries from the earliest times. Undoubtedly men of the Paleolithic age, fifty thousand years ago, knew and hunted him. Then, after forty thousand years had rolled by, men entered the Neolithic age, when they learned to polish the stone used in their tools and weapons. It was during this period that man, among other things, took the all-important first steps toward domesticating plants and animals. These momentous events probably took place about 10,000 to 12,000 B.C. The burro was doubtless among the animals chosen to be tamed.

It is generally believed that agriculture and animal husbandry were developed in river valleys. One authority conjectures that the fertile Jordan Valley was the home of the very first farmers,[1] and the Middle Eastern burro may have been domesticated by the farmers of that region as early as 8000 B.C.

The Tigris-Euphrates Valley was also the scene of early farming activities. The wild ass had been hunted in this region from time immemorial and was unquestionably tamed very early. The oldest extant writings of the Middle East—poems, records, legends, folklore—all make reference to the native wild ass. When the Ashurbanipal Palace in Nineveh was excavated, a bas-relief was found showing men roping onagers—an ancient species that later became extinct (this ancient work of art is now in the British Museum). Situated on the east bank of the Tigris (opposite modern Mosul, Iraq), Nineveh was one of the oldest and most populous cities of Assyria.

Every country seems to have a national epic. The now-famous library unearthed in Nineveh was founded by Ashurbanipal (669–626 B.C.), the last of the great kings of Assyria. He ordered his scribes to collect, copy, and translate ancient Sumerian texts throughout the country, and among this vast collection of cuneiform tablets was found a Babylonian epic, perhaps the earliest recorded epic—the Sumerian *Gilgamesh*. This story, written on twelve clay tablets consisting of three thousand lines, tells about Gilgamesh, a demigod and legendary ruler-hero of the ancient city-state of Uruk, in the lower part of Sumer (now Iraq). Gilgamesh was the fifth king of Uruk. From the epic we know that the wild onager, game of the ancients, was hunted in Sumer. Enkidu, a wild man who became the friend of Gilgamesh, was referred to as the slayer of the wild ass and the leopard.[2]

It is well known that in 480 B.C. the Persian forces under Xerxes moved into battle against the Greeks in onager-drawn chariots,[3] and nearly two millenniums earlier the warriors of Sumer, in the southern Tigris-Euphrates Valley (later southern Babylonia), fought from chariots pulled by onagers. A sled mounted on four solid wheels is one of the characters in the Sumerian script.[4] It is the first picture we have of the wheeled vehicle, and it dates from about 3500 B.C. A Sumerian plaque uncovered by an archaeological expedition portrays a cart which appears to be constructed of wood and reeds and covered with an animal skin. The covering is probably onager hide, which was elastic and durable, as is the hide of its descendants. Two onagers are shown drawing the cart. The onager was doubtless used to transport the raw clay for the tablets. We can visualize him standing patiently while the raw clay from the deposits was loaded into panniers strapped to his sides, and then taking it to the tablet makers. Later he packed the heavy clay

Roping wild onagers. Scene from Ashurbanipal Library (669–626 B.C.), Nineveh. Courtesy of British Museum.

tablets to various regions under the jurisdiction of the city-state.

The ancient land of Sumer included the important city-states of Ur and Uruk; as mentioned above, the latter was the dominion of the legendary Gilgamesh. When and where the burro joined the Sumerian farmers is not known. It may be that the Sumerians arrived on the Tigris-Euphrates Plain during the latter part of the Neolithic age, between 6000 and 5000 B.C. They probably came from the mountainous region of southern Armenia on the north. The Sumerians were tillers of the soil, possessing livestock—goats, sheep, cattle, hogs, and asses. It may be that these people were the first to domesticate animals; certainly they expanded domestication. They may also have been the first to hitch the burro to a sled and later to chariots and wheeled carts.

The Sumerians left records of their use of the ass both in warfare and in peaceful pursuits. One vivid illustration is pictured on the

Domesticated onagers pulling four-wheeled war chariots in a scene on one side of an inlaid panel, Ur, Mesopotamia (3000–2700 B.C.). Courtesy of Iraq Museum of Antiquities, Baghdad (Trustees of British Museum).

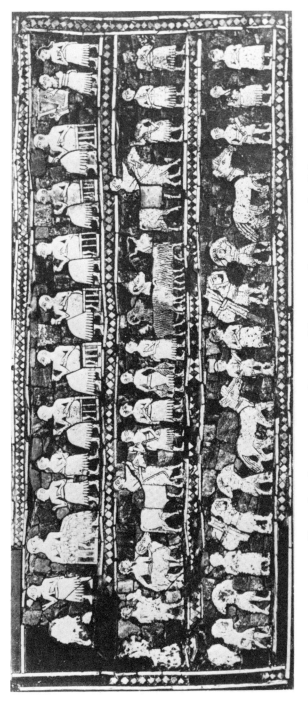

Domesticated onagers engaged in peaceful pursuits, the reverse side of the inlaid panel shown in the previous illustration. Courtesy of Iraq Museum of Antiquities, Baghdad (Trustees of British Museum).

Standard of Ur, a metal-and-shell mosaic which portrays the Sumerians' activities and may have served in the ceremonies of the
citizens of Ur. The standard, discovered in a royal grave in the
1920's by archaeologists under the leadership of Sir Leonard Wool-
ley, presents a panorama of the activities of the people. On one side
of the standard an onager is shown hitched to a war chariot. On the
other side he is pictured engaged in peaceful tasks more compatible with the nature of the domesticated animal.

The Sumerians, an innovative and creative people, may also have
invented the wheel. We know that in farming they used a combination plow and seeder. A tube was attached to a box that fed
seed into the furrow behind the plow, much as the lister drill oper-
ates today. The Sumerians hitched an ox or a burro, or both, to this
implement, which may also have been supplied with a rotating
shaft and wheel.

The Sumerians were grain and vegetable farmers living in a
communal society. Most of the land was owned by the temples.
The farmer owned his home and a small parcel of land. He also
owned the small tools of his trade. He grew barley and wheat. The
grain was cut with obsidian knives and threshed by burros and
oxen, who trampled the whole-grain stalks on circular harvest floors
of hard-packed earth. The farmer separated the grain kernels from
the chaff by tossing them up into a slight wind; the heavier grain fell
straight down, and the chaff blew to the side. At first the grain was
ground in hand-fashioned mortars made of volcanic rock. Later a
revolving stone wheel or roller moving around on a second, sta-
tionary stone was used. Burros or oxen pulled this heavy stone,
grinding the grain into flour. Monotonously, round and round they
would circle, usually blindfolded. In rural areas of the Middle East
and the Orient this method of threshing and milling is still common
today.

The Middle Eastern burro had other duties than those related to
agriculture. He helped in the construction of the ancient Sumerian
ziggurats. The ziggurat was a massive pyramidlike structure with

A modern scene in the biblical Middle East, comparable to one of Abraham's day. Reproduced by permission from *Atlas of the Bible*, by Luke Grollenberg.

an altar and idols at the top and wide stairways leading up from the ground below. The little four-footed animal carried the sun-dried bricks for these structures, as well as for houses, walls, and irrigation canals. He also provided milk, along with the goat, sheep, and cow (and later the mare and the camel).

With all his uses the burro became an important part of the economy. As early as 3000 B.C. the ancient Sumerians had established values for items of trade, including animals. Cattle, sheep,

Chariot drawn by four onagers, Mesopotamia, copper, ca. 2800 B.C. Now in the Iraq Museum, Baghdad. Courtesy of Oriental Institute, University of Chicago.

goats, hogs, and burros were used in the exchange system. Later copper, bronze, and silver were added.[5] A burro of good quality and strength could be purchased for fifteen shekels, or around fifteen dollars (incidentally, the amount I paid for Catrino, my burro, a few years ago—about which more later on).

The interest of ancient peoples in animals was reflected in their art. They were sketching, sculpturing, and painting the likenesses of animals thousands of years before they invented writing. They painted the walls of rock shelters and caves and sculptured figures

Silver and electrum rein ring with the figure of an onager on top. From the tomb of Queen Pu-Abi at Ur, ca. 2500 B.C. Courtesy of British Museum.

An inlay from Ur, ca. 2600 B.C. From H. W. Janson and Dora Jane Janson, *History of Art*, Englewood Cliffs, N.J., Prentice-Hall, Inc., 1964.

of the animals. They decorated their clay pottery with pictures and designs and thereby left us an enduring and universal key to their accomplishments. The peoples of the Middle East especially excelled in their portrayal of animals. An inlay from Ur, dating from about 2800 B.C., pictures a burro, a bear, and a deer performing on musical instruments (nearly four thousand years later in Europe the burro and the harp were similarly portrayed in medieval sculpture).[6]

The glory of Sumer faded, and about 2000 B.C. the warlike Elamites from the east and the Amorites from the west invaded the city-states. The new peoples brought their burros, and for two centuries they were sovereign. The Amorites had many interesting customs and institutions. Among them was the use made of the burro in contractual agreements, a practice established by the earlier Sumerians. The Amorites regarded the animal highly. To validate a major pact, they would sacrifice a burro in a ritual that solemnized the agreement.

Then from Babylon, itself of Sumerian origin, came the great King Hammurabi, leading his onager-drawn chariots of warriors to take Sumer and later the land of the Elamites. He made the city-state of Babylon the capital of his kingdom. Babylon was a religious center and one of the most famous cities of antiquity. It was situated on the Euphrates River just north of the modern town of Hilla, in central Iraq. It is likely that during the first several centuries of its existence the work animals of Babylon were the burro and the ox.

Perhaps the first formal attempt at a treatise on animal husbandry was written, in cuneiform, by a Sumerian. The work concerned the horse and not surprisingly, was written by a woman.[7] For many years after their arrival in the Middle East, horses were few in number. The horse was first mentioned on a clay tablet found in Sumer and dating from about 2000 B.C. It referred to the horse as "the ass of the mountain." The horse continued to be scarce for some time, chiefly because he was expensive to buy and to feed. In time his duties became chiefly those of war—pulling the chariot.

He was not employed for riding until later. Thus the horse became an animal of war, while the burro continued chiefly as one of farming, trade, and industry. When called upon to serve in war, the burro exerted his energies in packing equipment and supplies.

The camel too became identified with war, though ultimately his most important contribution lay in greatly extending the caravan routes; he could carry heavy burdens and go for long periods without water. But the burro was not supplanted—merely complemented. His usefulness continued.

The early peoples of the Twin Rivers area were close observers of their domesticated animals, much more so than the peoples who were to follow them. Perhaps they were closer to the period of domestication and were appreciative of the animal, whereas later generations took tame animals for granted. The famous Code of Hammurabi (written about 2000 B.C.) tells us of this interest. The code was a collection of laws, rules, and regulations, derived from the Sumerian Code of Ur-Nammu, of 2300 B.C. In the code were listed the fees to be paid for the hiring of an ox, a goat, or an ass. The ass, although smaller than the ox, was assigned an equal fee, twenty measures of grain; the goat, one measure. The code also prescribed the fees to be paid veterinarians for their services in ministering to sick animals. Commercial transactions were given major importance in the code. Among the articles of commerce were listed burro hides.

The Babylonians adopted many customs of the Sumerians and embodied them in the code. Among the rules was one prescribing that in the taverns dark beer was to be drunk by people engaged in heavy work; light-colored beer was to be served to those doing lighter tasks.[8] The ass delivered to the taverns the huge leather jars containing both.

The long strip of land at the eastern end of the Mediterranean Sea (now Syria, Israel, and Lebanon) was the meeting place of the domesticated African and Asiatic asses. From the Nubian

Desert by way of Egypt came *Equus asinus africanus*, with a bray and a length of ears superior to all. This species may have been supplemented by crossbreeding with the species from Somali, *Equus asinus somalicus*. In the Sinai Desert, in Syria, and in Israel these burros met two principal working species of Asiatic asses, the Syrian, *Equus hemonicus hemippus*, and the more widely distributed and better known *Equus hemionus onagra*. Crossbreeding of the African and Asiatic animals occurred in Egypt, as well as in Israel, Syria, and adjacent lands. Columella, a Roman writer on agriculture of the first century A.D., reported that onager males were being crossed with female African asses (incidentally, Columella also recommended the use of burro manure as a soil enricher). Petronius, a Roman of about the same period, mentioned that male onagers were crossed with female horses to produce mules.[9]

Observation of the present-day multitudes of working burros in the Middle East indicates that the African species was the dominant one. The ears, the volume of the voice, and the transverse stripe are everywhere evident. Crossbreeding began at least as early as 3000 B.C., and possibly even earlier. In Syria, Egypt, and Israel, traders and herdsmen met, exchanged wares, and "burro-traded." The blood of the African and Syrian animals and the onagers flowed in the burros that traversed the caravan routes running north, south, and east from Damascus, the Syrian "Pearl of the Plains."

Damascus is believed to be the oldest continuously populated city in the world. It was a thriving agricultural and commercial center when the biblical patriarch Abraham passed through on his way to the Promised Land. In ancient times it was known as the "City of the Asses" because of their numbers and importance to the city. It was to Damascus that they came, laden with vegetables, fruits, and other produce. There they were loaded with articles of trade and sent on caravans to distant markets.

Eight hundred miles stretch from the banks of the Euphrates River in Iraq to the Nile River in Egypt. While much of this re-

gion is desert, perhaps no other area compares with it in significance in the history of commerce. Caravans have crossed and criss-
crossed the vast expanse ever since animals were domesticated. The
burro was the first tamed animal to traverse the desert bearing
trading items. The hard hoofs of the little sun-loving animal cut the
trails to and from the trade centers. Many of those trails are still
in use today. The burro was also the first animal to be hitched to a
plow on farms in the scattered oases. True, the ox was domesticated early and pulled the plow and other heavy loads. However,
the larger animal was put to work in the river valleys and in areas
of greater rainfall than the desert regions enjoyed. He was not as
well adapted to drier places. He also ate more—a disadvantage in
regions of scanty food. Traditionally the burro has been the puller
of lighter farm implements and the bearer of loads, while the ox
has done much of the heavy pulling. Rabbinical literature prescribed that the ass was to carry loads; the ox, to drag them.

There is an old belief that animals (and also plants) talk to each
other and that man can understand them, provided his ears have
been licked by a serpent. One of the tales from the *Arabian Nights*
tells about a burro who lived well while his barnyard companion,
an ox, worked hard, pulling a plow in the fields. One night, following a hard day of toil, the ox complained to the burro about his
lot in life. The cagey burro suggested that the ox feign sickness.
The ox followed his advice. But the farmer overheard the burro's
advice, and the following morning he hitched the burro to the plow
in the ox's place. The burro, after a long day of hard work, had a
sore neck, and his legs were weary. He was all but exhausted when
the farmer turned him into the barnyard. The ox thanked him for
taking his place, adding that he had enjoyed the day of rest and
planned to play sick the next morning. The smart burro replied that
he had overheard their master say that if the ox was not feeling
well the next morning he would be taken to the butcher. The story
had its effect, for the ox was up early the coming morning, eager to
pull the plow.[10]

Banner bearers and trumpeters. From a Hariri manuscript, Baghdad, A.D.
1237. (The animal bearing the drums may be a mule rather than a burro.)
Courtesy of Bibliothèque Nationale, Paris.

The peoples of the Twin Rivers region were somewhat ahead of the Egyptians in metallurgy. The Armenians of Hayasa on the north were probably the first successful smelters of iron ore. Their Hittite relatives borrowed the process and maintained an advantage in war with their iron weapons. The burro was a part of these beginnings and developments in mining, carrying the prospector's primitive tools and supplies. With their superiority in metallurgy, the Hittites eventually conquered the Middle East and ruled supreme until the advent of the Phrygians.

The Phoenicians who lived in what is now Lebanon were merchants, traders, craftsmen, and seafarers. Their culture was especially active around 1000 B.C. They relied upon the pack burro on their trade routes and at their seaports. Similarly, the Cappadocians of Asia Minor relied on the burro for their trade in the poppy plant.[11] Burros packed women into the poppy fields; the women grooved the pods and collected the dried juice.

The ancient cities of the Middle East were walled for protection from siege. The walls posed a problem of water supply. Engineers solved the problem by having tunnels dug from inside the walls to distant springs. Burros were employed to carry the earth taken from the excavations. An extensive and impressive domestic water supply devised by the ancient peoples who inhabited northern Israel has been revealed by archaeologist Yigael Yodin. One day while Yodin's workmen were removing rubble at the bottom of a shaft, a twelve-foot-high tunnel was opened that had been sealed off since biblical times. About 850 B.C. engineers, scorning to depend on a spring, had dug deep to tap the natural ground-water reservoir. According to Yodin, the stonework shaft stairways, ten feet wide, sloped gently down to the tunnel mouth and were roomy enough to accommodate two columns of donkeys, one carrying water jars up from the bottom, the other returning with empty jars. If proposed restoration is carried out, tourists will one day be able to see this impressive work, including the underground passageway that strings of burros once trod.

A burro pulling a plow for a modern Palestinian Arab, a scene virtually unchanged from ancient times. From Nathan Ausubel, *Pictorial History of the Jewish People* (Crown Publishers, Inc., 1967). Reproduced by permission.

Unearthed ruins of old cities also indicate that civil engineers of the ancient Middle East took the pack burro into consideration when laying out city streets. The widths of the streets were set to allow two loaded pack burros to pass without obstructing each other's load.

As mentioned earlier, the Assyrians ultimately captured much of the Middle East. They reached their cultural peak between 750 and 612 B.C. They were specialists in war and masters of war psychology. Their advance agents, or infiltrators, were adept at propaganda. They warned of the invincibility of the Assyrians, stressing the brutal and terrifying techniques the army would employ if any resistance was made.

The Assyrians may have been the first to convert from war chariots to cavalry, thus gaining greater mobility. But the burden-bearing burro plodded on, doing his traditional work, regardless of the banner that happened to be flying in the breeze above his head. Some of his clan continued to pack wood, pull the plow, and bear trade items. Others were conscripted for military duties, bearing equipment and supplies for the campaigns, tents for the generals, wood for fires, and food for the soldiers.

Burros also helped Nebuchadnezzar II, the most illustrious ruler of the New Babylonian, or Chaldean, Kingdom, who held the throne from 605 to 562 B.C. The little animals did their share in Nebuchadnezzar's efforts to rebuild Babylon after he took it from the Assyrians. Burros also contributed their legs and backs to the building of the massive, more than fifty-mile-long wall surrounding the city. They helped with the building of the elaborate Hanging Gardens, a gift from Nebuchadnezzar to his Median wife, who was homesick for her land in the hills on the north. The laboring, braying burros of Babylon were well represented at the scene.

To the Greek historian Herodotus, Babylon was a fascinating city. One of the scenes that particularly interested him was the arrival of boats from Armenia. He described the boats as round, like shields, and made of hide. The framework was made of withies, and the skins were stretched taut on the underside. The boats were filled with cargo, mostly wine in palm-wood casks, and loaded on top of a filling of straw. The boats were carried downstream by the current, each boat guided by two men with paddles. The boats varied a great deal in size, the largest having a capacity of fourteen tons. Every boat carried at least one live burro, and the larger boats carried several of the animals. When the casks of wine and other cargo had been sold, the boats were dismantled, the straw and frames were disposed of, and then the hides were loaded on the burros for the return journey by land to Armenia. The strength of the current of the Euphrates was so strong that the boats could not be paddled or rowed upstream. Back in Armenia with their burros, the men repeated the boat-building process, again using the hides carried back by the burros.

A pack burro resting in a Turkish farmyard, 1970. Courtesy of Harry R. Varney, agricultural attaché, Ankara, Turkey.

Burro hide itself was prized in the Middle East from earliest times. It was tanned and shaped into footware. Shagreen, specially processed and tooled untanned leather, was made of burro hide (the word *shagreen* is derived from the Turkish *sāgri*, meaning "rump," and the best-quality shagreen comes from the rump of the burro). The process used in preparing shagreen is countless ages old. It consists of covering the hide with small round granulations by pressing seeds or grains of wheat into the hair side of the skin while it is still wet or green—freshly skinned or preserved in a moist state. The hide is then soaked to allow the kernels to expand. When the hide has dried, the roughness is scraped off, and the seed or grain has swollen into a relief effect. It is dyed various bright colors, with green dominating. Purses are one end-product of the craftsman's skill.

Burro hides were used for many other purposes. Perforated with holes, they served as sieves for separating grain from chaff. The hides became harnesses, parts of packsaddles, panniers, and other gear. The leather served as reinforcements for crates and furniture, seats for chairs, and hinges for swinging doors. Massive wall-smashing war machines made of heavy timbers were tied together with straps of leather cut from burro hide. These battering rams were used by the invading Crusaders in the Middle Ages during their wars with the Moslems. In fact, a one-armed torsion stone thrower was given the name "onager" because of its ruggedness.

Victorious Babylonian kings delighted in having their captives sewed up live in fresh or still-moist burro hides and then placed in the hot sun, where the hides slowly shrank, strangling or suffocating the victims. A strip cut from a tanned burro hide was used to whip criminals. Drumheads were made from the burro's hide, and flutes from his bones. Amulets of his hide and hair hung from the necks of children as charms to ensure that they would be strong, brave adults. Bile from the burro's body was sought as a cure for jaundice, and in some areas it was rubbed over the eyes of the blind to restore eyesight. Burro urine served as a disinfectant. Middle Eastern mothers rubbed the caul of a burro on the head of a newborn child to bring it good luck. The peasant used burro manure to enrich his farm plot. Burro droppings were used as fuel in lands where wood was scarce.

Many thousands of years have passed since the burro first made an appearance in the Middle East. His descendants' lives have not changed very much. He continues today, carrying burdens of all kinds, but none so precious as those two scarce necessities, water and wood. He is as familiar a sight as he was centuries ago, helping the women and peasant farmers of the region all the way to northern Iraq, the home of the Kurds.

The Kurdish women are stalwart and proud, and their lot is a hard one. They lead their burros long distances to secure firewood, spending the nights sleeping on the ground with curled ropes serving as pillows. While riding or walking behind the burros, often over rough trails, they spin yarn and sing. They sometimes spend two or three days on the journey, sitting around campfires at night, singing folksongs as they spin or make sandals, while their burros graze nearby.[12]

7. Bearing Religion

The burro was an important element in all three of the great monotheistic religions born in the Middle East—Judaism, Christianity, and Islam. The pastoral patriarchs who prepared the Scriptures recognized the importance of this helper of man at a time when desert herdsmen and livestock owners reckoned their wealth in numbers. The burros were an important part of this capital accumulation. One concordance to the Bible lists 153 references to the burro; no other animal is referred to as often. Genesis leads with 18 references; Exodus follows with 12.[1]

Because of their importance to the Jews, the animals were well cared for. Jewish law prescribed that both the ass and the ox were to rest on the seventh day, like their owners (Exodus 23:12). Jewish law also, perhaps inadvertently gave the burro further protection. Unlike other ancient peoples, the Jews did not eat the flesh of the burro; Mosaic law considered it unclean. But in dire emergencies such as the famine in Sumeria, a burro's head was sold for eighty pieces of silver (2 Kings 6:25), and presumably it was eaten.

The first burros mentioned in the Old Testament were those given to Abraham by Pharaoh (Genesis 12:16). A drought had driven Abraham, a desert chief, from Canaan into the Nile Valley. As he neared Egypt, Abraham cautioned his wife, Sarah, that because of her great beauty she must be known as his sister rather than as his wife. Otherwise he would be murdered by jealous men who desired her. The Egyptian princes noted her beauty and took her before Pharaoh, who, because he had been told that she was Abraham's sister, added her to his harem. The king paid Abraham well for her, giving him burros, sheep, oxen, and camels.

To punish Pharaoh for taking Abraham's wife, the Lord sent a plague to Egypt. When Pharaoh finally learned the truth, he returned Sarah to Abraham, reprimanded him for his lie, and ordered him to depart from Egypt.

Biblical lands were not enclosed with fences in ancient times (nor have they been since). Genesis 13:6–18 tells of a conflict between Abraham and his nephew Lot over pasture and water holes. To resolve the conflict, Abraham gave Lot his preference of nature's bounty. Lot chose the Plain of Jordan and its verdant river valley. Abraham took Canaan for himself. However, God told Abraham to look in every direction, saying that all the land that Abraham could see was his and that he was to claim it. Abraham and his family pulled tent stakes; packed the mohair tents, carpets, bedding, food supplies, and other items on burros, and headed toward the Plain of Mamre. There Abraham claimed large areas of grazing land for his herds.

Years later God tested Abraham's loyalty (Genesis 22:1–13), asking him to offer up his beloved son, Isaac, in sacrifice. Abraham obediently saddled a burro for the three-day journey to Mount Moriah. When Abraham reached the hill, he left the burro with two servants and climbed to the top. There he prepared the sacrificial altar. As everyone knows, of course, God spared Isaac, and a ram was sacrificed in his stead. According to Jewish tradition, the burro that served Abraham on the journey to Moriah was the same animal on which Moses placed his wife and sons and took them to Egypt (Exodus 4:20).[2]

In still another famous story in Genesis burros played an important role. Joseph, the son of Jacob, was sold into slavery in Egypt by his older brothers (Genesis 37:28). Joseph rose to power and influence with Pharaoh. Some years later, during a drought in Canaan, Jacob sent Joseph's brothers with strings of burros to Egypt to purchase grain (Genesis 42:25–26). Later a second trip was made. This time Jacob sent to Pharaoh's governor (unaware that Joseph was his long-lost son), presents of balm, honey, spices, myrrh, nuts, almonds, and gold in payment for grain (Genesis 43:1–11). In Egypt strings of pack burros were once more loaded with grain and other good things, and the return journey was started. However, this time, shortly after it departed, Joseph ordered the burro train and the Israelites to return for questioning about a silver cup missing from Joseph's home. It was found in a sack belonging to Benjamin, one of Joseph's brothers. At his home Joseph revealed that he had ordered the cup placed in the sack as a test. He also let his identity be known to the brothers who had sold him into slavery. All was forgiven, and Joseph sent his brothers on their way with "ten asses laden with the good things of Egypt, and ten she asses laden with corn and bread and meat . . ." (Genesis 45:23).

Another reference to the burro—one of the oldest and most famous in the Bible—is found in Numbers (22:21–33). Balaam, a prophet, was hired by a Moabite king to curse the Jews as they marched through Moab toward Palestine. But the Lord appeared to Balaam in the night and commanded him to bless the Israelites instead. Balaam, however, was unwilling to follow the Lord's instructions. The next morning he saddled his she ass and prepared to meet the Israelites. Along the way the burro Balaam was riding left the road and turned into a vineyard, mashing Balaam's foot against a wall. Balaam, exasperated, struck the burro repeatedly. The burro (presumably speaking in fluent Hebrew) defended herself by saying that she had seen an angel of the Lord. Then Balaam himself saw the angel and, convinced that he must obey the Lord, followed his orders.

According to Jewish tradition, Balaam's ass was a special one. She was carefully nourished and kept in a secluded place, for she was destined to play a special role in Jewish history: she was to carry the long-awaited Messiah, who would go forth to rule the earth.

Balaam's jenny and the serpent of Eden were the only two animals in the Bible that talked. However, there were other burros

The Burro Talking Back to Balaam, a portion of a painting by Rembrandt, A.D. 1626. Courtesy of Museé Cognacq-Jay, Paris.

that, according to legend, spoke in human tongue, among them a burro owned by the Queen of Sheba; and the burro of Bethpage who carried Jesus into Jerusalem.[3]

Another reference to the ass is famous in biblical lore. Samson, a judge of the Israelites, was endowed with supernatural strength. In a famous battle with the Philistines, Samson picked up the jawbone of an ass and put away a thousand of his enemies. This considerable effort left the warrior thirsty. He called upon God to provide him with water. God responded by cleaving a hollow place in the jawbone of the ass. Water gurgled forth, and Samson drank his fill and was revived.

According to Mosaic law, unlike things were not to be mixed. For example, barley and wheat were not to be planted in the same field; two animals of different species, such as the burro and ox, were not to be hitched together for plowing; and the crossbreeding of animals was prohibited. Though mules are often mentioned in the Bible, the Jews did not breed them. They were probably imported from the East. Nor did the horse figure largely in ancient Jewish economy. It was the ass whose importance, together with that of the ox, was sufficient to merit mention in the Ten Commandments: "Thou shalt not covet thy neighbour's house, thou shalt not covet thy neighbour's wife, nor his manservant, nor his maidservant, nor his ox, nor his ass, nor any thing that is thy neighbour's" (Exodus 20:17). The Pentateuch, the Talmud, and other collections of Jewish traditions and laws abound in reference to animal life, and again and again throughout Hebrew history and literature the burro is included. He was of enormous importance to this closely knit religious group.

The golden age of Israel dawned around 1,000 B.C., during the times of Saul, David, and David's son, Solomon. Those were energetic decades. Improved ways of doing things were developed. New techniques were applied in tilling. Burros pulled plows with improved points made of iron, and new tree- and vine-pruning knives came into use, as well as sickles for cutting grain. Excavated cities of the era are surrounded by massive fortified walls of stone and mud, large water-conveying tunnels, and other advanced construction. These structures vividly demonstrate the enormous labor required to build them, both human labor and that of animals—the ox and the burro.[4]

Saul, the first king of Israel and the ruler who inaugurated Israel's golden age, slipped into a state of melancholy. He sent word of his condition to Jesse, the father of David, who lived in Bethlehem. Thereupon Jesse loaded some burros with bread, wine, and kid goats and directed his talented young son, David, to mount another burro and take the gifts to King Saul. David was to remain, sing, and play his harp to relieve Saul's despondency (1 Samuel 16–20). David was successful and after many famous exploits was destined to become king himself.

In the meantime David became a desert raider. Abigail, the wife of Nabal, who lived in Carmel, acted to forestall David's plundering of her husband's herds of sheep. Without her husband's knowledge she had servants load pack burros with loaves of bread, skins of wine, and other food. She then mounted her riding burro and went to David's encampment, not far distant. She presented David and his followers with the gifts and asked them not to do harm to Nabal's domain. David, musician, poet, and lover, was impressed by Abigail's appeal—and perhaps by her beauty. He promised not to attack. Ten days later Nabal died. David asked Abigail to be his wife. She accepted (1 Samuel 25:2–42).

After Saul's death David was anointed king in Hebron. He consolidated the tribes of Israel and Judah, and upon his death his son, Solomon inherited a rich domain. Solomon, a wise man and an astute politician, raised taxes and demanded more tribute from subject peoples, rallying them around a grandiose public building project for the glory of God.

Because of Hebrew strictures against images and adornments, Israel had few craftsmen. Therefore Solomon secured skilled workmen from Phoenicia to design, build, and embellish the new temple at Jerusalem. His recruitment program brought together architects, engineers, carpenters, plumbers, masons, and unskilled laborers—153,000 in all (II Chronicles 2:17). Thousands of pack burros were used to haul timber from the forests of Lebanon. Solomon did not neglect his animals, however, for he had stables and corrals built for them. The temple was seven years in the building (959–52 B.C.), and when it was finished it was a wonder to behold.

Solomon had farflung economic and political interests, and gold flowed into his treasury in a steady stream. At ports on the Red Sea cargoes of valuable products from India, South Arabia, and Africa were unloaded. Spices, perfumes, ivory, jewels, and other merchandise were placed on pack burros by Jewish merchants with a monopoly on many inland trade routes. The trains of burros transported the products to trade centers throughout the Middle East. Solomon received tax revenue from many of these commercial transactions.

One of the most famous incidents in the Old Testament is the story of the visit the Queen of Sheba paid to Solomon to seek his counsel. Jewish tradition has it that she arrived in Palestine riding on a burro.

Man has always gained basic knowledge from observing the beasts, birds, and insects. Early man learned much about crafts from watching and imitating the creatures of his environment. Of special importance were the social and behavioral patterns of non-human life. Rabbinical literature points out that many advantages await the human being who thinks upon the chastity of the dove, observes the decency of the cat, copies the cheerfulness of the grasshopper, and emulates the honesty of the ant. Ants do not steal from each other. To borrow from the Hebrew, they would say, "We will not steal until the burro climbs a ladder."

Among the desert patriarchs Job was probably the most observant of the animal life about him. In Job 39:7–8 he reported God's description of the wild ass as one who preferred the open spaces, who "scorneth the multitude of the city, neither regardeth

he the crying of the driver" (the last comment an early acknowl-
edgment of the burro's preferred rate of travel). Job also under-
stood the effect of droughts on wild asses: "The range of the mountains is his pasture, and he searcheth after every green thing."

Drought was ever the specter hovering over the nomads and
their animals. The lack of sufficient rainfall meant that desert
dwellers and their herds preyed upon the farms in the river valleys.
The lush green fields of grain, legumes, and other crops growing on
irrigated land were (and are) irresistibly tempting to the drought-
starved animals from the parched desert.

Other ancients observed the habits of wild asses. Not only the
uninhabited regions but the ruins of once-great cities were their
habitation. As Isaiah commented: " . . . the palaces shall be for-
saken; the multitude of the city shall be left, the forts and towers
shall be for dens for ever, a joy of wild asses, a pasture of flocks . . .
(Isaiah 32:14). Conflicts of interest arose, principally over the
infringement of livestock from the desert upon the cultivated fields
of the peasant. The Scriptures make reference to the perils of
drought: "Because the ground is chapt, for there was no rain in the
earth, the plowmen were ashamed, they covered their heads. Yea,
the hind also calved in the field and forsook it, because there was
no grass. And the wild asses did stand in the high places, they
snuffed up the wind like dragons; their eyes did fail, because there
was no grass" (Jeremiah 14:4–6). The inference is that the animals
were blinded by sand and dust storms.

Fondness for animals and concern for their welfare permeate the
Old Testament and became part of the Judeo-Christian heritage, as
illustrated in medieval times in the custom of blessing animals. In
Rome on Saint Anthony's Day animals, including burros, were
blessed and sprinkled with holy water. Owners ranging from popes
to peasants led their animals to the altar.[5]

The custom of blessing animals spread over Europe and the
Western Hemisphere and continued into the modern times. Louis
Simond, who toured Italy and Sicily in the 1800's, mentioned seeing

domestic livestock—oxen, calves, horses, pigs, and burros—brought to the church to be blessed.[6] While living in Cuernavaca, Mexico, Mrs. Robert Louis Stevenson described attending the cathedral and observing the ritual of the blessing of the animals—burros, horses, cows, dogs, cats, and fowl. The animals had been dyed brilliant colors for the occasion.[7]

With some variations the ritual still prevails in Latin-American countries, though church blessings are less common today. On June 24, Saint John's Day, the people paint their animals bright colors and place colored cloths and pompons on the necks and horns of the smaller ones. These embellishments are usually added at the owners' homes and are a form of blessing to assure fertility in the coming year. The blessing of animals, a custom brought to the southwestern United States by the Spaniards, gradually ceased. Today, however, there are signs of a revival of this medieval ceremony in areas of Spanish influence and culture.

Other practices relating to animals established during biblical times were carried over to the Middle Ages. One was the animal trial. Precedents were written into Jewish law: "If an ox gore a man or a woman, that they die: then the ox shall be surely stoned . . ." (Exodus 21:28). Animal trials were common during the Middle Ages in Europe. The trials were formal, and the proceedings were serious. Both prosecuting and defense lawyers argued their cases. In time two schools of thought developed. Churchmen held that trials of animals for misdeeds were valid because they were based upon long-established custom that dated from the Old Testament. The other theory held that animals do not have intelligence and that it was therefore ludicrous to bring them to trial. The latter theory placed the authority of the church in jeopardy. Then the question arose, Could the biblical argument prevail when the church anathematized those whom it did not undertake to baptize? (Perhaps a wise omission on the part of the church fathers. A burro hates to enter water, and a burro baptism requiring immersion would have been an event to witness.)

Nativity (illuminated page from an antiphonary), Siena, Italy, fourteenth century. Note the donkey in the stable behind the newborn Jesus. Courtesy of Montreal Museum of Fine Arts.

Flight into Egypt, etching by Claude Henri Watelet (1718–86), after Rembrandt. Courtesy of Museum of Art, University of Oklahoma.

Yet the practice continued into the eighteenth century. French court records between 1542 and 1741 indicate that 332 hogs, 18 horses, and 8 burros were convicted of crimes.[8]

The burro is important in Christian tradition and legend, as well as in the New Testament accounts of the life of Christ. Countless paintings show Mary riding an ass on the journey to Bethlehem, in the stable, and on the flight to Egypt after Jesus' birth.

The road to Bethlehem has been trod by countless burros through the centuries. But it was an American of the twentieth century who immortalized one of the little animals, who served a very special purpose on that ancient road almost two thousand years ago.

In 1947, Charles Tazewell wrote what was destined to become

an enduringly popular Christmas story, *The Small One*. The story is about an emaciated but proud little burro and his loving boy protector, Pablo. The Small One had grown old and weak from long years of toil, and Pablo's father decided to have him slaughtered. It fell to Pablo to take the old burro to the slaughterhouse. Pablo, saddened by his mission, desperately sought an alternative. He took The Small One to the horse auction, but only jests and laughter greeted his pleas for a kind buyer for the burro. Finally, after continued rebuffs, a man on the street paid Pablo one piece of silver for the animal. The man assured Pablo that he would take good care of The Small One—and that he was badly needed, for he was to carry the man's wife, Mary, to Bethlehem.

The appealing story has become a favorite of readers and audiences at Yuletide. For eight years it was broadcast annually on Kate Smith's radio program, with Ethel Barrymore as the first narrator. In time it was recorded, with Bing Crosby as principal narrator.

The story of Jesus' birth in the stable in Bethlehem has given rise to countless legends and traditions. Legend has it that an ox and an ass were in the stable when Jesus was born and that at midnight every Christmas Eve the oxen and burros of the Christian world kneel in their stables.

In his early years as a carpenter Jesus doubtless owned a burro for riding and transporting the tools of his trade. Countless paintings and sculptures portray Christ astride a burro. And, of course, the most famous of all New Testament burros is the ass on which Jesus rode in his triumphal entry into Jerusalem on Palm Sunday. Jesus chose a burro to ride to signify his humility: "Behold, thy King cometh unto thee, meek, and sitting upon an ass . . ." (Matthew 21:5).

In later years Church dignitaries, politicians, and businessmen imitated Jesus' ride. Sculptured reliefs on public buildings show men of importance riding burros to impress the common people and to symbolize peace and good will.[9] This pattern has lasted to

Entry into Jerusalem. Portion of a painted manuscript. Armenian, fifteenth century. Courtesy of Montreal Museum of Fine Arts.

the present day. On Palm Sunday and on Easter burros are used in ceremonies throughout Christian lands. A rider with a beard and wearing clothing simulating Christ's is often a part of the ritual. Tradition holds that the cross on the withers of the burro appeared because Jesus chose him to ride. Another tradition claims that Christ's burro is one of the three burros permitted in heaven, the other two being Balaam's ass and the burro the Queen of Sheba rode when she visited Solomon.

Unfortunately, Jesus' entry into Jerusalem was caricatured by early enemies of the Christians. Tacitus and other Roman writers accused the Jews of worshiping the ass.[10] Later the Christians were

Entry into Jerusalem, Palm Sunday. From an early manuscript. Courtesy of
Freer Gallery of Art, Washington, D.C.

also accused of the practice. Tertullian wrote that one day a man
appeared on the streets of Carthage, carrying a figure with the
hoofs and ears of a burro, clothed in a toga and bearing a sign "The
God of the Christians Begotten by an Ass."

Fragments of terra cotta illustrate the calumny of onalatry, or
ass worship, of which the Christians were accused. One fragment,
dating from the first century A.D. and discovered in 1881 in Naples,
shows a Christian boy worshiping a crucified figure with the head

Entry into Jerusalem. Portion of diptych portraying scenes from the life of Christ. French, fourteenth century. Courtesy of Montreal Museum of Fine Arts.

of a burro. Another fragment, discovered in Syria, represents Christ with the ears of a burro and with a book in his hand.

Other corruptions arose. The ass, and also the pig, came to be symbols of heresy or of the devil. A fresco, probably executed in the third century A.D., in the Catacomb of Praetextatus (near a main highway leading into Rome), shows Christ as the Good Shepherd protecting his herd of sheep from the evil influence of these two animals.[11]

But these corruptions, inspired by malice or ignorance, did not prevail, and though the burro was destined to remain an object of scorn and abuse for countless generations, man never ceased to call upon him. From the times of Christ and Mohammed the burro has carried disciples, priests, and missionaries, bearing religion throughout the world.

Out of Syria comes an old story about a great sheik, Ali, who maintained a holy tomb. The tomb, which supposedly contained the remains of an ancient, unnamed prophet, was simply called the Tomb of the Prophet. A lamp burned on the mount both day and night.

Travelers, invalids, cripples, rich, and poor stopped before the tomb. There they rested, meditated, and paid homage to the venerable one. Over the years Ali became wealthy from the offerings left at the tomb. One day a servant of Ali wearied of his job and asked permission to leave and seek new adventures. Ali, an understanding master, consented and gave the servant a burro for his journey.

Many miles away and with the passage of time, the burro died. The saddened owner covered the grave of his faithful friend with sand and stones. While the servant lay grief-stricken on the mound, a wealthy hadji (pilgrim) came upon the scene and, believing the grave to be the tomb of a wise man, left a sum of money. An idea was born in the servant's mind; his tears dried. He remained at the burial place, and when travelers stopped, he referred to the mound as the Tomb of the Prophet. His scheme caught on. After a lapse of time he became rich from the money left at the tomb, and the sacred place became well known across the desert expanse. At last it attracted the attention of the servant's former master, Sheik Ali, who paid a visit to the tomb. The keeper, seeing his former master, was stricken with guilt at his deed and confessed what he had done. The great sheik was sympathetic and forgiving. He told his former servant not to worry, adding that the tomb that he himself had maintained actually contained a burro, the father of the "prophet"

Saint Francis in Ecstasy, by Giovanni Bellini. Note the donkey in the upper-left portion of the painting. Courtesy of the Frick Collection, New York.

in the second tomb.[12] And so the "philosopher of the desert" became a prophet of the desert.

According to Moslem legend only a few nonhumans are allowed in the Garden of Allah, Islam's heaven. They are Jonah's whale; the ram that was substituted for Isaac; a lapwing (crested plover) be-

longing to the Queen of Sheba; an ox belonging to Moses; the dog
of Kratin, or Katmir of the Seven Sleepers; Al-Borak, Mohammed's
horse; the camel of the prophet Saleh, Solomon's ant; Noah's dove;
Balaam's ass; and Mohammed's burro. In the list of animals only
the burro appears twice. Perhaps rightly so, for the burro contributed to the spread of Islam and the territorial gain of the Moslems.
Wealth—extreme wealth—flowed through the hands of the Moslems, especially to the caliphs (the successors of Mohammed), and
the emirs, who served in administrative positions. Burros carried
silk from China, porcelain and steel from India, glassware and em-
broidery from Aleppo, and cotton goods, as well as innumerable
other items of trade, from everywhere. They became important
agents in the Moslems' strivings for conquest of land and religious
conversion, an onrush that began in the two desert towns of Mecca
and Medina, in western Arabia. From these two holy cities the followers of Islam made their influence felt through the entire Middle
East, eastward into India, across Persia, into Turkey, and southward from Mecca to cover all of the Arabian Peninsula, crossing
the Straits of Eden and embracing virtually all of eastern Africa,
including Egypt. Northern Africa accepted the fiery Crescent, and
its Moors, encouraged by the Arabs, crossed the Straits of Gibraltar
and ruled the people of Spain for several centuries. Sicily also heard
the muezzin's call to prayer.

For more than thirteen centuries now the burro has also heard
the muezzin's call. Five times a day Islam's followers respond, their
first call sounding when daylight is just beginning to break—when
it is light enough for one to distinguish a black strand of wool from
a white one. The last prayer comes at bedtime. Neither is of much
concern to the Moslem burro. Generally the first call occurs before
his toil begins, and the last after the day's work is done. But he may
well look forward to those that fall within the day. While his master
is performing his ablutions and praying, the burro gets to rest his
tired body.

The Koran does not stipulate a specific day of rest. It does require an extra prayer on Friday, Islam's holy day. However, Friday is also a market day, and so there is no rest for the burro. He must carry the peasant's produce to market, and perhaps also the wife and the children. He does, however, snatch some time to rest while his master visits and exchanges news in the *souk*, or marketplace. On the return trip the burro packs the purchases of the day —coffee, tea, rice, dates, and perhaps some cloth. Riding or leading the burro, the Arab may "count his beads," ninety-nine in number, using the various names assigned to Allah (legend has it that only the camel knows the one-hundredth, but he won't tell).

The Encyclopedia of Islam devotes much space to *Al-Himar*, the burro, in both the wild and the domestic state. The wild jacks are described as jealous creatures. They reduce competition in the herd by seeking out the newborn males and emasculating them with their teeth. The pregnant jenny, aware of the danger, finds seclusion in remote places to bear her young. After the colt's hoofs are hard enough to allow him to run over the gravelly plain, the mother returns with him to the herd.

It is reported that some Arabs are ashamed to ride on burros. They also object to his voice, saying that it is repulsive, that dogs howl in pain when they hear it, and that the burro brays when it sees the devil (whereas the rooster crows when it sees an angel).[13] Perhaps these Arabs never heard that their prophet, Mohammed, had no such aversion to the animal. Islam's Messenger had one of his own, and furthermore he rode him. The name of his burro was Yofur.[14]

When one considers the traditional speed of a burro, it is doubtful that Mohammed was riding Yofur when he fled from enemies on the day he ducked into a cave not far from Mecca. Mohammed was saved by a spider that quickly wove a web over the entrance to the cave. Shortly thereafter, when his enemies reached the entrance of the cave, they saw the web and reasoned that no one had entered or the web would have been broken. They continued looking elsewhere. The spider, whose quick work saved Mohammed's life, is given a special place in Islamic legend, as are other animals. Mohammed was sympathetic toward animals, birds, and insects. Legend has it that doves perched on his shoulder and ate wheat from his ear. Burros have been carrying pilgrims to Mecca since the time of Mohammed, as for centuries before the birth of Islam they took worshipers from the desert to the innumerable shrines and idols of Arabia. One can visualize the animals plodding along in the heat and sand, heads lowered, ears drooping, crossing an unfriendly desert, bearing the poor, the crippled, the aged. Burros also carried the hafiz—those persons who knew the Koran and the Hadith (the body of Islamic traditions) by heart. These reverent ones would often sit crossways on their burros discussing Islam while the animals rested.

Not only has the burro performed his duties in Hebrew, Christian, and Moslem lands, but he has taken part in the spread of other religious sects as well, including the Zoroastrians of Persia, the Buddhists of China, and the Hindus and Parsis of India. The Parsis' religious code, alone among the eastern religions, directly enjoins humane and considerate treatment of all animals, including burros.

Religions have always had sects and schisms. Abu Said Abi'al Khayer (A.D. 967–1049) was a Persian ascetic who advocated Sufism, a mystical branch of Islam. Abu Said's teachings attracted ardent followers. Before receiving his blessing, they smeared the manure of his burro over their faces.[15]

Throughout Moslem history the burro played an important, if sometimes shameful, part. In the Middle Ages, after the Crusaders captured Palestine and adjacent areas, one contingent turned southward. Their purpose was to raid Mecca. They moved down the west side of Arabia, very likely using burros to carry equipment and supplies. As the Crusaders approached Medina, the Moslems rode into the ranks of the invaders and routed them. All but a few were massacred, and only one Crusader escaped. Two of the captured men were escorted to Mecca and executed there. Some were placed on burros, facing backwards, and sent on a long journey to Cairo. This was a typical form of humiliation forced upon nonbelievers. As late as 1890 a Jew of Morocco, a Moslem country, was not permitted to ride any animal except the burro. He was also forced to face toward the tail of the animal and to remove his sandals.[16]

The already burdened burro also became entangled in the doctrine of the transmigration of souls. The ancient Armenians of western Asia had a custom of sacrificing a burro at the grave of an ancestor of a living person who owed an overdue debt. It was be-

A Pilgrim on His Travels, a Buddhist cave painting, ca. A.D. 660, western China. Courtesy of Tun-huang Institute. Reproduced in *A Pilgrim on His Travels*, by Basil Gray (Faber and Faber, London, 1959). Reproduced by permission.

lieved that if the debt was not paid the soul of the man's ancestor
would pass into the sacrificed burro.[17] Needless to say, the practice
placed tremendous pressure on the delinquent debtor—a sort of
Armenian merchants' credit bureau. (In at least one Jewish tradition the burro fared better than the Armenian animal. This knowing burro did all that he could to encourage the prompt payment
of a tithe on a crop: he refused to eat the fodder until his owner
paid the tithe.)

The burro continues to bear man's sins. On the rugged volcanic
island of Santorin, about sixty miles north of Crete, tourists explore
the island on burros. (These animals may well be descendants of
burros brought to the island during the Mycenean age more than
three milleniums ago.) Every day the burros pack visitors up a
steep hairpin road leading to a mountaintop village and then down
again. The natives of Santorin explain that the burros spend their
lives bearing sightseers up and down the mountain because they
are the repositories of transmigrated souls of dead sinners who are
now working off their purgatory. The burro toils for the sins of man.

So far I have dwelled on the burro's role in religions as they were
and are practiced in the East. The American Southwest has rich
religious traditions, too, and from those traditions two tales have
arisen, in both of which the burro plays his role.

The first story takes place in Santa Fe, New Mexico, in the 1870's.
Our Lady of Light Chapel had just been completed. Mother Magdalen, mother superior of the Loretta Sisters, was concerned about
the high, isolated choir loft. The sisters used a tall ladder to climb
to it, but they had to make the climb long before services to preserve
their dignity. Experienced builders had told Mother Magdalen that
no carpenter on earth could build a stairway up to the loft. There
was not enough room for the structure, they told her. But she and
the other sisters kept praying for a solution.

One day someone knocked at the door. When the door was
opened, there stood a burly old man with a bearded face and frost-

colored hair. Behind him was a heavily loaded burro. The man told
the sisters that he had heard that a carpenter was wanted at the
chapel. He was of that craft and had his own tools. The sisters invited the man to consider the problem. He stood silently, looking
up at the choir loft twenty-five feet above and then down at the
scant floor space available. Finally he said that he would begin
work as soon as he had provided for his burro.

The old carpenter did not give his name. He worked alone, and
his tools were few and simple. The sisters wondered what kind of
staircase he would build. After a few days he departed with his
burro for a load of lumber. The sisters could not wait; they peeked
through the door but could not understand what they saw. Three
steps were completed—but they were facing the side wall, not the
loft!

The carpenter and his burro returned, and for eight months the
chapel echoed to the sawing and hammering of the mysterious
craftsman. Then one morning there was silence. The carpenter had
vanished. He had asked for no pay, no expression of gratitude.
When Mother Magdalen saw their memorial—the impossible stairs
—she was awed. The staircase was designed in a spiral. As it rose,
it completed two 360-degree turns. No central pole or other means
of support was visible. The stairway seemed to be floating. She sank
to her knees and began counting the steps . . . 29, 30, 31, 32, 33—one
for each year of Christ's life!

Today the stairs are still intact. Banisters were added later. But
the work remains a masterpiece and a monument to prayer and
devotion.[18]

There was once a burro with a very cruel master. He was given
only stale food and water and not enough of those, and he was
overworked and beaten every day. He never got enough rest at
night. At best he was always hungry, thirsty, and tired. On Christmas Eve his master rode him a long distance to a Christmas party.
The burro had been ailing for some time and was very sick that

An Algerian burro, 1971. Courtesy of Louis Giménez.

night, but that made no difference to his owner. By constant beating he forced the burro to stagger on. At their destination he tied the animal to the hitching rail and went in to the party. The burro stood still, trying to rest for the trip home by not moving a single muscle, but he just grew more tired. Resting did not seem to help a bit. The night grew colder. Suddenly he heard a loud, musical bray, and out of the darkness came a *burro platero*, a silver burro. His coat was the color of a newly minted silver dollar and just as shiny even in total darkness. His eyes were like twinkling stars, his bray was like the laughter of children at play, and his hoofs made a musical tinkle every time they touched the ground.

"Come with me," the silver burro brayed.

"I cannot," said the sick burro. "I must wait to take my master home."

"Come with me," urged the silver burro.

"I cannot, I am too tired, and besides I am tied to this rail."

"Come with me," the other insisted, and finally the old burro followed. He walked away as if the rope were not there. The saddle slid from his back, and with it his great weariness left, and he felt wonderful. He bounded across the country with the silver burro and actually enjoyed it. Suddenly there seemed to be many more stars than before, not only in the sky but on the ground, all huge and bright, some silver and some gold.

All at once, night was gone and it was day. He was in a field of belly-deep green grass, stretching to the horizon in all directions, with countless springs of cold, crystal-clear water. Thousands of burros were there. There was no sun, just light that seemed to come from everywhere. It was a heavenly place.

But who was the silver burro so different from the rest? The burros nearby had common burro colors, but the silver burro was very glossy, more so than the finest racehorse. The burro's curiosity got the best of him and he asked, "Who are you? Where are you from?" The silver burro brayed like the laughter of children and said, "I am the burro of Belén [Bethlehem]. I went to Belén with San José and Santa María, carrying the virgin on my back. I was there when the Niño Cristo was born."

The Christmas party lasted until after midnight. The burro's owner sang and danced, ate his fill of good food, and drank more tequila than he should have. When he came out, he found his burro lying dead where he had tied him. His starved, worn-out body was cold and stiff, but the silvery burro of Bethlehem had taken his spirit to burro heaven.[19]

8. Burros, Camels, and Some Arabs

Arabia is a huge peninsula, an immense plateau that rises to 12,000 feet near the Red Sea on the west and then slopes through escarpments, hills, gravel plains, and sand dunes to the Persian Gulf on the east. It is about 1,250 miles wide and 1,400 miles long. It is chiefly desert country. Several sheikdoms and independent countries are scattered along the coast of Arabia, but Saudi Arabia makes up most of the land mass. Rub' al Khali, the "Great Sandy Desert," covers most of southeastern Arabia.

A Saudi Arab.

Wild asses once roamed over the Arabian terrain and drank from natural water holes, for permanent streams of running water are nonexistent. The wild asses were eliminated by hunters long ago.

Scattered across the peninsula are isolated farming oases. There in humble clay-brick houses live the Moslem farmers, closely clustered near a village centering around a *souk* and a mosque. Both are scenes of great activity on Friday, the chief day of both worship and commerce.

It is in and around these farming communities that the domesticated Arab burro is most often seen at work. He is the beast of burden for the Moslem farmer, while the camel serves the desert Bedouin and the caravan trader. The horse is of little importance in the desert economy of Arabia.

Pack burros in the Tassili, Sahara Desert, Algeria, 1971. Courtesy of U.S. Information Service, Algiers.

It is not known which of the work and pack animals was first domesticated in Arabia. In the northern part the burro appears to have been serving man much longer than the camel; in the central region the camel may have been packing for man before the burro. Along the southern fringe of the peninsula both animals were domesticated very early, and some persons believe that the dromedary (the one-humped species of camel) may have been domesticated by dwellers of central Arabia as early as the fourth millennium.[1]

Records can be as deceptive as a desert mirage. Evidence in the form of stone implements found in the southern and central parts of the peninsula indicates that man was chipping away there one hundred thousand years ago. However, adverse changes in climate and the resultant migrations of the culture destroyed most clues to man's prehistory on the peninsula. The desert Bedouin, with his black tent and herds of camels, moved up and down the wadis, leaving few traces for archaeologists.

In ancient times the Minaeans, a Semitic race, ruled in the southwestern region of the peninsula. This civilization was overthrown by the Sabeans about 650 B.C., who also conquered portions of eastern Africa across the Red Sea. The Sabeans used both the camel and the burro. The Nabateans, Arabs who ruled a kingdom east of Palestine, were masters of the great caravan terminal of early Arabia Petraea in the northwest and monopolized the lucrative trade routes extending into central Arabia. Burros, as well as camels, have been carrying packs on those sandy trails since long before the Christian era began.

Frankincense, the resin of the Boswellia, a tree of south Arabia, Africa, and India, was eagerly sought by merchants of the Middle East and of Rome. When the resin is burned, it gives off a fragrant odor. In ancient times great quantities of frankincense were used in temples and on funeral pyres. The resin was used also in medicines, in cosmetics, and in embalming preparations. To supply this market, strings of burros plodded to the hills, were loaded with resin collected from the forty-foot-tall trees and packed in skins and returned to the trade centers. Camels also served in this trade.

Coffee was first cultivated in southern Arabia. The coffee bean and the drink made from it are surrounded with legend. One tradition has it that the drink was revealed to Mohammed in a dream by the angel Gabriel. Another tale—and one that is commonly accepted (because great discoveries are often made by accident)—is the story of a ninth-century Arab goatherd named Kaldi. One day as he was tending his flock he noticed that they were frisking about in ungoatlike antics. Kaldi observed that the goats were eating berries of an evergreen bush. He tasted them himself and soon was experiencing a feeling of exhilaration and mild intoxication. He soon dashed off to spread the word of his discovery. A variant of this tale claims that Kaldi was a part-time mullah, or teacher, and that he gave the berries to his followers during evening devotions to keep them awake.

Coffee roasting and brewing spread rapidly throughout the Middle East, and by the sixteenth century it was appearing in European countries, shipped from Middle Eastern ports, to which it had been carried by burros. Coffee is still one of the most important burdens borne by Arabian burros.

The oil hidden under the sands of the desert countries was first discovered in the 1930's and after World War II became Arabia's most valuable export. Black gold has modified the pattern of life for many persons, particularly in coastal towns in oil-production areas and in a few of the population centers of the interior. However, for the desert Bedouins, the farmers, and the caravan traders, their daily lives move along in old, well-established customs. Burros, camels, goats, sheep, and a few cows remain important to their existence.

On the farms of the desert oases burros have among other tasks the job of "manning" the irrigation pumps. It is a monotonous duty that the burro has performed throughout the Middle East ever since the wheel came into use and man devised irrigation to water

Three white burros drawing irrigation water near Hofuf, Al-Hasa Province, Saudi Arabia, 1955. The practice still prevails. Photograph by author.

his croplands. The typical Arabian well is an open, hand-dug well, twenty-five to seventy-five feet deep. At the deeper wells, such as those in the Hejaz, three or more burros and sometimes camels are used. A wheel about three feet in diameter, usually made from the trunk of the date tree, is placed over the well on an axle crosspiece ten or twelve feet high. A groove or channel is provided for the pull rope, which is made of twisted *leif,* the fiber that grows around the trunk and between the *jareeds,* or branches, of the date palm. On the lip of the water container are fastened two or more short ropes that are tied to the pull rope. Another rope is tied to the bottom of the container and adjusted so that, as the burro pulls the container to the surface of the well, the rope tightens, tilts the container, and discharges the water into a hollowed-out date-palm log or a rock-lined ditch.

Also attached to the bottom of the container is a weight that pulls it below the surface of the water for refilling. The container may be a goatskin or, more recently, a used inner tube of a truck tire or a five-gallon oil can. The experienced burro knows within an inch or two where to stop, turn, and return to the well for the next trip. His harness is crude, made of straps, ropes, and scraps of cloth. More often than not, a small boy or girl has the chore of keeping the burro working—not leading or driving him back and forth, for he knows what to do, but keeping him working. If he pauses to rest, his youthful master will send a clod or a stick his way.

During the summers additional water is needed, and night shifts operate at the wells. The hubs turning on the wooden shafts create hard, smooth surfaces for both the wheel and the axle, and the resulting friction produces loud squeaks as the wheels revolve (they are never lubricated). This condition created a problem one night for two foreign oil-company employees who were camped near a date grove where the night shift was underway. The continuous squeaking of the wheel kept them from sleeping. Disgusted, they arose, dressed, took a squirt can full of oil and headed for the well. One climbed the wheel-supporting framework and gave the inside of the hub a good lubrication. The squeaking stopped—but so did the sleep of the Arab farmer in his home nearby. He arose and went out to see why his night-shift boy and burro were not working. To his surprise, they were. The boy told his master what had happened. The following morning the farmer proceeded to clean the oil from the wheel so that the squeak would continue to play its historic role—to notify the owner, day or night, that all is well.

The Saudi Arabian burro toils in a "three-H" code of existence—hot, hard, and humiliating. His lot is to be born hungry in a harsh environment and to remain poorly fed throughout his laborious life, seldom if ever enjoying a rewarding meal. While he strives on the little farms, pumping water for the grain and alfalfa fields, the vegetable plots, and the thirsty date trees (the Arab farmer has a saying: "The date tree likes to sit with its feet in cool water"), he is permitted to partake but sparingly of the fruits of his labors. He

is allowed only enough to hold his abused hide over his tired bones
and to provide enough tough sinew to keep him going. His spirit
is gone; he is far removed from his freedom-loving ancestors who
once roamed the same sands.

In the mid-1940's, King Abdul-Aziz Ibn Saud of Saudi Arabia
ordered his farms modernized. Tractors replaced animals, and the
burro's life became somewhat easier. But many of the king's employees, numbering about one thousand, continued to ride their
burros to work in the mornings. The animals were tethered on the
banks of irrigation canals and ditches to nibble at any herbage that
might grow a half-inch or so above the surface. Competition was
keen among the burros for what little vegetation was to be had
at the edges of the king's property. After work, on days off, and
even, unless they were closely supervised, during work the burros'
owners would dig up the roots of the native grasses for their animals. After shaking the soil from the stubble and roots, they would
tie them into large bundles and place them on the burros for the
homeward journey.

One of the burros was a little white one. At some time early in
his life he had fractured a front leg near the knee joint. Apparently
little or no attention was given to the injury, for the white burro's
leg was bowed and crooked, though it did not hamper his work, or
inspire mercy in his hard-driving master. The foreign supervisor
at the farm, who became fond of him, called him Crooked Knee.
In digging the grass roots along the canal banks the Arabs sometimes endangered the canal's water-holding capacity. Crooked
Knee's owner had been warned a time or two about it. One day the
supervisor drove by in a pickup, stopped, and got out to reprimand
the Arab again. An argument ensued—partly because of the language barrier. At one point the Arab raised his *mahaush* (sickle)
in the air to punctuate his remarks. He was standing on the bank
with his back to the canal, and the temptation was too great: a
quick, slight push keeled the Arab backward into the five-foot deep
water. He went under and came up sputtering, spitting water,
waving the sickle, and swearing. Crooked Knee had been standing

White burros on the royal family farm, Saudi Arabia, 1955. Photograph by author.

quietly with his head lowered, observing the scene. When his master landed in the canal, Crooked Knee merely bent one ear forward, but his sad, sunken eyes seemed to sparkle with delight. For a brief interval in a lifetime of one of monotonous days, Crooked Knee was avenged—and, one likes to think, amused.

Other foreigners have had their encounters with Arabs and their donkeys. In the 1950's the International Locust Control Mission was invited to the Hejaz to conduct a campaign against the locusts. One day an Englishman with the mission was spreading

Yemen burros, 1971. Courtesy of U.S. Foreign Service, Sanaa, Yemen Arab Republic.

locust poison in wheat bran when the local emir and a farmer came to him and reported that a burro belonging to the farmer had died from eating the poisoned bran. The Englishman protested that this could not be true, for the formula used in the mixture was not injurious to men or animals. However, the emir and the farmer were persistent and demanded that he pay for the burro. They climbed into his Land Rover and took him to where the burro lay. They pointed as evidence to some of the poisoned bran mixture in the burro's mouth. The Englishman said that perhaps the emir would be satisfied that the bran was not the cause of the animal's death if he himself would eat some in the emir's presence. The emir agreed. The Englishman then took a tin plate from his camping equipment, filled it with the bran, and ate it. The emir was convinced. The Englishman was sure that the Arab farmer had placed a handful of the bran in the dead burro's mouth to recover his financial loss. The poor burro had most likely died from starvation and overwork.

Ibn Saud was a colorful king, and he ruled forcefully from his palace at Riyadh. Once in 1949 he ordered the head farmers on his farms fifty miles south to send him a large supply of watermelons. Of course, the farmers could not refuse the king's bidding, but they were resentful about what they considered an unreasonable request. Mohammed Sedais, their spokesman, framed a reply to the king: "Your Majesty, we are already working as hard as donkeys to supply Your Majesty's needs." The old warrior shot back the terse command, "Send more *hub hub* [watermelons], or I'll come down to my farms with my sword and cut the tails off you donkeys."

Al-Hasa, a district in Saudi Arabia, is a center for the breeding of white asses. In early times they were sent to Mecca (another breeding center) for riding purposes and for ceremonial occasions. Muscat and Oman, a sultanate on the Gulf of Oman, was also famous for its breed of large white burros. It was from that country that until recently the sultans of Zanzibar obtained the white asses used in royal processions.[2]

There is a gypsy tribe of Arabia, the Suluba (or Slaib) that is not of Islam but is believed to be Christian. The people of the tribe neither ride nor own camels but employ only burros. They are smiths, knife and saw sharpeners, and tinkers. They roam from place to place offering their services. In early times they did not engage in the holy wars but were called upon to make and repair swords and other equipment.

The Sulubas are best known for the white asses they breed. The burros are noted for their hardiness, and ability to withstand thirst. The Sulubas present a colorful picture as they cross the sand dunes riding and leading their white burros.

In contrast to the desert farmer, the true Bedouin does not generally own burros, and he scoffs at those who do. His is a camel-oriented culture. The short, wiry Bedouins of Arabia are intelligent, freedom-loving, and extremely resourceful. They must be so, to endure and prosper in the hot, harsh, barren desert expanses. In ancient times these Semitic tribes moved northward from the desert in successive waves. The first waves used the pack burro to carry their tents and other possessions. After 1000 B.C. they were riding camels in their raids and on their migrations to the Tigris-Euphrates Valley, where their descendants lived a more settled life.

Today the Semitic Bedouin of central Arabia still lives the kind of life that his ancestors lived millenniums ago. His family still lives in the black tents made of strips of goat hair, the handiwork of the women. He and his family continue to roam over the broad desert expanse, seeking the grass or shrubbery that sustains his camel. For the Bedouin's life depends upon his camel. He provides transportation, and from his belly the women pull the hair to card, spin, and weave into blankets, carpets, bags, and wearing apparel. The camel also provides milk, meat, and skin.

In order to ration the baby camel so that a supply of milk will be available for her children, the Bedouin mother ties a string of soft yarn around six-inch sticks of a desert shrub alongside two or

Arabian camels at work and at rest. Photographs by author.

more of the camel mother's four teats. The sticks project beyond the teats and prevent humped-back baby from taking all of its mother's milk. At night the yarn is removed, and the woman milks into a bowl, perhaps one hulled from a date-tree trunk.

The camel's skin is converted into leather that serves many purposes. Urine from the female animal is used as a shampoo and as a disinfectant, as well as a gargle for a sore throat and a medicine for stomach pains. Bedouin mothers and midwives bathe newborn babies in the urine and pulverize the hard, dry camel droppings for a native "talcum."

Without the camel the Bedouins could not survive. In emergencies the Bedouin pushes his camel stick down the animal's throat and drinks the vomited water. If the animal has drunk more than two days previously, the water is not drinkable.

The women of ancient Arabia had more freedom and influence than those who followed the birth of Islam. They accumulated herds of camels, goats, sheep, and burros, and it was their preroga-

A Bedouin on his camel, Saudi Arabia, 1950 (the boy in the picture ulti-mately became a tractor driver on the king's farm).

A working burro in Algeria. Courtesy of Louis Giménez.

tive to order the men to take the herds into the desert for grazing. In time tribal wars and blood feuds killed off many males. Because of their scarcity men became more important than women. The male and his procreative powers became all-important. Evidence of the dominant role of men is still seen today in many aspects of Bedouin life. The camel brand (*wasm*) of Saudi Arabian royalty represents in outline form the human penis and testicles burned on the hindquarters. Castration of animals is almost unheard of in Arabia.

Hunting was and remains an important aspect of Bedouin culture. But, like the American Indian of earlier years, the Bedouin hunts out of necessity and kills only what he needs for food and provisions. It is not he but the Western hunter who destroyed the wild ass and threatens the graceful gazelle and the noble oryx. The typical modern-day Bedouin uses a century-old muzzle-loader for his hunting. He inserts the powder and then pours in the end of the muzzle a handful of dry, pulverized camel or burro manure and packs it down with a ramrod. Next he inserts some tiny scraps of metal (or, if metal is not available, some gravel) and then packs in more manure to hold it. Now he is ready to hunt birds, rabbits, or gazelles. It need hardly be said that wholesale and wanton slaughter is impossible with such arms and ammunition.

The collection of taxes from the desert Bedouin poses problems. For the settled Arab the tax is imposed in the form of livestock—a certain percentage of burros, camels, goats, sheep, and cattle. Bedouins, moving across the desert from wadi to wadi, are not easy to tax. Their need for water helps. The tax officials perform their annual duties during the hottest parts of the year. They ride their camels to the few water holes in the desert and there camp to await the Bedouin herdsmen's arrival with their animals—to levy the taxes in kind.

9. Persian and Hindu Trails

The wild onager roamed throughout southwestern Asia. His domain was extensive and varied:

> He trampled Bahram's unremembered grave
> When he fled the hunters on the Persian plain,
> Escaped them in the salt-choked Persian marshes,
> Eluded their horses in the folds of hills,
> In the shadow of rain . . . .[1]

The Asiatic wild ass has been saddled with several common names. Depending on his range and physical characteristics, he is called kiang, koulan, khur, dziggetai, ghorkhar, and onager. One or another of these animals ranged from Mongolia to Arabia and were hunted and eaten by both prehistoric and historic man for thousands of years up to modern times, when their ranks were decimated by the gun, the Jeep, the Land Rover, the pickup, the airplane, and other relentless means of the chase.

As late as the 1930's the graceful onager was hunted in Persia (modern-day Iran) but in pathetically dwindling numbers. An article that appeared in August, 1931, told of a hunting trip made to seek a kill of Persian onager. The article described the animal as smart, crafty, and speedy.[2] The onager could cope with man when he hunted on foot with bow and arrow or spear and used weight traps and even concealed pits; he could compete with the hunter after man mounted a horse. But when the gun and the mechanical age appeared, his days of survival were numbered. Yet he hung on in Iran, where he may still be found. Ernst Schwartz has commented on the animal's great speed—thirty miles an hour. Schwartz, not himself a hunter, condemned the wanton shooting of the animal and stressed the imperative of conservation.[3]

Fortunately, since the later 1930's (when a low point was reached in the census of the onager in Persia and perhaps in adjoining Afghanistan and the Soviet Union) there are indications that the species will survive. The establishment of the Badkhyz Reserve by the Soviets across the border from Iran, has undoubtedly contributed to the animal's new lease on life. The numbers are also increasing in Iran, according to the 1966 edition of the *Red Data Book* (published by the International Union for the Conservation of Nature and Natural Resources).

The onager has figured in Persian writings throughout recorded history. Adam Olearius, a seventeenth-century German traveler, wrote of a journey to Persia and his visit with the king. One incident that occurred during his stay demonstrates the equally long history of man's brutality to animals. The king provided "entertainment" for Olearius and other guests with an afternoon of slaughter. The entertainment involved thirty-two wild onagers held in a small enclosure. Men equipped with guns and bows and arrows released their weapons at the confined and helpless animals. The arrows protruded from the sides of the onagers, and the bullets punctured their bodies. The animals, in pain, running, kicking, and biting each other, finally fell mortally wounded. Apparently the guests of the king enjoyed the event, and at the evening feast the roasted flesh of the animals was the entree.

Persian royalty indulged in sumptuous banquets. They took advantage of almost any event as an excuse to hold a feast. Herodotus recorded that they celebrated their special days with extraordinary magnificence and, "despising the poverty of Grecian entertainments, where the cheer provided was not sufficient to fill the bellies of the invited guests," served animals roasted whole—horses, camels, and, the choicest of all, the onager.[4] The flesh was washed down with rich red wine drunk from cups made from the hard hoofs of onagers. During the feast poetry was read, and belly dancers performed to the accompaniment of music.

The Persian poet Omar Khayyám described the ancient scene in his *Rubáiyát*, while telling of Bahram, a Persian prince who lost his life while hunting the wild onager:

> They say the Lion and the Lizard keep
> The Courts where Jamshijd glorified and drank deep;
> And Bahram, that great hunter,
> The Wild Ass stamps o'er his Head,
> But cannot break his sleep.

The Persians gave us the word *paradise*, meaning "hunting preserve." Such a place, with a plentiful supply of wild onagers, was indeed an Eastern hunter's paradise. So swift and courageous were these animals that rulers proudly wore their tanned hides as apparel.[5]

The Persians loved poetry, and Persia has produced some of the world's greatest poets. One of their favorite subjects was animals, both wild and domesticated. Many a verse, couplet, or quatrain was devised while the poet rode along, rhyming to the easy gait of the burro, whose quiet and peaceful manner produced serenity and invited meditation. When they halted, the rider-poet sat crosswise on the burro's back, composing while the burro rested.

It is believed that the domesticated burro of Persia worked his way from south to north. He was serving man at a very early date in the Zagros Mountains and in adjacent lands bordering on the Persian Gulf. The ancient Medes and Persians made use of the burro long before the Scythians did. The Scythians adopted the tame burro from contacts both warlike and peaceful (generally the former) with the Medes and then the Persians. These nomads respected the animal, and because of his courage and stamina they made him a god of battle and adopted burro milk as a staple food.

There appears to be no evidence that the ass was domesticated in central Asia or the southwestern steppes at a very early age. The animal that came into use in those areas at a later time was a descendant of the African species.[6] A Soviet Russian palaeontological expedition into central Asia failed to uncover ancient bones or fossils of the African species, though the scientists did find bones of domesticated cattle, sheep, goats, hogs, camels, dogs, and what were possibly remains of the domesticated Oriental onager. All these remains dated from about 2000 B.C. Excavations in caves and other likely locations in south Kazakhstan uncovered bones of burros dating from between A.D. 500 and 1400, and the Soviet scientists concluded that the African ass appeared in west-central Asia between 200 B.C. and A.D. 300. Near Kaunchi burro bones were found dating from 300 B.C. The paleontologists did not find any clues to the first appearance of the burro in the Caucasus, though they maintained that the animal had been known in Europe since the eleventh century B.C. This report and others seem to confirm the fact that the burro shunned the colder temperatures—and also that the horse culture was strongly entrenched in west-central Asia.[7]

The burro has been a basic element in very early times of the Iranian economy for many centuries. As mentioned earlier, he pulled war chariots for the Persians. However, as always, his peaceful contributions were, and remain today, much greater and more enduring. He is a familiar figure in the Iranian village and among the desert nomads. He pulls the plow, carries women and children, hauls water, and transports farm produce—wood, hides, fruit, gums, cotton, alfalfa, rice, wheat, barley, and millet. He has borne countless Persian rugs to market. And Persian turquoise, gold, and silver have also been loaded on his strong and willing back.

The Persians were skilled and innovative irrigation engineers. They laid out efficient underground *quanats*, or canals, which are still used to convey water from its source for many miles to parched but fertile lands. Much human and burro labor must have been necessary for this work. The channels had to be tunneled and then covered. In places it was necessary to line the channels with stone, and the manholes, or shafts, six to eight feet deep and three feet in diameter, also had to be lined. The shafts, which rise about three feet above the surface, are spaced one to two hundred feet apart. They were devised to provide entrance to the channels during construction and for repair operations. This method of canal construction has important virtues: the underground route prevents evaporation, an important factor in a hot, dry country; it makes theft of precious water difficult; and it avoids the problem of blowing sands, which quickly fill an open canal. The Persians introduced their method of canal construction into the arid lands they conquered, notably in the eastern and central regions of Arabia, where they are still in use.

Like other early peoples, the Persians found many uses for the burro. They considered the bile of the burro a useful medicine for failing sight and also, according to Thomas Pennant, an eighteenth-century traveler, for "disorders of the kidneys." Pennant, who referred to the wild kiang of central Asia as a "mule," notes that the Tartars had never tamed the kiang but that "they shoot and eat him and prefer this meat to that of the wild boar or horse." He also observed that the speed of the kiang exceeded that of the antelope, and in an aside explained that out of admiration and respect for this quality the Tibetans (who referred to the animal as "The Eared") symbolically mounted their god of fire on his back.[8]

Like the burros of virtually every other age and land, the Persian burro suffered from abuse. Persian folklore tells about one burro who did something about the matter: he went to the king. This ruler, unlike most rulers of his time, was opposed to abuse of the peasants by nobles and officials. To make himself readily available to his people, he had a large bell installed on the palace grounds. A long rope was attached to the bell. He assured his people that anyone who believed himself unfairly treated was to come to the palace and pull the rope three times. The king promised to come down from his rooms and listen to the case. One night, after a day of overwork and abuse by his master, a burro went to the palace, grasped the rope with his teeth, and pulled it three times. The king responded and went down to the courtyard. The burro led the way to the home of his cruel master. The king ordered the owner punished for mistreatment of the burro.

As in other countries, the burro is represented in Persian art and sculpture. A bas-relief from a stairway in Persepolis, the ancient capital of Persia, shows a lion attacking an ass—probably a wild onager. Marco Polo crossed Persia on his journey to China in 1271. He was much impressed with what he observed. He told in his book of travels about the fine domesticated burros that he saw there. They were, he commented, the "handsomest" in the world and brought higher prices than horses did. He concluded that merchants, traders, and caravan masters preferred pack burros because of their economy: they ate less than a horse but would travel farther in a day.[9]

The Persian items of trade in Marco Polo's time were primarily gold, silk, cotton, wheat, barley, millet, grapes, and fruit, all carried by the "handsomest" burros. These commodities were sought by the Tartars from the east, who in return provided dried milk, ermine, and sable skins.

Today the old Persia meets the new. In 1965 an Associated Press release from Tehran, the capital of present-day Iran, reported that a light plane carrying a local police chief made a forced landing near a Turkish border town and crashed into a pack burro and his master. The owner of the burro died in the accident, but the animal survived. Well, no burro would crash into a plane.

Today it is only an hour by jet from the Iranian border to India, whereas on a burro it takes forty days and forty nights. But many early travelers made the journey this way, observing as they went the countryside, the people, the wildlife, and the geography. Strabo, the Greek geographer, was one of the early travelers and observers. He visited Persia and India almost two thousand years ago. He wrote in his geography of the burro's contributions to the people of Carmania (today the Iranian province of Kerman). He reported that horses were scarce but that burros were very much in evidence on the farms and on irrigation projects. The Carmanians made

Burros of India, about 1955. Note the sparse grazing. Courtesy of Horace Holmes.

many uses of the burro, some relating to warfare, for they were a warlike people and worshiped only one deity, a god of war, to whom they offered up the burro in sacrifice.

East of Iran lies India, the vast subcontinent of Asia, with a pre-history lost in antiquity. Indian mythology has it that one of the "vital airs" entered a large body of water, and from that union an egg was produced. The embryo of the egg became Agni, the God of Fire; its cry (the bray) became the burro; its tear became the horse; and the shell of the egg became the earth. Then a priest addressed the burro, saying, "Ample be thou, and well to sit upon, bearer of the earth."[10]

Thus the burro, and his special usefulness as a bearer of burdens, entered the mythology of India. Another tale, this one from the sacred books of the Parsis, tells of a three-legged burro with six enormous eyes who performed extraordinary deeds. When the animal held its neck in the ocean, its ears terrified everything, and the ocean shook. When he brayed, every female water creature of Aûharmazd became pregnant. His droppings turned to ambergris. He also pacified the turbulent sea.[11]

Later the burro's status was demythologized in the sacred literature of India. There it was prescribed that a peasant was to address his burro upon preparing to mount him: "A Sudra [worker] art thou, a Sudra by birth. To Agni thou belongest with two-fold sperm. Make me arrive safely."[12] In the India of mythology the burro was divine, benign, and prized. But something went wrong, and since those ancient days the animal has been condemned to low status. In India as elsewhere the burro was the loser when he came under the subjugation of man. His spirit was broken, his dignity crushed—even his physical size was shrunken. What few asses remain in the wild—most, if not all, in the Little Rann of Kutch (a salt marsh in northwestern India)—average a foot taller than their domesticated kin, according to the *Red Data Book*. Some of the ill-fed domestic animals are not much bigger than a large dog.

John Lockwood Kipling summed up the relationship of the Indian to his animals:

> The Hindu worships the cow, and as a rule is reluctant to take the life of any animal except in sacrifice. But this does not preserve the ox, the horse, and the ass from being unmercifully beaten, over-driven, over-laden, underfed, and worked with sores under their harness; nor does it save them from abandonment to starvation when unfit for work, and to a lingering death which is made a long torture by birds of prey whose beaks, powerless to kill outright, inflict undeserved torment.[13]

Kipling's observations, made more than three-quarters of a century ago, generally hold true today. There has been little improvement in the treatment of animals, except for the cow, which is still considered sacred. The Buddhist religion, which originated in India, pleaded for merciful treatment of animals, but that faith is all but dead in the India of today.

Thus the caste system affected the burro too. The Brahmans were too pure to lower themselves by riding the animals. Today, as elsewhere, his name, his appearance, his work, his bray (the Hindu peasant calls him Gedha, "Roarer") are derided. Regardless of his behavior he is sure to be criticized. If he works hard and does his duty, he is stupid. If he is slow responding to the wish of his rider or driver, he is lazy. If he displays natural good sense and caution, he is stubborn. An Afghan folk tale illustrates the lot of the Indian burro:

> At a Punjab River ferry a crowd of passengers and animals were assembled. When the boat came, all went aboard without hesitation, excepting a donkey which refused to move. His driver pushed and the boatman hauled without effect, until at last an Afghan among the waiting passengers drew his *churra*, the long and heavy Khyber knife, and smote the poor beast's head off at a blow, crying, "Obstinacy like this may be permitted to an Afghan, but to a donkey, never."[14]

Occasionally, of course, the donkey's "obstinacy" was respected. Among the Bilocks, neighbors of the Afghans, when a male child was born, "asses' dung in water, symbolical of pertinacity, [was] dropped into his mouth from the point of a sword before he [was] given the breast."[15]

Yet, despite the burro's status in India—which was the lowest—Indian doctors did not hesitate to prescribe milk from the jenny for the ailing and for babies. Her foal was cheated, while those who despised the burro grew stronger.

Superstitions have always plagued the burro. However, in some isolated areas of India at one time the burro enjoyed, for a time at least, a bit of prestige and honor. Young bridegrooms about to enter upon the wedding ceremony would mount a male burro for an instant as an appeasement to the dreaded goddess of smallpox, Sitala.[16]

The burro bore the brunt of other superstitions. When a peasant wanted to visit harm on an enemy, he would say, "May your land be plowed by asses!" The land could be cleansed or restored by hitching a lordly elephant to the plow.

The burro was commonly used in sacrifice. When a Hindu student had broken the vow of chastity, he was required to offer to Sitala a burro for sacrifice. Then members of the lowest caste would be compelled to eat the remainder of the offering. A Brahman named Daja who had broken his vow of chastity was ordered to kill, skin, and sacrifice a black burro to Sitala. Then he was forced to wear the burro hide for a year and during that time beg and confess his sins.

Burro carrying a load through a village, India, 1970. Courtesy of U.S. Information Service, New Delhi.

The Buddhists followed a similar practice. Nolanda University was a famous Buddhist school in ancient India. At one time it had an enrollment of ten thousand students, all male, living in six blocks of dormitories four stories high and studying in one hundred lecture rooms. They too were required to remain chaste. If a student approached a woman, he was ordered to go to a spot in a forest where four roads met and there sacrifice a burro to the gods.

The caste system of India also had a rigid code of behavior that amounted to segregation. If a male Vaisya, a member of a lower caste, had intercourse with a Brahman woman, he forfeited his property and was also fined. Then he was shaved with lather whipped from the urine of a burro (perhaps the greatest insult to an Indian was to be sprinkled with burro urine). Should a Brahman woman be approached by a Sudra, a member of the lowest working caste, the man was burned. The woman's head was shaved, her body was anointed with butter (which is repulsive to the Indian), and she was placed naked on a burro. After riding along the highway for a distance, she again became pure.

Once the burro had lost his status, he became a vehicle of contempt, as illustrated by the punishment meted out to a husband who left his wife without cause. The penalty exacted against the husband was that he had to put on a burro's hide with the hair turned outside and then beg for six months. Burros also carried robbers and those judged guilty of manslaughter. The guilty one's head was shaved, he was branded on the forehead, and then he was made to straddle a burro, to be paraded through the streets, a severe and face-losing form of punishment—worse than the hangman's noose.

The court jesters of India were quick to compare the likes and dislikes of people with those of burros. Roja Birbal was a jester in the court of Akbar the Great (A.D. 1542–1605), the greatest of the Mogul emperors of India. One day Akbar and Birbal were sitting on a terrace of the royal palace. Opposite them was a tobacco field in which a burro was standing. Birbal was fond of both smoking and chewing tobacco. Akbar, calling attention to the burro in the field, said, "See, tobacco is such a bad thing even a burro does not like it." The jester replied, smiling, "Only people who are like the burro refuse to use the fragrant leaf."[17] (Birbal would have enjoyed the story of the Colorado miner's burro who refused to pull loaded ore cars unless he was given a good slice of chewing tobacco each morning.)

Menander (or Milinda), a Greek king of India, was once taught a lesson by a burro. During a discussion with the philosopher Nagasena, Menander asked him which of the many attributes of the burro he should assume. The wise Nagasena replied, "The hard lot of the burro, for seldom is he permitted rest."[18]

In lands of warm climate, such as India, two crops a year are a common pattern. This pattern poses a hardship on the farmer and his work animals and also depletes the soil. Indian farmers, most of whom are sharecroppers, have for centuries been hard pressed to earn a living, even a meager one. When famine strikes, they fall

Karachi burros at work, 1970. Opposite: Barrels containing 250 pounds of powdered milk being loaded on a burro cart from the godown (warehouse). Above: Powdered milk being transported to distribution centers in Karachi. Saint Patrick's Church is in the background. Courtesy of U.S. Foreign Agriculture Service, Karachi, West Pakistan.

below the minimum needed for survival, and many die of starvation. The burro has shared this lot with his owner, and over the centuries the animal has become more emaciated—while, ironically, the cow has become more sacred. India is second in human population in the world and perhaps first in cattle population. The lack of adequate food had caught the burro short, and few care.

In years of plenty the farm produce is carried or pulled to market by the burro. Wheat, barley, vegetables, fruits, nuts, jute, and sugar cane are representative crops. Tea leaves from the tea gar-

dens, wood, and water are also packed on his back. Before trucks
arrived, many products of the forests were borne by the burro,
notably teakwood and white sandalwood.

The latter tree is a small, partly parasitic evergreen. The Indian
lumberjack had unusual assistance in harvesting and processing
it. He felled the trees, trimmed off the small branches, and then
left the wood lying on the ground. White ants ate the worthless
sapwood down to the heartwood, which they did not relish because
of the aromatic oil with which it was impregnated. Then the lumberjack would return with his burro to collect the wood.

Indian sandalwood has been an exportable item from before the
fifth century A.D. The oil was sometimes distilled and used in perfumes and medicines. Romans and especially the Chinese used
the wood for clothes closets, chests, carvings, fans, and jewel boxes.
Its lasting aroma and insect-repellent qualities made it so highly
desirable that today it is virtually nonexistent in the native state.
It is cultivated in southern India, and is used in ceremonial crema-
tions, in Buddhist rituals, and as incense by those who can afford it.

The maharajahs of India grew enormously wealthy from the
products of the mines—diamonds, onyx, amethysts, gold, silver, lead,
and antimony, dug from nature's storehouse. The labor was performed by poorly paid men and poorly fed animals—the latter included burros. They also carried precious salt from the coast and
from the mines of the interior.

Coal in Bengal and iron ore aplenty were carried by the burro.
Indians were among the first skilled smelters; they were smelting
ingots as early as the sixth century A.D. Ingots two inches in diameter were processed and transported on the backs of burros and
other animals to smelters, where they were converted into high-
quality steel. Among the important products made from it were
steel shoes for burros, horses, and mules. Without the protective
shoes, animal transportation, which played so important a part in
the development of civilization, would have been reduced to a
crawl.

Today the little burro of India carries everything but the Indian elephant—and he even transports portions of that animal. He packs the tusks on his back and the ivories, or dice, used in games of chance, invented in India. Chessmen made of ivory may be found in the burro's pannier.

The lowly burro has served in virtually every enterprise, noble and ignoble, undertaken by man in India. He was employed in the construction of the incomparable Taj Mahal, built in the seventeenth century by Shah Jahan as a memorial to his beloved wife— and he also bore on his back the stones used to build the fort at Agra in which Shah Jahan was held until his death by his faithless son, Aurangzeb.

Burros transporting bricks to a building site in West Pakistan, 1970. Courtesy of U.S. Information Service, Rawalpindi, West Pakistan.

10. Lu-tzu (the Chinese Burro)

"A wife can be had for five dollars; an ass costs fifteen." This old Chinese proverb emphasizes the importance of the burro in the economy of China.

The People's Republic of China (Mainland China) has more burros than any other country in the world. *The FAO Production Yearbook* for 1971 estimates that there are 11,622,000 burros in the country, out of a total world population of 42,700,000.

It is likely that the Chinese burro is descended from the African species. In a reference to the burro in Shu Wen's *Dictionary of the Chinese Language as It Appeared at the Close of the First Century, A.D.*, the animal's long ears are emphasized, a characteristic of the African, not the Asiatic, burro.

Oddly enough, though the burro must have been a part of the Chinese scene from ancient times, he was seldom mentioned by writers of antiquity. The rulers of the Shang Dynasty (ca. 1776–1122 B.C.) of Honan Province, who governed a people of high culture, apparently were not acquainted with the burro. Bones of domesticated horses, oxen, sheep, hogs, and dogs from this period have been uncovered, but not those of the burro.[1]

The philosopher Confucius, of the fifth century B.C., mentioned in his writings the use of horses in pulling war chariots, but made no reference to the burro. Of course, absence of any reference to him does not mean that he was not present. The burro was not a symbol of royalty, of wealth, or of war, as was the noble horse.

Lao-tzu, a great Chinese philosopher born about 604 B.C., held views compatible with the burro's nature though he made no mention of the animal:

All things in nature do their work quietly. . . . They fulfill their
purposes and crave nothing. . . . When they have reached their
prime, they return to their source. This withdrawal is peace, and
the fulfillment of destiny. This ebb and flow is an eternal law. To
know that law is wisdom.[2]

One finds it almost impossible to believe that Lao-tzu was unac-
quainted with the burro.

We learn from Mo Ti (ca. 480–390 B.C.), a philosopher of humble origins, about heaven's punishments for people who fail to
identify themselves with the phenomena of nature: "Heaven sends
down immoderate cold and heat and unseasonable snow, frost, rain
and dew. The five grains do not ripen, and the six domestic animals
do not mature. There are diseases, epidemics, and pestilence."[3] Unfortunately, Mo Ti did not identify the six domestic animals, but
the burro was doubtless one of them.

Centuries later, when this animal was a common worker in China,
writers continued to overlook him. Not until the time of Chu Yuan
(332–295 B.C.), was the burro referred to in Chinese writing. Chu
Yuan, a poet, commented:

> . . . drive feeble burro
> With no whip
> How long will it take
> To reach end of journey?[4]

These few lines leave no doubt that the animal was well known in
the poet's locality—and that he was emaciated from overwork and
underfeeding.

After Chu Yuan's time, references to the burro became more
common. Shih Chi, an early biographer, recorded the comments of
the historian Ssŭ-ma Ch'ien (145–87 B.C.), who said that the
"strangest" animals of the invading Huns were the ass and the mule.

For centuries the Mongols, who lived north and west of China,
pressed on the borders of China and raided frontier towns and
farms for food, livestock, money, and women. In the third century

B.C. the Chinese began building the Great Wall to hold back the invaders. The construction continued intermittently for several centuries, carried on by prisoners of war and forced labor. The burro contributed his efforts to this project, the largest structure on earth.

Early Chinese art did not slight animals. In fact, Chinese artists tended to make more use of nature and animals than of human beings. The wild ass is especially common in sculptured works, where he is portrayed as graceful, active, and dignified. One piece of bronze sculpture uncovered from the Han Period (ca. 200 B.C.) shows a tiger and a wild ass fighting. Another work portrays an attack on the animal by two of his natural enemies (one is a bear, the other has not been identified).[5]

While the Hans were sculpturing bronze works of animals in China, Buddhist monks were beginning to spread their faith be-

Burro grinding grain, Anhwei Province, China, 1948. Photograph by author.

yond the borders of India. At about the time the Christian era
began, the Buddhists were moving eastward and north into Turkistan. From there Buddhism spread along the caravan route to
China.

Indian burros accompanied the monks, packing their food, clothing, art, and religious writings. The Buddhist faith ultimately
linked the cultures of India, China, Japan, and Southeast Asia.
However, it had a more lasting influence on other Eastern countries than it did on India, its birthplace. In Tibet, Turkistan, Mongolia, and China the burro carried materials, laborers, and monks
across desert wastes and into the mountains, where Buddhist temples and monasteries were built. It is to be expected that these
burros, at least, were well treated. Buddhism is one of the few religions of Eastern origin that is sympathetic to animals.

One emperor of the earlier Han Dynasty (ca. 206 B.C.–A.D. 9)
was partial to white burros: four of them pulled his carriage. This
practice set a style, and the noblemen imitated him. Then others
followed suit, and the custom became widespread. The use of the
burro both for pulling carriages and for riding continued beyond
the Han period.

Seldom do government officials seriously consider reducing ex-
penses, but Ming Ti, a ruler of the first century A.D., ordered a
burro substituted for a horse to pull the royal buggy. Ming Ti knew
that the burro was much more economical to feed and care for
than a horse.

A few centuries later a historian of the Wei Kingdom (ca. A.D.
424–451), reported that Emperor T'sin issued a proclamation or-
dering officials of the kingdom to ride burros—an economy move
such as Ming Ti had initiated. Another ruler made use of burros
in transporting army provisions when he moved his military forces
from one part of the realm to another. One Emperor Ling (A.D. 508–
554) was also fond of burros, especially white ones, and kept several hundred of them. He himself enjoyed driving four white burros
on outings and on trips to the market. Yao, a dethroned ruler of the

Pack burros, Anhwei Province, China, 1948. Photograph by author.

period, became a groom for Emperor Ling's burros—and perhaps enjoyed his simple duties more than those of royalty.

While attending to the transportation needs of Chinese royalty was a part of Lu-tzu's chores, he had more important tasks in the Chinese economy.

Pack burros probably carried bags of coal out of the Chinese mountains in the second century B.C., for coal mining was an industry as early as the Han Dynasty. (It was not until the thirteenth century A.D. that coal was mined in Europe.) At some time following the Han period the burros and the coal miners were relieved of their work. Opposition developed among the people against disturbing Mother Earth by digging into her privacy and removing her coal. When the Sungs assumed control of the country in A.D. 960, the miners and the burros returned to their labors.

One hundred and fifty years before the Christian era began, the Chinese burro was carrying small mulberry branches, bamboo, and leaves to be used in papermaking. Later he carried the paper to outlets to be sold for writing, wrapping, and packaging.

The caravan route extending for more than fifteen hundred miles east and west across Turkistan was far from an easy one. Much of the expanse was barren desert. The burro became a part of the traffic across the inhospitable land, packing the prized lapis lazuli, gold, silver, and other items of commerce.

The burro also traversed the Silk Road, the route that led from eastern China to India and Turkistan. The Chinese founded the silk industry, and for many centuries silk was one of their most important items of trade. An ancient mural depicts a caravansary at which burros and camels stand patiently waiting as their owners, the traders, haggle over prices.[6] On their return journey the burros packed items traded from the Persians and the Arabs. Among the products was opium, which was introduced into China by the Arabs.

Marco Polo, the Venetian traveler, opened China to the Western world and gave us the first account of the remarkable Kublai Khan. The Mongol ruler had inherited the large domain conquered by his grandfather Genghis Khan, and had added more land and people to the territory. During his aggressions Genghis Khan, a stern disciplinarian, had carried with him a wooden statue of a burro. A prisoner or rebel was put astride the burro, nailed to it, and then flayed alive or chopped to pieces.

But there were other sides to the khans: they were excellent administrators, made the long trade routes safe for the caravans, and encouraged trade and relations with foreign countries. Kublai Khan, whom Marco came to know, was less warlike than his grandfather. He was a patron of the arts and tolerant of foreigners. Consuls and ambassadors were given considerable freedom of action, and Kublai provided them with many courtesies, including horses, spiced wine, and beautiful women.

The customs and practices of the Chinese fascinated Marco Polo. He told of a ritual involving milk from white mares, part of a herd of horses kept by the great khan. Only descendants of Genghis Khan were allowed to drink the milk of these mares—with one exception. A family named Horiad was allowed to share in the royal milk because members of the family had especially fought valiantly for the khan. In August of each year on the twenty-eighth day of the moon, astrologers would scatter on the wind milk from the white mares to honor the idols and spirits cherished by the people.[7] Apparently the burro was not a part of this ritual, but he was contributing in a more practical and realistic manner for the "common soul." As elsewhere, he did his traditional work, his jenny provided milk for babies and invalids, and after death their hides were converted into shoes and also into medicinal gelatine of great repute throughout China.[8]

While the ass was plodding his domestic course in China, his kin the kiang was still running wild in the Gobi Desert and surrounding hills. In 1925 the naturalist Roy Chapman Andrews, who led many expeditions to the Gobi Desert in search of earliest man, took time off from his work to chase bands of kiangs. He finally got close enough to take some pictures of them and also to shoot one and capture a baby that soon became a pet around camp. Andrews clocked the speed of a wild jack at forty miles an hour for a mile, and then at thirty-five. The kiang was finally run down after being pursued for twenty-nine miles. For sixteen miles of the twenty-nine the kiang averaged a speedometer rate of thirty miles an hour.[9]

Sven Hedin, a Swedish explorer who led an expedition into Tibet early in the twentieth century, told of capturing two wild baby kiangs. The weather was very cold, and the little ones were wrapped in blankets, loaded on camels, and taken to camp. There they were fed a diet of flour and porridge—an abrupt change from their mothers' milk. Naturally they cried for their mothers. Hedin thought it best to turn them loose, but one of his native guides said that it would be of no use, since the scent of human beings on their babies would cause the mothers to reject them. The guide's argument prevailed, and the two little captives were slain and eaten.[10]

Sir Charles Bell, another traveler who visited Tibet in the 1920's, wrote that the herdsmen in the grazing area along the Tibetan and Sikkim frontiers had domesticated burros. The aconite plant that grew there was poisonous to burros, though not necessarily fatally. The herdsmen claimed that the remedy was to slit the afflicted animal's ears and pinch his hindquarters.[11]

The Mosaic law forbidding the association of unlikes was unknown to the Chinese farmer. The ox and the burro worked side by side or in tandem pulling the plow for the peasant who could afford to own both animals. They are similar in a number of ways; they are slow, steady, patient, and consistent in temperament. However, they are decidedly unequal in weight, a fact that works to the disadvantage of the burro, unless a proper adjustment is made on the evener to which the singletrees are hooked. The ox and the burro of rural China did the same kinds of farm work—plowing, harrowing, pulling drills, hauling carts, and carrying the harvests from the fields. Then as in other Eastern countries, they trampled the grain loose from the sheaths on circular, hard-packed earth floors and pulled the heavy stone roller round and round, grinding soybeans, millet, wheat, and other grains. The burro transported farm products—vegetables, eggs, grain, soybeans, rice, tobacco, chickens, ducks, pigs, fruits, nuts, and fodder—to the markets. He packed on his back sesame oil for cooking and the residue, or pulp, which had been converted into cakes to be used as fertilizer.

For China to feed its immense population, the maintenance of soil fertility is imperative. Every effort is made to keep the soil in balance. Sesame and soybean-oil cakes are used, and some chemical fertilizers are applied, but the farmers still rely heavily upon the manure of livestock and fowl and upon "night soil" (human excreta). Children are assigned the tasks of collecting animal drop-

Pack burro, Anhwei Province, China, 1948. Photograph by author.

pings. Early in the morning during autumn, after wild geese have grazed in the young growing winter wheat, children may be seen with their baskets picking up the goose droppings, to be added to the compost pile. This organic heap is an important part of Chinese farming, as it is for all Oriental—and European—farming. Over the centuries Chinese farmers and burros have carried countless tons of night soil from population centers to the farms. Without this human fertilizer the feeding of China's millions would hardly be possible. Everything comes directly or indirectly from the earth; the Chinese sees no reason why everything should not return to it—and the more directly the better. When large foreign concessions were operated in China before the Communists came to power, night soil from the foreign compounds commanded a premium price. The diet of the foreigners was superior to and more varied than that of the average Chinese citizen, and there was more of it.

The northern Chinese use more burros than do the rice farmers south of them. Burros and water-covered rice paddies are not compatible. In those regions the water buffalo takes over cultivation.

The water buffalo cannot thrive without water, and the burro cannot thrive with it. Yet the burro is at work in the southern portions of China. He can be seen on the roads and trails and in the village streets. He climbs the mountain trails with farm produce, merchandise, and wood.

The Hwai River, north of and roughly parallel to the mighty Yangtze, serves in a general way as a dividing line between northern and southern farming. The north produces millet, wheat, rye, soybeans, kaoliang, and vegetables. Kaoliang is a member of the sorghum family and grows from six to eight feet tall. Like the soybean it is put to a variety of uses by the innovative Chinese. The grain is used for poultry and animal feed, and it is also fermented and converted into a potent wine. The stalks and leaves are used as animal roughage, for fuel, and in construction work. Countless tons

Farm boy with his pack burro, Anhwei Province, China, 1947. Photograph by author.

of kaoliang have been strapped to the sides and backs of burros for transport from farm to market. So much of his body is covered by the stalks that the little burro is hardly discernible as he carries his load along the road.

Shortly after the end of World War II, I was appointed an agricultural rehabilitation officer ("agrehab") with the United Nations Relief and Rehabilitation Administration (UNRRA). A small group of employees from other countries and I were stationed at Pengpu, a town in a large agricultural region on the Hwai River in Anhwei Province. Our duties were to assist people of the area by channeling supplies and offering our services to those who had suffered as a result of the recent flooding of the croplands by the Huang-Ho (Yellow) River, and also as a result of the Japanese occupation. The sufferings during the occupation had been greatly exaggerated, as is common, by wartime hysteria and propaganda. One Chinese co-worker in the program said: "The Japanese occupation did us more good than harm. They had organization, worked hard themselves, and provided leadership that we didn't have. They had us performing tasks that we should have been doing—constructing buildings, railroads, highways, and generally improving all around."

We foreign workers lived in a compound that had formerly quartered Japanese army officers stationed in Pengpu. Life sometimes became monotonous for us in our walled-in compound. One day we acquired a pet—a year-old female burro, gray in color, small in stature, and emaciated from hunger. We named her Maggie. She quickly adapted herself to the yard of the compound. She was provided kaoliang grain, fodder, vegetables from the kitchen, and table scraps. One of the workers was an Australian, a former Royal Air Force pilot. He grew especially fond of Maggie. Sometimes he would open the door leading from the dining room to the yard and with his arm around Maggie's neck bring her inside to the table. Then he would feed her choice morsels from the menu. Maggie ate very daintily—to be honest about it, making less noise than some of

Maggie and friend, Anhwei Province, China, 1948. Photograph by author.

us seated around the table. Maggie soon became so fond of the dining room that she needed no formal invitation and was on the alert for any opportunity to make an entrance. However, some of the people objected to her presence at the table, and she finally was forbidden to come indoors.

The Australian greatly sympathized with Maggie and objected to her ostracism. He decided that something should be done to resolve these sorrows—and that was to drown them. Returning to the compound one evening about sundown, we noticed that the Australian and Maggie were sharing a bottle of kaoliang wine. The Australian had one arm around Maggie's neck for support and was holding the bottle in the other hand. But Maggie needed assistance too; without a doubt it was her first experience with wine. However, she seemed to have no objection to it, and she never col-

Burro, Taiwan, 1970. Courtesy of Taiwan Government Agency.

Sightseeing, Taiwanese fashion, 1970. Courtesy of Taiwan Government Agency.

A Korean astride his burro, painted on silk by Ham Yundok, eighteenth century. Courtesy of National Museum of Korea.

lapsed—though she did drop to one knee occasionally. At last we persuaded the two that there had been enough drowning of sorrows. Maggie was given her ration of kaoliang grain (unfermented) to stabilize her legs and constitution, and the Australian went to bed.

Soon afterward the Chinese Communists moved into Pengpu, and we went to Shanghai and embarked for our homes. We left

Korean servant and master on burro, painted on paper, by Paik Unbai (b. 1820). Owned by private collector, Seoul, Korea.

Maggie with a Chinese boy, who promised to find her a home with a farmer. Today the lot of the Chinese burro remains the same—with a change in the names of masters, from Nationalists to Communists, the burro plods on.

Burros were early transported from the mainland to Japan and Korea, probably in junks. They were present in Japan at least as

Ichimonji, photographed in 1963, when he was twenty-nine years old. Note his gold-filled teeth. He died a year after this photograph was taken. Courtesy of Ueno Zoo, Tokyo, Japan.

early as the twelfth century, for a Chinese customs official saw them there. Chau Ju-Kua, performing duties for his country, was for a while stationed in Japan and reported seeing water buffaloes, sheep, and asses.[12]

In May, 1963, a special Japanese burro was the subject of an Associated Press wirephoto. He was Ichimonji, a twenty-nine-year-old burro at Tokyo's Ueno Zoo. Ichimonji was a veteran of the war between China and Japan in the mid-1930's. Over the years visitors to the zoo had provided Ichimonji with too much candy, and his teeth had decayed. Dentists, aware of his popularity with the people of Tokyo, filled his teeth with gold. Sadly, a year later, this lovable burro died.

11. The Greco-Roman Theater

The Greeks were familiar with the ass from ancient times. Homer, the legendary writer of *The Iliad* and *The Odyssey*, favorably compared Ajax, the strong man of the Trojan War, with the ass. Ajax was likened to the animal in his stubborn resistance against his enemies. About mules Homer was less complimentary, calling them "savage" (one wonders whether the poet may have been kicked by one). The philosopher Aristotle later disagreed: "Man and mule are always tame."

Midas, a legendary king of Phrygia, was noted for his golden touch and also for his ass's ears. As the story goes, Apollo gave the ears to Midas as punishment for designating Pan's music superior to Apollo's. Hence the expression the "ears of Midas," used to describe an unqualified music critic.

The mule was mentioned in an ancient poem of Lydia. The poem was written to alleviate the worries of King Croesus about his hold on his throne. The king consulted an oracle to learn whether his reign would be of long duration. The oracle reassured him that he would remain king until a mule was monarch of Media, the land of his enemies.[1]

The ass was early associated with Greek economy. A gold intaglio dating from the fourth century B.C. portrays a burro. He is a pathetic sight, emaciated, his bones protruding, a symbol of resignation twenty-four centuries old. Yet monetary values were early assigned to him, for he was pictured on coins of the fourth and fifth centuries B.C.[2]

Gold ring with engraved bezel, Greek, fourth century B.C. Courtesy of Museum of Fine Arts, Boston.

The Silk Road mentioned earlier was not confined to land. In time silk was brought by ship to Ceos, an island in the Aegean Sea, where artisans made it into dresses for the ladies of Athens and later of Rome.

Ceos is noted for other things than the manufacture of silk clothing. Simonides (556–468 B.C.), a famous Greek lyric poet, was born there. Simonides had some ungallant comments to make about women. In his work he compared them with the fox, the pig, and the burro, adding that women were as changeable as waves on an ocean.

As elsewhere, the burro played a prominent part in the mythology of Greece and Rome. In Greece the skull of a burro was sacred to Priapus, the god of male procreative powers and guardian of vineyards and gardens. The practice of placing the skull of an ass on something elevated to keep evil at a distance was also common in Egypt and across northern Africa to the Atlantic Ocean.[3] In some areas farmers placed the skin from the head of the burro in a field to ensure a good crop.

Silenus, a woodland deity, was a teacher and companion of Dionysus, or Bacchus, the Greek god of wine. The burro came to be the symbol of Silenus' wisdom and of his extraordinary powers as a prophet. Silenus was commonly pictured with the ears and legs of a horse, astride a burro with the infant Dionysus in his arms.

Silenus' burro is the subject of still another myth. Zeus, the chief god, had taken possession of Mount Olympus. Men asked him to grant them a permanent springtime. Zeus agreed and delegated the burro of Silenus to carry the precious treasure to earth. During his long journey the burro became thirsty and approached a fountain for a drink. The fountain was guarded by a snake, who refused him a drink unless he would give up the treasure entrusted to him by Zeus. The burro agreed, trading the gift of heaven for a skin of water. Ever since that time, the story goes, when snakes grow old, they can change their skins and become young again, for they have the gift of eternal spring.[4]

Silenus on his burro, from a mosaic at Chebba, Tunisia, ca. third century
A.D. Courtesy of Musée du Bardo, Le Bardo, Tunisia.

Many people have difficulty distinguishing between the burro
and the mule, but the Athenian philosopher Socrates (470?–399
B.C.) had no such problem. During his trial for impiety and cor-
ruption of youth, Socrates commented: "You say first that I do not
believe in gods, and then again that I believe in demigods. You
might as well affirm the existence of mules and deny that of horses
and asses."[5]

Demosthenes (385?–322 B.C.), the greatest orator of ancient
Greece, made use of the burro in fables designed as object lessons.
To illustrate the foolishness of arguing over insignificant matters,
he told the following story:

A man hired a burro to ride on a journey to a neighboring town. Along the way the sun grew hot, and the traveler dismounted and sat in the shade of his mount. The burro's owner came by and objected to the man taking the liberty of enjoying the shadow of the hired animal, saying that he had rented only the burro, not the shadow, and therefore would exercise his prerogative by occupying the sun-protected spot himself. A heated argument occurred over this shadowy trifle. (The burro did not join in the battle. He rested.)[6]

It seems that burros were not common in the colder regions north and east of Greece in the time of Aristotle (384–322 B.C.). In his *History of Animals*, Aristotle said that the burro was not known in Thrace (a country now divided between Greece and Turkey), because the climate there was too cold.[7] Obviously the burro's dislike for cold weather was known to the ancients. Yet there is evidence that the burro had been living for centuries across the Bosporus Strait in Asiatic Turkey. Incidentally, in discussing the burro, Aristotle advised his readers that the jenny and jack should not be mated until each was thirty months old but added that both were capable of procreating young at an earlier age.[8]

Euclid, the Greek geometer who lived in Alexandria, Egypt, in the fourth century B.C., devised a difficult proposition for his students. In Book I of his *Geometry* the fifth proposition presents an obstacle for many students. It has been referred to as *pons asinorium*, or "ass's bridge." The name is fitting and indicates some acquaintance with the burro, who frequently stops before crossing a bridge and, reluctant to proceed, often requires a shove—likewise students confronted with the fifth proposition.

Whether associated with poets, philosophers, or geometricians, the burro was an important part of ancient Greek culture. In Alexandria, where prominent Greek scholars gathered, Ammonius Saccas, a fourth-century, A.D. grammarian who was fond of poetry, owned a burro. The burro earned a place in history because he enjoyed listening to his master read poetry, somewhat like his latter-day counterpart, Juan Ramón Jiménez.

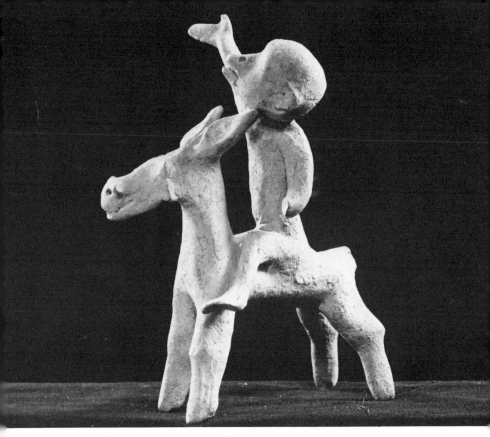

Ape riding on a donkey, terracota, Boeotian, Late Archaic period. Courtesy of Museum of Fine Arts, Boston.

How did the burro reach Greece? Victor Hehn believed that the burro came to Greece from Asia Minor.[9] That is a good guess, it seems, for there are many islands that may have served as stepping-stones to Cyprus, Crete, and the mainland of Greece. As late as 1895 wild burros were reported in the Dodecanese Islands off the coast of Turkey. In fact, the islands, because of the long presence of these animals, were once called the Gaidaronisi, meaning "Asses." The asses were descendants of domesticated animals.[10] It is pos-

Ass bearing packsaddle, red-figured, Attic period. Courtesy of Museum of Fine Arts, Boston.

sible that the spread of the grape and olive cultures of those regions gave impetus to the burro's journeyings.

Chiefly because of the rugged topography of Greece, the burro and the mule have been more important than the horse among the rural people of that land. They are better adapted to steep mountain trails. Because of a shortage of burros resulting from severe economic conditions, following World War II large numbers of burros were imported into Greece. The UNRRA purchased one thousand burros in the West Indies and sent them to the mountainous areas of northern Greece. The burro is still as important in twentieth-century Greece as he was in Homer's day.

The packsaddles of Greek burros have held many products, among them bolts of silk and linen, wine, oil, honey, drugs, perfumes, timber, olives, grapes, grain, and fruits. Burros were a familiar sight on the islands of the Aegean and the Mediterranean, and in the many ports of Greece, where the little animals waited to receive cargoes from ships and carry them inland. Greek commerce, the lifeblood of the Hellenistic world, was ultimately dependent on the burro.

The burro was also a feature of the Roman scene, both in commerce and in the arts. Legend has it that it was a burro who made the grandfather of the financier politician Marcus Licinius Crassus (115?–53 B.C.) laugh for the first time in his life. Watching a burro eat a thistle, he laughed and declared, "Like lips, like lettuce." He coined a phrase that has been used ever since, meaning that the burro's mouth is tough and such plants as the thistle pose no problem for him.

Murrius, who wrote a very early work on farming in Italy, indicated that wild asses—probably onagers—could be found in Phrygia and Asiatic Turkey. Murrius also passed along to his readers hints on how to produce fine-quality breeding jacks, suggesting that they should be raised on mare's milk. He seemed to think that such nourishment resulted in a vigorous animal that would command a good market price. Cato (234–149 B.C.), the author of *De Agri Cultura*, and Varro (116–27 B.C.), who wrote *De Re Rustica*, agreed with Murrius. Incidentally, Varro's treatise is considered to be the best ancient work on agriculture. Both Cato and Varro commented that the ass was common throughout Italy.[11]

Cato did some surveys of agricultural economics. One farmer told him that on his farm he had three burros to haul manure from the stables to the fields, a fourth to turn the mill, and a fifth to operate the wine press. Two more were employed to help a yoke of oxen cart manure from the stables to the vineyard.[12]

The difference between the size and strength of oxen and burros was considered by the farmers. In areas where the land was of light or loose texture, burros were hitched to lightweight plows. Oxen were reserved for tight or heavy soils, which required heavier and sturdier plows. Where possible, burros were selected for the varied tasks on the farms because they consumed less food than oxen or mules. Cato emphasized this advantage.[13]

Roman emperors came and went, but for the peasant and his burro life altered but little. The Roman writer Phaedrus, of the first century A.D., told the following fable:

A driver exhorted his burro to flee, for the enemy was near. The burro, unimpressed, calmly asked, "Will the approaching enemy place a double burden on my back?"

"No," said the owner.

"Then," replied the burro, "what do I care whether you die as my master or someone else does?"

In his *Natural History*, Pliny the Elder (A.D. 23–79) devoted much attention to animals, among them the burro. He praised the jenny as a devoted mother and named three uses of burro milk in addition to sustenance for the foal—as a drink for human beings, as a cosmetic, and as an antidote for poison. The breeding of good-quality jennies was highly profitable, he wrote, and, among the desirable attributes of a quality female, "thc hair of the ears and of the eye-lids is an important point." Pliny shared some unscientific

Terracotta burro. Classical Greek period (1000–600 B.C.). Courtesy of Metropolitan Museum of Art, Cesnola Collection, New York.

notions with his contemporaries. To assure that the foal was female, he said, the breeder must see to it that the jenny faced northward while being serviced by the jack. He warned also that the jenny must be made to gallop after copulation; otherwise the "genital fluid" would be lost.[14]

Symbols have an important place in the culture of a civilization. Representations of the burro's attributes were of special significance in Rome. Again it was Pliny who noted that Roman married couples had carvings of burros' heads mounted on their bedposts,[15] presumably to assure potency. The sex life of the male burro has long been considered spectacular and clothed in an abundance of temperament.[16] Certainly the burro jack is combative. Though smaller than a horse stallion, a jack can give a splendid account of himself when the two clash over the favors of a mare. The result is a bruising, bloody, kicking, biting contest.

But in Rome as elsewhere, the burro came in for more than his share of ill-repute. There is a Roman proverb that says, "When one meets a burro, bad luck will occur." To express the impossible, the Roman said, "It will be done when the burro climbs to the tiles," meaning "to the roof."

The burro was the subject of one of the most famous Roman satires, *The Golden Ass*, by Lucius Apuleius. In the story Lucius temporarily was transformed into an ass. He underwent many of the humiliations the burro has had to suffer from time immemorial.

As in other early cultures, Romans ate the flesh of the burro. It may have been Maecenas (70?–8 B.C.), a Roman statesman, who popularized burro meat. He arranged for it to be served as the entree on the banquet circuits of Rome. He was fond of burro meat and apparently had conducted some experiments to determine the best feed for an animal that was raised for meat. Maecenas recommended a diet of biscuits soaked in milk.[17]

The infamous emperor Nero (A.D. 37–68) began his rule in a sensible manner. Later he became cruel and probably mad. But he treated his mules well: they were shod with silver shoes. His

Burro depicted on Roman coin, fourth or fifth century B.C.
Courtesy of British Museum.

empress, Poppaea, went him one better: her
driving mules were fitted with golden sandals.

Poppaea was an enchantress. She was meticulous in appearance,
taking hours for her toilette. Of course, being the wife of an emperor, she set the pattern for the noblewomen of Rome. She recognized the cosmetic value of burro milk, as had that earlier sensuous
queen, Cleopatra of the Nile. To ensure a plentiful supply of milk
for her marble bath, Poppaea maintained five hundred burros.
Jennies accompanied her on her journeys.

However, beauty cannot always soothe the savage beast, and
Nero in one of his fits of rage kicked Poppaea in the stomach. Poppaea, who was pregnant, died from the blow. Nero fancied himself
an orator and delivered the funeral oration. He heaped on her pyre
quantities of incense and perfumes that probably took southern
Arabia a whole season to produce and many strings of pack burros
to transport.[18]

The Roman Empire and its invincible legions conquered and
plundered vast territories and grew rich in booty and commerce.
The generals confiscated gold, silver, and other valuables. They
killed or enslaved prisoners of war and monopolized trade. Many
of the slaves were sent to Italy, and in time the slave population
became enormous. Italy was largely an importing nation but paid
for its imports with the wealth of conquered countries. The Romans
chiefly imported finished goods, among which were many luxuries.
Pack burros delivered these products, some of which came from the
farthest reaches of the known world. Burros carried grain, wool,
hides, and casks of wine from Sicily; ivory, apes, rare marble, spices,
obsidian, and tortoise shells from Ethiopia; grain and oil from

northern Africa; wool, gold, silver, lead, tin, copper, iron, cinnabar, grain, cork, and olive oil from Spain (Rome's richest province); wine, oil, marble, and gold from Greece; fabrics, figs, honey, carpets, and wood from Asia Minor; glass, fabrics, oil, fruits, and nuts from Syria; incense, gums, myrrh, ginger, cinnamon, and precious stones from southern Arabia; grain, glass, dates, cotton, and alabaster from Egypt.

Roman politicians knew how to please the masses: give them bread for their stomachs and plenty of entertainment. Five thousand animals died in combat with men as a part of the dedication of the Colosseum in Rome.[19] The emperor Sulla (138–78 B.C.) arranged for one hundred hungry lions to be used in the gladiator games. Caesar arranged a similar game with four hundred lions, and Pompey turned loose six hundred lions in the Colosseum. Claudius (10 B.C.–A.D. 54) ordered a division of the praetorian guard to fight panthers, while Nero had a division do combat with four hundred bears and three hundred lions. The wild onager, a favorite combatant, was probably introduced to the games some time between 27 B.C. and A.D. 117.[20] The onager was matched against all comers and was cheered on—though he was no doubt far less interested in the tributes than in his survival.

The tremendous numbers of wild animals needed for the carnage of the Roman games made heavy demands on traders and buyers. Ropers and trappers earned their livelihoods supplying the emperors' needs. Cicero, writing in 50 B.C., reported meeting a fellow Roman citizen named Vedues, during a journey. Vedues, who presumably was a buyer and trader for the promoters of the Roman games, had chariots, slaves, and wild asses destined for Rome. The art of roping an animal did not originate with the American cowboy. A painting of a scene at Bona, Numidia (a Roman province in North Africa), shows a horseback rider attempting to lasso a wild ass.[21]

Like other early cultures Romans made use of the "by-products" of the burro. Parmesan cheese was made from burro milk. Some

A burro in modern-day Italy. Note his burden. Courtesy of Giuseppe Primavera.

bologna sausage was composed of burro meat rather than pork. The blood, the sweat, and the urine of the burro were used as medicines. He was sacrificed in rituals. Before entering upon their official duties, Roman officials, praetors, consuls, and dictators would offer up a burro in sacrifice at Lanuvium.

After the advent of the Christian era and the establishment of the papacy in Rome, the burro's lot remained little changed. He

continued to be an object of scorn and a symbol of humiliation. In
A.D. 997 Emperor Otto III deposed Pope John XVI. To complete the
brutal act, Otto shortened the pope's tongue and nose with a sharp
knife, gouged out his eyes, placed him on a burro, facing backward,
and paraded the two through the streets of Rome.[22]

Today Greek and Italian burros are still doing much the same
work that their ancestors did in the Greco-Roman period, though
the products they carry have changed. In their panniers one may
find, in addition to traditional items, such things as car parts and
radios. A recent issue of *Time* included a photograph of a peasant
and his burro on a trail somewhere in southern Italy. They were
homeward bound from the market, and on the back of the burro?
A television set.[23] He has spanned the millenniums in transportation and communication.

12. Spreading Trails

The burro beat trails with his durable hoofs throughout the continent of Europe. He became an all-important factor in transportation, in food production, in folklore, and in proverbs from Spain to Poland and beyond. The burro found a home in the Balkans, and his trails extended from the Bosporus to the English Channel and across to England, Scotland, and Ireland.

While he is found in virtually all parts of Europe, his like prefer some areas to others. He thrives best in the warm Mediterranean climate. It is within this region that he has served the longest time.

No one knows for certain when the first burros arrived in Europe. There is some evidence that the domesticated African ass arrived in France as early as 2000 B.C. In 1883 it was reported that "M. Boucher Perthes has found in the peats of the Somme [River], some fifteen or sixteen feet below the level of the stream, an equoid skull which M. Sanson has recognized as that of an African or Nilotic ass."[1]

Apparently man had taken the animal to that region of northwestern France. Prehistoric rock carvings of the wild ass found in Spain and in Switzerland are likely those of the onager or kiang. No drawings resembling the African species have been discovered in those countries. A study by Rossel I. Vilá claims that the animal was in Europe in Neolithic times. According to Vilá, the animal is indigenous to Catalonia in northeastern Spain. This area is noted for its excellent Catalonian jacks, which have sired good mules in many countries. It was a member of this breed that the king of Spain sent as a gift to President George Washington in 1785.[2]

It can be assumed that pack burros served on portions of the Amber Route, which extended through eastern Europe from the

Baltic Sea to the Aegean and Adriatic seas. While yellow amber was the chief article that passed along this trail, other items of trade also moved on it.

One nineteenth-century authority traced the burro's migration into northern Europe through study of languages. The animal was closely associated with the words for *burden, load, carry, pack,* and *transport.* A name for the burro entered the language of the Lithuanians and of three Germanic tribes during the early part of the rule of the Gothic king Ermanaric (A.D. 350–376), who established a great kingdom extending from the Gulf of Bothnia and the North Sea south to the Black Sea. Traders, peddlers, and gamblers were accompanied by burros through the Gothic lands.[3]

The early Christian missionaries also rode or led burros along the spreading trails of Europe. They very likely used the animals not only because Jesus did but also because of their easy gait, packing ability, patience, and inexpensive keep.

There may have been a stepped-up migration of the burro northward in Europe in the third and fourth centuries A.D., but there is little recorded information about him during the decline of the Roman Empire and throughout the Middle Ages. It is also unknown whether the burro was present in England in Roman times, but it would indeed be strange had the Romans not brought the useful burro with them.

Burros were serving the traders and farmers of southern Gaul during the fifth century, and the Anglo-Saxons may have brought some of the animals to England during that century. There had been trade between the people of England and Gaul centuries before the Roman domination of southern England, perhaps as early as 1860 B.C.[4]

According to Thomas Pennant, an eighteenth-century English naturalist, the donkey was mentioned during the time of Ethelred II (A.D. 968?–1016), which may be the earliest record of the burro in England. Pennant also claimed that the donkey died out in England during the reign of Elizabeth (1533–1603) and quoted

A Portuguese burro resting. Courtesy of U.S. Information Service, Lisbon.

Another Portuguese burro resting. Courtesy of 1968 Kodak International Newspaper Snapshot Awards.

the sixteenth-century English chronicler Raphael Holinshed as saying that, in his time, "our lands did yealde no asses." Pennant stressed the donkey's age-old usefulness in the mines of England.[5]

Saint Nicholas, of the fourth century, A.D., the patron saint of Russia, also became the patron of an unlikely group composed of sailors, thieves, scholars, virgins, and children. He was, moreover, a benefactor of the burro. Among his many good deeds Saint Nicholas is supposed to have come to the rescue of two burros whose heads had been wickedly sliced off. Taking pity on the ani-

Burro operating wheel at Carisbrook Castle, England. He is drawing water from a well 161 feet deep, sunk in 1150 A.D. For 150 years burros have been used to work the pump. Three burros are used, and they work one hour on and two hours off. The wheel, made of oak, is nearly 400 years old. Courtesy of Ministry of Public Buildings and Works, London.

mals, the saint sewed their heads on again. Over the centuries Saint Nicholas became part of the Christmas celebration in the Netherlands, Belgium, and other northern European countries (and in time, as Santa Claus, in America). Saint Nicholas was said to make his gift-giving journeys either on a white horse or astride a white burro (the reindeer were an American innovation). A Dutch legend has it that if the weather is misty on Saint Nicholas' Day (December 6), it is because Saint Nicholas is baking his Christmas cakes. These cakes, still made by Dutchwomen during the Christmas season, are adorned with various shapes. When children ask about them, they are told that the marks are made by Saint Nicholas' white donkey as he steps over the cakes on his way through the mist.

The donkey early entered European folklore, proverb, and literature. In England, when the police failed to catch a thief, it was a common bit of sarcasm to ask, "Who stole the donkey?" The answer was, "The man with the white hat." White hats were made from the hides of white burros, which were sometimes stolen and sold to hat manufacturers.[6] The English have an old proverb: "Donkeys as well as pitchers have ears," a warning that uninvited listeners are overhearing the conversation. An evil man was said to "ride a black donkey." France contributed this proverb: "If hard work made riches, the donkey's packsaddle would be made of gold." From Spain we learn: "The burro endures the load but not the overload." The Genoese observed: "The ass carries wine but drinks water."

The French writer Honoré de Balzac (1799–1850), in one of his novels, *La Peau de chagrin* (*The Skin of Sorrow*), wrote about the symbolic power of a wild onager skin. The chief character of the story is Raphael, a young man dejected by ill fortune in gambling and other ventures. He enters a dingy store and visits with the old proprietor. The merchant perceives Raphael's discouragement and tells him about his talisman, the hide that hangs on the wall behind his chair. He explains that he received it from a Brahman and that it is shagreen. When the merchant says, "It will make you richer and more powerful than a king," the young man is immediately interested and carefully examines the piece of skin. He notices a seal, called in the East the "Signet of Solomon," and also a mysterious message written in Sanskrit:

> Possessing me thou shalt possess all things
> But thou life is mine, for God has so willed it.
> Wish and thou wishes shall be fulfilled;
> But measure thy desires, according to the

Life that is in thee.
This is thy life
With each wish I must shrink
Even as thy own days.
Wilt thou have me? Take me,
God will harken unto thee.
    So be it!

The aged merchant offers Raphael some advice: "To will and to have your will covers life. To will consumes us. To have our will destroys us." Then he warns the young man that the skin will contract according to the strength and number of his desires. Nevertheless Raphael takes the skin and departs, saying in substance, "A short life but a merry one." He begins to enjoy life to its fullest, indulging himself in every pleasure. The hide shrinks steadily. At last, Raphael tries desperately to find some means to stretch what is left of the skin, but in vain. He dies a young man.[7]

The Dutch scholar Erasmus (1466–1536) alluded to the burro in his attacks on the scholastics. He scorned them for their theories about how the Virgin Mary conceived the Savior in her womb: "God, who took our nature upon Him in the form of man, could as well have become a woman, a devil, an ass."[8]

The Turks also have their proverbs. A child of Turkey will say, when he loses a baby tooth, "Go away little burro; come big burro." Then he throws the tooth over his right shoulder.

The Germans have many tales, proverbs, and customs that involve the burro. At Frikhausen in Württemberg the peasants kept a wooden replica of a burro as the tutelary deity of the village. When explaining a bad crop of grapes from their vinyards, the people of Silesia said that the peasants had eaten the head of the burro on which Silenus rode. Upon being asked by a child where babies come from, the German mother of olden times replied that they came from the burro pond.[9] To the German boasting of a journey he was about to take, his friends would issue a warning: "If a burro goes atraveling, he will not return a horse."

A modern-day Turkish burro. Courtesy of Harry R. Varney, agricultural attaché, Ankara.

The Portuguese farmer placed the skull of a burro in a prominent place in his field to divert the evil eye.

The people of Wales say, "If a donkey turns round and faces you, it is a sign of good fortune; if it turns its back on you and runs away, it is a sign of misfortune." They also say, "If you have a donkey with you in a dangerous place, you will come to no harm." To be followed by a jenny and her colt is also a good sign. And in still another proverb we are assured, "If a burro's bray is the first thing you hear in the morning, make a wish and it will come true."

The Bulgarians, knowing the disadvantages of quarreling, say, "While the stallions kick each other, the donkeys eat hay."

At the close of the Middle Ages the burro was used as a symbol by a schoolmaster at the University of Paris in what became a heated controversy over free will. Tradition has it that the teacher, Jean Buridan (1300?–1358?), posed this problem: If an ass is placed at an equal distance between two bundles of hay, will he

A Portuguese burro. Courtesy of U.S. Information Service, Lisbon.

Bremen Town Musicians, bronze by Gerhard Marcks, 1951. Courtesy of Mrs. Harry Lynde Bradley, Milwaukee, Wisconsin.

choose one to feed from, or will he be so confused by the opposite
attractions of the bundles that he will find it impossible to make a
choice between the two and die of starvation?[10] The problem became known as "Buridan's ass."[11] (The professor and his students
did not know the burro very well. Anyone who understands the
animal knows that he will walk to one bundle and eat his fill and
save the other one for supper.)

One of the most famous donkeys of European folklore was an
old German donkey who became the organizer and leader of the
famous little group known as the Four Musicians of Bremen, later
immortalized in one of *Grimm's Fairy-Tales*. The old donkey, no
longer able to work, realized that his master was planning to do
away with him. One night he quietly left the barnyard and headed
for Bremen. On the way he met a dog, a cat, and a rooster, all of
whom were old and fearful of being put to death by their masters.
The donkey persuaded them to go to Bremen with him and become street musicians.

When night came, the four hungry animals settled down, not
too comfortably, in a forest. The rooster, perched high on a limb,
saw a light coming from a house. The old burro suggested that they
investigate the house in search of better quarters. When they arrived at the house, the burro, the tallest of the four, walked quietly
to the window and peered in. He reported to his three friends that
several robbers were sitting around a table laden with food. The
hungry friends decided to chase the thieves away.

The burro placed himself under the window, the dog jumped
upon his back, the cat climbed upon the dog, and the rooster flew
up and perched on the back of the cat. Then, on a signal from the
donkey, each of them sent forth his distinctive music. The terrified
robbers fled. The musicians of Bremen went into the house and ate
their fill. Then they blew out the light and settled down for the
night.

Later that night the robbers returned to the house. Seeing no
light, the leader sent one of his band to investigate. The robber,

finding all quiet, entered the kitchen to light the lamp. He mistook the glowing eyes of the cat for smoldering embers and held out a match to kindle them. The cat spat and scratched him. The frightened robber made for the door, where the dog bit him on the leg. As he ran through the yard where the burro had been lying, he got a hefty kick. From the roof the rooster, thinking it was morning because of all the activity, cried out "Keekerikee! Keekerikee!"

The mauled and terrified robber ran to his chief and reported:

In the house, by the fire sits a fiendish witch; she breathed her hot breath on me, and scratched my face with her long fingernails. In front of the kitchen door lies a man with a knife; he stabbed my leg as I passed by. Out in the barnyard lurks a black monster; he gave me a whack with a heavy club. Up on the roof sits a judge, and as I ran by he screamed: "See the thief flee! See the thief flee!"

He vowed never to go back, nor did the other robbers ever return. And the musicians? They did not continue to Bremen but remained contentedly in their new home till the end of their days.

In medieval Germany the burro was the symbol of Saint Thomas, the doubting apostle. Among German boys it was common to deride the last one to enter the schoolroom and dub him "Saint Thomas the Donkey."[12]

In the Swiss Alps a burro, it is said, was killed and quartered for having drunk up the moon's reflection in a bucket of water.[13]

The manners and customs of mankind are varied and often unfathomable. Peasants of Île de Ré, an island just off La Rochelle, France, had the curious custom of putting a pair of trousers on the front legs of their burros. And the Dulanis of the Yarkand region (of western Sinkiang Province, China) tied a garter on each leg of a newborn baby burro. This custom, the people thought, would keep devils at a safe distance.[14]

The donkey was never plentiful in the northern reaches of Rus-

Burros in Russia. Top: A burro and his rider herding browsing camels on the barren Kara Kum ("Black Desert"), U.S.S.R. Courtesy of Davis Thomas. Below: Russian burros and boys entertaining tourists on the Kara Kum, near Ashkhabab. Reproduced from *Sports Illustrated*, September 8, 1969. Courtesy of Davis Thomas.

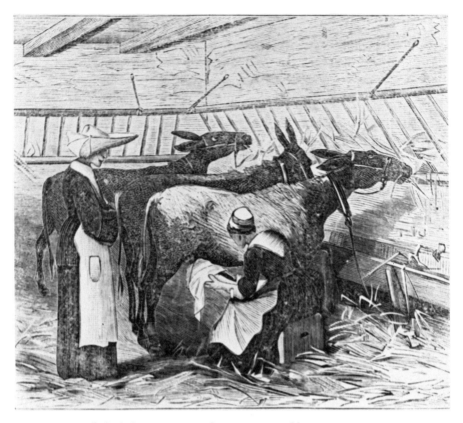

Burro milk for babies. From *Popular Science Monthly*, January, 1883.

sia, but he was common enough to be a vehicle of ridicule. Peter Ulrich, grandson of Peter the Great and heir to the throne, was a sickly child and evidently not a star pupil. He was often slighted and made fun of by his tutor, a man named Brümmer. One of the punishments meted out to the young prince was to deny him food. Brümmer would make the boy stand inside the entrance to the dining room at mealtime with a picture of a donkey hanging around his neck.[15]

Not only burro milk but also burro flesh were long prized as food in France. The French king Francis I (1494–1547), weary of war, returned to Paris to recuperate. But his health did not improve, and his doctors were unable to help him regain his strength. Then a Jew recently arrived from Constantinople was consulted. He suggested that the ailing king drink burro milk. Soon the king was well and strong again. The practice of drinking burro milk caught on. Paris and other large centers became markets for the milk, and dairy herds came to be common around population centers.

Three and a half centuries later a scientific experiment conducted in Paris proved that burro milk was indeed beneficial. The results of the experiment were reported by W. Parrot, physician at the Hospital for Assisted Children in Paris. Babies born diseased were in turn causing infections in their wet nurses. Some milk burros were placed in the hospital garden, and the nurses held the infants under the udders of the jennies and allowed them to nurse directly from the animals' teats. The experiment was carried on for one year with eighty-six babies affected with congenital and contagious diseases. Six were fed cows' milk from a bottle; only one of the six recovered. Forty-two were nursed at the teats of goats; eight recovered, and thirty-four died. Thirty-eight nursed at the teats of jennies; twenty-eight recovered, and ten died.[16]

In 1877, Philip Gilbert Hamerton devoted a section of his *Chapter on Animals* to burros. At royal picnics in Lyons, France, a dish called *seucisse*, composed of burro meat, was served. Hamerton gave the burro credit for its contributions to civilization, commenting that artists and writers learned philosophy from him. But Hamerton believed that the animal's chief value lay in his edibility: "His flesh was so compounded by the chemistry of nature as to be perfect food for man, but his brain was contrived with such bumps of obstinacy and resistance that he is the most vexatious of all our servants." It was a mistake to ride or drive one, said Hamerton; he should be eaten instead.[17]

At other times and in other places burro meat was eaten not as a delicacy but out of desperation. The Siege of Paris and of Malta by the British in the early nineteenth century forced the people to the edge of starvation. They ate horse and burro meat, and were even reduced to eating dogs, cats, and rats.[18]

The Romans had their bloody games in the Colosseum, and the French had theirs in the Paris Bear Garden. In Paris dogs were set on captive bears, and there were also battles between dogs and burros. Pennant, a spectator at one of the animal contests in the garden, reported seeing a fight between a dog and a burro. The latter won.[19]

Other by-products of the burro were in demand in Europe just as they had been in ancient times. During the Middle Ages fresh burro manure was used to treat diseases of the eyes. The cure for gout was to bind the hoofs of the animal on the patient's lower extremities—the left hoof on the left foot and the right hoof on the right foot. Burro blood was said to have prophetical powers, and it was used in rituals to foretell the direction in which the fickle finger of fate might be pointing.

On September 23, 1878, several European donkeys achieved modest fame. One, a French burro named Modestine, passed into the ownership of a young writer who wanted to do some traveling for adventure, for literary material, and for his health. Robert Louis Stevenson wrote of his efforts to secure the little animal from an old man of unsound intellect known as Father Adam. Modestine was "a diminutive she-ass, not much bigger than a dog, the colour of a mouse, with a kindly eye. There was something meet and high-bred, a Quakerish elegance, about the rogue that hit my fancy on the spot."[20]

Stevenson bargained long and hard for Modestine in a market-place. Before the transaction was completed, he had acquired a plentiful supply of advisers. At last she became his property for the consideration of sixty-five francs and a glass of brandy for Father Adam. According to Stevenson, the little burro was the least expensive of Stevenson's traveling supplies. Both men shed tears when they parted from the pack animal, Father Adam when Stev-

A modern-day Modestine. This is Philomène, looking over her enclosure. This little Corsican burro is in a clean, comfortable stall in the middle of a popular restaurant in Paris, 1971. Photograph by author.

enson led her away, and the author upon parting from her after he had completed his journey.

During the twelve days of vagabond travel over ridges, rocky trails, and byroads, Stevenson thought that he disliked Modestine, chiefly because of her slow speed. But, he wrote: "As for her, poor soul! She had come to regard me as a god. She was patient, elegant in form, the colour of an ideal mouse, and inimitably small. Her faults were those of her race and sex; her virtues were her own." Stevenson commented about their parting: "Up to that moment I had thought I hated her; but now she was gone, and oh, the difference to me!"[21]

Jack Burroughs, in his tender little poem "A Friend in Need," told how a hungry little French burro was saved from punishment:

> There is a public garden in Bordeaux
>   Where, carved in true, compelling lines of stone,
>   Rosa Bonheur, calm visaged and alone,
>   Looks ever down upon the endless flow
>
> Of life in the less rugged flesh. A slow,
>   Ungainly little donkey, as, wind-blown,
>   A weed into a garden drifts, unknown,
>   Stole in one day to feed where flowers grow.
>
> A keeper, shocked that this dull beast should browse
>   Before the statue of the mighty dead,
>   Rushed up, with blows the sinner to arouse.
>   He stops, club poised above shaggy head;
> Calm eyes seem watching him; his head he bows,
>   And leads the dumb brute gently forth instead.[22]

While the donkey may have died out in England at one time or another, Ireland has uninterruptedly been his home since he was introduced there, and the Irish have bred and exported thousands of the animals to England, to South Africa, and to other countries. One observer at the close of the nineteenth century had this to say about Irish donkeys: "They are small, stunted animals, but with

plenty of endurance which a donkey never loses, but they show all
the worse results of neglect in breeding."[23] The people of Ireland
have had a close affinity with the little animal and in fact have made
him a symbol of good luck.

Cruelty to animals was common in England as in all countries.
In 1835, Parliament enacted a law designed to protect domesticated animals, but the law was seldom enforced. Neglect was common, as was deliberate, brutal, and sadistic cruelty. Of the few
cases ever brought to trial, two were heard in the court of Rockford.
One involved a man who boasted that he could knock one down
with a blow of his fist (doubtless a starved, emaciated, and weak
animal). The other case involved several men "who rode a donkey
around a field until it fell from exhaustion; then they beat it with
sticks, tore out its tongue, and otherwise mutilated it." The men
were convicted and sentenced to six weeks at hard labor.[24]

Such events were not uncommon. An article in *Blackwood's
Edinburgh Magazine* reported that the donkey was "mistreated in
England, unfed, homeless, vagrant, unpitied, untended, kicked,
lashed, spurred, tormented, troubled, thumped, and thrashed."[25]

Historically, the lot of the English donkey has been an unhappy
one. An early English botanist told how donkeys sometimes lost
their hides while they were still living:

If asses chaunce to feed much upon hemlock [a poisonous herb],
they will fall so fast asleep that they will seem to be deade, inso-
much that some thinking them to be deade indeed have flayed
off their skins, yet after the hemlock has done operating, they
have stirred and awakened out of their sleep to the grief and
amazement of the owners, and to the laughter of the others.[26]

Brutality often took the guise of "scientific experiment." London
scientists had become interested in the secrets of the witch doctors
of the Amazon Basin, and specifically in the process used to prepare
curare, a poison applied to the tips of arrows. Several experiments
were undertaken with this poison, one of which involved a female

donkey. She was injected in the shoulder and within ten minutes appeared dead. Then an incision was made in her windpipe, and with a pair of bellows the experimenters inflated her lungs for two hours. She regained consciousness, held up her head, and looked around. However, when lung inflation was discontinued, she again sank into apparent death. At last, after two more hours of work with the bellows, the donkey got to her feet. She did not seem to be in pain, and the wound made by the injection healed satisfactorily. But for a whole year she was lean and sickly. Finally, when summer came, she regained her weight and health. Then a sympathetic scientist sent her to more comfortable quarters near Wakefield, England.[27]

At least one nineteenth-century Frenchman protested the lot of the donkey. He suggested that, in lieu of fines for cruelty to animals, the culprits should be compelled to serve as donkeys for a while and to receive abuse in return. The author admitted that such a sentence would be "contrary to progress and civilization"—but not contrary to justice, civilized or uncivilized.

In his plea the Frenchman told of a dream he had once had concerning the matter of cruelty to animals. In his dream he gave a thistle to a donkey, who ate it and then requested another. Then the donkey told how he once had been a butcher and had starved and beaten a donkey. Now, likewise, he was tied, starved, and beaten.[28]

As mentioned earlier, the donkey was maligned by some of England's celebrated poets. Chaucer's works are permeated with barbs, as are those of Shakespeare. Byron also cast aspersions in his direction. One of the few English poets to appreciate the loyalty of the donkey was William Wordsworth, who revealed his compassion for the patient, faithful animal in his long poem *Peter Bell*. One night Bell, a rough, renegade potter, came upon a gaunt, weak donkey alongside a stream. Thinking of saving his legs, the rogue mounted the animal, who stood motionless, heavy head lowered, gazing into the stream:

His head is with a halter bound;
The halter seizing, Peter leapt
Upon the Creature's back, and plied
With ready heels his shaggy side;
But still the Ass his station kept.

Repeated urgings by Peter had no effect on the burro, who merely

Stood just as he had stood before!
. . . .
All, all is silent—rocks and woods,
All still and silent—far and near!
Only the Ass, with motion dull,
Upon the pivot of his skull
Turns round his long left ear.

Thought Peter, What can mean all this?
Some ugly witchcraft must be here!
—Once more the Ass, with motion dull,
Upon the pivot of his skull
Turned round his long left ear.

Then Peter, exasperated by the animal's refusal to move, beat the
little donkey with his staff until the animal fell, first to his knees
and then on his side, moaning and braying, all the while keeping
his head pointed toward the edge of the water. Belatedly Peter saw
in the moonlight the body of a man in the water. Peter fainted from
shock. When he came to, the beaten donkey was still lying beside
the river. But as the dazed Peter walked to the river and with his
staff tested the depth, the donkey arose and came to his side:

His staring bones all shake with joy,
And close by Peter's side he stands:
While Peter o'er the river bends,
The little Ass his neck extends,
And fondly licks his hands.

. . . .

The Ass looks on . . . .
. . . .
And Peter draws him to dry land;
And through the brain of Peter pass
Some poignant twitches, fast and faster;
"No doubt," quoth he, "he is the Master
Of this poor miserable Ass!"[29]

Other British poets expressed sympathy for the donkey. In that regard the Scottish Robert Burns had an explanation for the thick hide of the burro: "The donkey's thick hide was given it by a compassionate Providence as a provision against pre-ordained cudgelling."[30]

Donkey derbies were being staged in England more than ten years before the first Kentucky Derby was held in 1875. Donkey derbies were advertised as charity benefits, but in reality they were held strictly for the amusement of the spectators and at the expense of the animals. The spectators made fun of the animals forced to run in the races.[31] The custom of holding such races crossed the Atlantic and can be found in one form or another today in the western states, as well as in Alaska and Hawaii.

In the last quarter of the nineteenth century the burro's status was an inferior one, as indicated by the fact that no tax was imposed on his owner. The burro was the "child of Ham, the slave of the household, and . . . attached to the poor and the gypsy."[32] Today, however, England has excellent animal-welfare laws and enforces them vigorously. The English are ahead of the Americans in this regard and frown upon our liberal use of dogs, monkeys, and other animals, including burros, in scientific experiments. In this country burros have been subjected to experiments to determine the quantities of carbon monoxide and other smog fumes that can be inhaled before fatalities result—an unthinkable practice in England.

Farmers, traders, craftsmen, and merchants of the British Isles have long made use of the burro. He has served the costermonger in the produce markets of London; he has labored on the fertile farms of England, Scotland, and Ireland; he has done his duty in Wales; he has carried or pulled carts of delighted children at coastal resort areas; he has provided amusement for spectators at Derby races (though that duty he has performed but indifferently); he has served as an export for Ireland; and he has been a popular exhibit at zoos. Today he is beginning to come into his own in still another function—as a family pet. Let Robin Borwick, formerly a professional donkey breeder at Maidenhead, Berkshire, England, tell about Angelica:

> I have a friend who owns a country pub called the Bridge House. He only took this business over quite recently, and found he had a lovely old place with about an acre of brambles where the garden used to be. Not being the sort of man who has spent a lifetime with a scythe in his hand, he bought a donkey and called her Angelica. She is not the most beautiful of donkeys, but being large and partial to brambles, she completed the job very quickly. Angelica is intelligent and interested in all that goes on at the pub. Being part of the staff, she naturally takes her work seriously and does it very well . . . Other country pubs have gardens, where the children fret and get in the way while their parents have a well-earned drink after work, but the Bridge House is the pub where the children not only cry when they have to leave, but ask their parents to visit again. Like everyone who works at a pub, Angelica enjoys her pint of beer, and this does her no harm. . . . She is a strong donkey and her back is broad, she can easily carry a man, and many people do sit on her holding a tankard in the air while their wives take photographs. . . .
>
> Angelica's consumption of beer is carefully controlled. . . . She is much too valuable as an attraction and entertainer of children to be allowed to make an exhibition of herself by overindulgence. Beer is a good wholesome drink made entirely of vegetable ingredients, and just as appetizing to a horse or donkey as it is to me. It is interesting to note that alcohol first affects those parts of the brain which are most highly developed. In the

human brain, the center of intelligence is large in comparison with other mammals, so after too much beer man is even less intelligent than usual. Equines have well-developed centers of locomotion, and a donkey who has had one too many would have difficulty in walking down a white line even though it could still bray quite intelligently.[33]

As Britain grew, the donkey spread to the empire's far-flung possessions. In January, 1825, Richard Charlton loaded three donkeys on his brig, *Active*, and with a crew of ten left Falmouth, England, bound for the Sandwich (Hawaiian) Islands. The voyage was long, across the Atlantic, down the eastern coast of South America, through the storm-tossed waters of the Strait of Magellan, and across the Pacific to Honolulu. The *Active* arrived there in April, 1825, bearing Charlton, the first British consul appointed to the islands—and most likely the first donkeys seen by the natives.

It would seem logical that American burros from California should have arrived in Hawaii before English ones, for by that time Americans had acquired much of the island trade. During the early nineteenth century, however, there was a restriction in California against exporting breeding animals. Not until about 1879 did the first burros arrive from the United States.

A month after the *Active* docked in Honolulu with the burros, H.M.S. *Blonde*, captained by Lord Byron, a cousin of the famed poet, arrived from England. James Macrae, a botanist who accompanied Byron, kept a diary of the journey in which he mentioned Charlton's donkeys. Charlton insisted that the botanist take three donkeys on a scheduled trip into the forests to collect plant specimens. Macrae reluctantly settled for one of the animals; however, the donkey was soon discarded.[34] Though Macrae did not give the reason in his diary, it is likely that the donkey was fired for eating too many of the specimens.

For some years afterward the donkey failed to make much of an impression on Hawaiian economy. As late as 1835 human beings were pulling plows at Koloa, the first Hawaiian sugar plantation. However, by 1849 one Henry L. Sheldon reported that "the demand for livestock was very brisk in California, and the high prices realized led to the transportation thither from the [Hawaiian] Islands of horses, mules, bullocks, hogs, and fowl."[35] The mules were undoubtedly the progeny of male donkeys and mare horses in the islands.

By the 1850's donkeys had become a regular item of trade in the islands. In the columns of the *Pacific Commercial Advertiser* (published in Honolulu), which listed interisland trade, one finds mention of burros. The ship *Liholiho*, leaving Honolulu bound for Hilo on May 6, 1857, had as a part of its cargo "5 bbls. corn, 15 bbls. salt, 10 horses, 7 donkeys, . . . 2 brass clocks."

Why was the burro taken to Hawaii, Paradise of the Pacific? Not to enjoy a vacation or to attend a convention, but, as elsewhere, to bear burdens and to pull loads. Besides carrying firewood and water, his traditional chores, he transported coconuts, taro, rice, papayas, coffee, pineapples, sugar cane, cowhides, wool, sandalwood, and, of course, human cargo.

The first sugar mills in the Hawaiian Islands were animal- or water-powered. Very likely burros' feet beat out the paths around the two cylindrical stone rollers that ground the cane. It is known that one mill near Honolulu was dismantled, packed on burros, and carried to the Nuuanu Pali (a windswept mountain pass) and down a winding trail to a new location on the other side of the mountain.

As elsewhere, burro meat has served as an item in the diet of the people of the islands, and at one time was made into jerky.

Not only was Robert Louis Stevenson fond of the burro, as he admitted in *Travels with a Donkey*, but in the late 1880's his wife also enjoyed her burro, Dickey, who pulled her cart. The burro was given to her by the Golden Gate Park Commission before she and her family left San Francisco bound for Hawaii and Samoa. On the ship's deck a small stable was erected for Dickey. On the voyage to Honolulu, he became the ship's pet.

A Hawaiian burro. Courtesy of Paradise Publishing Company.

In the park at Waikiki Beach, Fanny drove Dickey hitched to a specially designed cart. Dickey had a mysterious work pattern. He would trot briskly for five minutes and then stop. Mrs. Stevenson would get out of the cart. When she got back in, he would continue for five minutes more, and then she must get out of the cart again before he would continue. It took Mrs. Stevenson quite a while to unravel the mystery of Dickey's starts and stops. Finally it was recalled that, at Golden Gate Park, Dickey had been taught to pull a cart with children for a five-minute ride. He was simply carrying on the custom.[36]

Apparently Dickey liked Waikiki Beach, for when the time arrived to board the ship for Samoa, he was reluctant to leave. Block and tackle were brought to hoist Dickey aboard. But he would not be led into this gear, though two, three, and finally half a dozen men tried to pull him into it. He stubbornly held back, much to the amusement of passengers at the ship's rail. Finally the captain shouted orders to the men to pull the burro in the opposite direction. The trick: Dickey, resisting, backed himself in the loading harness.[37]

The Samoans were entranced by Dickey. The Stevensons' maidservants took him along when they went to the fields to cut alfalfa for the cows. "They made a pretty picture coming through the forest, the girls in leaves and flowers, and Dickey a walking mountain of grass,"[38] commented Mrs. Stevenson.

Dickey was not the first of his line to graze or to pack bundles of grass in the Samoan Islands. More than twenty-five years earlier, in 1863, the *Kehrwieder* had on board, when it sailed for Apia, West Samoa, "12 bbls. potatoes, 3 asses, 12 sheep, 21 bbls. ale." Australia was another importer of asses. As early as July, 1858, the *Pacific Commercial Advertiser* reported that the *L. P. Foster* was departing for Portland, Victoria, Australia, with "175 bbls. Hawaiian beef, 15 kegs of sugar, 5 bbls. tallow, 30 jackasses." Two years later, in 1860, the *Mary Ellen* departed for Victoria with "75 bags of sweet potatoes, 2 jackasses, 2 whaleboats." In 1862 the *Benjamin Rush* left Honolulu for the same destination with "1 keg of whiskey, . . . 8 mules, 2 horses, lot of hay." A month later the *Constitution*, bound for southern Australia, logged "60 mules, 3 horses, 100 sheep, 10 goats, lot of hay." The Australians were good customers of the Hawaiian exporters.

The logs of these ships used "mules" and "asses" indiscriminantly, and we have no way of knowing how accurate they were. (People still confuse the two breeds. Some of my neighbors refer to Catrino,

A team of burros pulling wagons loaded with wool, Western Australia, ca. 1900. Courtesy of Bob Beattie.

my burro, as "that mule," and on my desk is an illustration from a magazine dated September, 1970, showing an unmistakable gray burro—with the transverse stripe across his withers—and a caption portraying him as representing "mule power.")

Thus the burro arrived in Australia and later in New Zealand and Tasmania. Whether the shipments from Hawaii were the first livestock importations to Australia and the adjacent islands is not known. However, we do know that during the last half of the nineteenth century and the early years of the twentieth the number of livestock of all kinds imported into Australia grew rapidly and that their offspring spread over that vast domain.

The burro of Australia performed much the same duties assigned him elsewhere. Traders, wood haulers, and water carriers made use of him. He was a familiar sight in villages and on farms. He was the prospector's friend and a partner in the ore fields.

Historically burros and sheep have been complementary—they go together. The burro was—and is—extremely useful on the large sheep stations in the outback. Not only did he bear burdens of equipment, supplies, wood, and water, but he also helped deliver wool, an all-important product of the sheep industry, to Australian railheads and ports. The wool was packed in large burlap bags and loaded on large wagons, to which were hitched teams of twenty burros.

Kirwan Ward, a columnist for the *Perth* (Australia) *Daily News* learned of my interest in burros from the American vice-consul in that city, William Gallagher. Ward mentioned in his column of September 2, 1970, that I was having difficulty securing a photograph of an Australian pack burro. Many readers obliged with photographs, and Ward reproduced two of them in his column. One photograph showed a twenty-burro team from Bamboo, a town in Western Australia. The picture brought the following comment from a reader, Bill Thompson:

"I drove that Bamboo team that you showed in your picture

for one day. Mick, the driver, took a load of wool into Marble Bar, unloaded it, loaded on about six tons of stores, let his donkeys go, and got on the grog. After a week or so I knew that Bamboo would be getting short of stores, so I got Mick's young offsider to muster the donkeys; then I yoked them up and put Mick on top of the load. Tied him down so he wouldn't fall off and drove the team to the 10-mile well and left him to it."

Burros are also used on cattle stations in Australia. North of Perth, in the far northern region of Western Australia, is the Kimberley Plateau, known to the Australians as the "Kimberleys." This extensive area contains very large cattle runs. Horses are not of much use in the area, being seriously affected by what is known as "Kimberley disease," which is attributed to a local poisonous plant. Burros, who do not eat the plant, take the place of horses, carrying water, food, bedding, and equipment to the mustering camps of the area.

Burros have their place in Australian folklore as elsewhere, but oddly enough it was an adopted Greek burro who achieved immortality in Australian history. The event took place at Gallipoli

Because horses are seriously affected by Kimberley disease, pack donkeys are used to carry gear for mustering (roundup) camps in the area. This scene is on the four thousand square miles of Gogo Station, the largest cattle run in the Kimberleys, the far northern region of Western Australia. Photograph by W. Pederson. Courtesy of Australian News and Information Bureau.

John Simpson Kirkpatrick (center) and Abdul, at Gallipoli, 1915. Australian War Memorial Photograph.

during World War I. In 1915, British soldiers, including Anzacs, landed on the peninsula in a campaign to take the Dardanelles. The campaign was unsuccessful, and British losses were heavy. In the retreat to the sea, an Australian, John Simpson Kirkpatrick, who came to be known as the Good Samaritan of Gallipoli," with a

Memorials to Abdul. Australian postage stamp depicting Kirkpatrick and his donkey, commemorating the fiftieth anniversary of the Gallipoli landing in 1915. Courtesy of postmaster general, Australia. Opposite: Bronze statue by Wallace Anderson commemorating *The Man with the Donkey* at the Shrine of Remembrance, Melbourne, Australia. Australian War Memorial photograph.

burro named Abdul, brought the wounded down murderous Shrapnel Gully to aid stations. Abdul and another burro had been taken aboard an Australian troop ship at the Greek island of Lemnos to carry pieces of artillery after the landing. During the landing, however, the burros were almost forgotten and were finally pushed overboard and swam to the beach. Later one of them showed up, following Kirkpatrick in his work as a stretcher bearer.

Both Kirkpatrick and Abdul worked day after day and into each night. The stretcher bearer would place a wounded soldier astride the burro, and the little animal would make his way out of firing range to the treatment centers. The two continued their rescue

work until Kirkpatrick was killed by an enemy bullet. Even then Abdul continued to rescue the wounded, continuing his by now familiar trail to the aid stations. Later Abdul, whose back was often stained with the blood of his wounded passengers, became a pet of the Sixth Mountain Battery Indians, who took him to India with them after the evacuation.[39]

Abdul was described as "a little mouse-coloured animal, no taller than a Newfoundland dog. . . . The donkey was a patient, sure-footed ally, with a capacity for bearing loads out of all proportion to his size."[40]

A memorial to Abdul and to his Anzac master stands in Melbourne, Australia. It is called *The Man with the Donkey.* In 1965 the Australian government issued three postage stamps portraying the statue to commemorate the fiftieth anniversary of the Gallipoli landings.

And so at least one burro achieved a measure of glory in wartime. But it was not a typical role for him. Much more common was the lot of two burros who sailed on the transport H.M.S. *Goslar* from New Zealand to Gallipoli. It was widely believed that burros will not drink impure or poisoned water, and it was the two burros' job to test the drinking water for the troops.[41]

13. Following the Conquistadors

Spanish and Portuguese literature is rich in folk tales and poetry. A recurring theme is one in which a clever rascal outwits a gullible soul. One story, a tale from the Portuguese, goes about as follows:

Two college students were walking along a country road when they met a poor merchant with a burro loaded with jars of cooking oil. The boys were without funds, and, seeing the burro with its profitable load, they had an idea. They would steal the burro, take him and his load to the neighboring fair, and sell them. As the merchant trudged along leading the burro, one student crept to the side of the animal's head. He carefully removed the halter and placed it on himself. His companion led the burro away. After a while the student stopped, and the merchant looked back and saw that he was leading a human being.

"Dear master," the student said, "thanks for beating me; it has dispelled enchantment that has held me for so many years in the form of a donkey." The bewildered trader replied that now he had lost his only means of support. He apologized for having beaten the burro but added that it had been necessary, for in his burro life he had been stupid and wayward, though he had been provided a handful of straw and a piece of bread after a day of hard work. The student forgave the merchant, telling him to go in peace.

The merchant went to his godfather, told his story, and was given money to buy another burro. At the fair the next day he saw the burro that had been stolen from him. He whispered into the burro's ear, "I tell you what, donkey, those that do not know what you are, are welcome to buy you if they choose."[1]

Two great classics of Spanish literature, *Don Quixote* and *Platero and I*, contain much praise for the burro. Juan Ramón Jiménez, in his philosophical conversations with his burro, Platero, grieves for the burros who are mistreated, beaten, and starved. Speaking of an aged and infirm burro that has been taken to the refuse pit and abandoned to die, he mourns: "Platero, tonight he will freeze to death in this high ravine, pierced by the north wind. . . . I do not know how to leave; I do not know what to do, Platero. . . ."[2]

Then he describes the lot of the sand dealers' donkeys, saying: "Look, Platero, at Quemado's donkeys; slow, drooping, with their pointed red load of wet sand, pierced, as a heart might be, by the green olive rod with which they are beaten. . . ." He observes gypsies who have come to town. A woman of their band is going to ask permission of the local authorities to set up camp behind the cemetery: "Look . . . How well she carries the memory of her beauty, gallant still, like an oak, her red kerchief round her body . . . . You remember the sordid tents of the gypsies, their fires, their gaudy women, their starving donkeys all around!" He tells

A Guatemalan burro carrying on with his traditional duties—here packing wood. Courtesy of Eduardo Trejo.

A Spanish burro laden with a tourist vendor's wares, near Toledo. Photograph by Florence Brookshier.

how the gypsies "dye their donkeys and give them arsenic and stick pins in their ears to keep them from drooping."[3]

Fortunate Platero, to belong to gentle Jiménez, who feeds him grapes and melons and talks with him as a friend.

Platero and I is more than the story of a man and his burro in remote Moguer, Spain. Jiménez' genius is reflected in his insight into the wonders of nature's creations. His warm attitude toward Platero and the anguish he feels about the mistreatment of other burros by their owners captures the sympathy of all but the most callous of souls. The poet and his burro are friends, ambling along together, the man talking tenderly to the silver-gray donkey as the

two wander among the hills or relax under a tree. The warm observations of Jiménez about his home, the people, the trees, grass,
crops, flowers, and animals, produce in the reader a sympathetic
response and a reverence for life—and an acceptance of all life,
with none to be rejected. The work is among the world's masterpieces in simplicity of manner joined with philosophic perception.

See how the author thinks of Platero as his equal:
Jiménez and Platero have traveled to the capital city. On an
earlier journey Jiménez saw a beautiful orchard in the city. Now
he wants Platero to see it and share his enjoyment. They walk together in the cool shade of the acacias and the banana trees. But
when they come to the gateway, the man who guards the entrance
says, "The donkey may not enter, sir." Surprised, Jiménez replies,
"The donkey? What donkey?" The gateman answers, "What donkey could I mean?" Then Jiménez realizes that the gateman means
his friend Platero. Refusing to enter the orchard without his companion, he pats Platero on the head, and they go on their way discussing other things.[4]

Spain and Portugal have long been the home and breeding
ground of the burro. The animal was laboring on the Iberian Peninsula during Roman times. And when the Moors took over Spain,
they brought additional burros from northern Africa to aid in the
conquest and to develop the country's resources and economy.

Climatically Iberia is healthful for the burro, but there as elsewhere his life has been an unhappy one. A poem inspired by a baby
Spanish burro illustrates his lot in life:

> Capering, he acts as wild
> As a naughty, wilful child
> Runs before his mother, then
> Kicks his heels and starts again,
> Leads her on with many wiles,
> Wagging ears she only smiles,
> Knowing in the future he
> Seldom e'er can happy be.[5]

Jiménez and Platero. From Juan Ramón Jiménez, *Platero and I* (tr. by Eloise Roach, drawing by Jo Alys Downs, Austin, University of Texas Press, 1957, 80). Reproduced by permission.

Yet despite mistreatment burros are loyal to their masters and have a homing instinct that has become legendary. Valiante, a nine-teenth-century Spanish burro, is a case in point.

Valiante was a prison burro. Holes had been punched in his ears to indicate his prison ownership. His chief duty was to serve as a form of whipping post. Recalcitrant inmates were placed upon his back and lashed with a whip. A double punishment was thus meted out—the humiliation of sitting astride a burro and being flogged. It seems likely that Valiante also felt the lash of the whip when it was wielded by an undiscriminating guard.

Valiante somehow gained his freedom and a new master, a Captain Dundas of the British navy stationed at Malta in the Mediterranean. For some time the burro was kept in a stable in British Gibraltar until Dundas could arrange to have him sent to Malta. In March, 1816, Valiante was placed on board the frigate *Ister*, bound for Malta. Off Cape Gata a storm blew up. The frigate was tossed and beaten by the waves. The crew, fearing that the ship would sink, pushed Valiante overboard into the rough, stormy sea in hopes that he would swim safely to shore.

Several days later Valiante showed up on Gibraltar unattended and went directly to his stall in the stable. The owner was surprised but assumed that for some reason the animal had not been put on board the ship. The mystery was solved when the *Ister* limped back into port for repairs. Valiante had swum to safety and without a guide or compass had made his way over mountains and across streams to reach his stall.

Why was Valiante not claimed by someone along the way? The holes in his ears were his passport. The peasants realized that he was a prison burro and, superstitious about such animals, let him go his way.[6]

Times have not changed too much. Valiante had holes punched in his ears, and today burros lose hairs from their tails to inmates of a prison near Alamos, in Sonora, Mexico. The prisoners fashion hatbands from the hairs. The burro cannot win, it seems—holes punched in his ears in Spain, and hairs plucked from his tail in Mexico.

The Moors took many good things to Spain, and during their long residence they accomplished much, using Middle Eastern scientific, medical, agricultural, and literary skills. The sons of Islam provided new ideas and kept the torch of learning aflame in medieval Spain. The Moslems replaced the oxen of the Spanish farmers with more versatile mules. They introduced the windmill into Spain, and from there it was brought to the American West. The Moors also introduced many new crops into Spain—rice, buckwheat, sugar cane, cotton, pomegranates, bananas, cherries, oranges, lemons, quince, grapefruit, peaches, apricots, dates, figs, and strawberries. All these products were carried to market by burros. Toledo became an important steel-manufacturing center, and burros helped haul the raw and finished products. The burro was thus a part of thriving economic activities—farming, crafts, trade. He carried fine silk, whose culture was introduced to Spain by the Arabs in the eighth century.

In the fifteenth century the flame of Islam grew dim in Spain. In 1486, Isabella la Católica assembled her forces to oust the Moors from their last stronghold, Granada. Supplies for the expedition were carried by a pack train made up of sixty thousand mules and burros—perhaps the largest number of animals ever assembled for purposes of war in Europe. Though it took another six years to assure her ascendancy in Spain, Isabella found time to turn her thoughts westward. Spanish housewives were complaining about the spoilage of their applesauce. Nutmeg was needed. Isabella dispatched Columbus in search of the Spice Islands. Poor, unlucky Christopher—he failed. All he discovered was America.

Then, after laboring for mankind more than five thousand years in the Middle East and for at least two thousand years in Europe, the burro sailed westward to labor in faraway lands.

He, along with his kin, the horse and the mule, accompanied the conquistadors to explore, settle, and develop the New World. Many historians believe that the transporting of these animals across the sea was the greatest single contribution that the Spaniards made in the Western Hemisphere. As Charles F. Lummis wrote, "The Spanish introduction of the horse, mule, burro, and ox to America marked the longest stride that so many people, in so short a time, have ever taken in the arts of transportation."[7]

Records of Spanish shipments of animals to the New World are sparse, but on April 9, 1495, Ferdinand II of Spain, Isabella's husband, wrote a letter of instruction to Juan de Fonseca, conveying the order that one Diego Carillo was to take some livestock to Columbus, who was then on his second voyage to the New World. The animals were to include six mares, four bull calves, two heifers, one hundred sheep and goats, four jacks, two jennies, twenty sows, and eighty boars.[8] Even earlier, on May 23, 1493, the secretary to the king and queen had been instructed to collect horses for the expedition. The horses waded to the shores of Hispaniola (today Haiti and Santo Domingo) in November of the same year.[9] When Columbus' fleet arrived at Gomera, in the Canaries, additional livestock, heifers, goats, ewes, and sows, were taken on board.[10]

The animals transported across the ocean in the small ships of the day endured a rough voyage. Horses and burros were swung in hammocks with only their hind feet touching the floor. Both water and feed often became scarce, especially during the calms in the horse latitudes. Sometimes the calms lasted for weeks, making it necessary to throw livestock overboard to conserve water.

Writing at the close of the sixteenth century, the Spanish missionary José de Acosta reported the healthy increase of horses and mules in the New World. He made little reference to burros, only saying there were not many (overlooking the fact that the mule is half burro). It is doubtful that Acosta was much of an observer, for the burro quickly became a valuable cog in the developing economy of New Spain.

The burro and the horse arrived in the West Indies a number of years before they set hoof on the mainland of America. Burros first trod the soil of Mexico very early in the history of the Conquest. One source says that Juan de Zumárraga, the first Roman Catholic bishop of Mexico, took a pair of burros with him and that they were first on the mainland.[11] About ten years after the arrival of Cortés in 1519, the bishop was recommending to the king of Spain the introduction of burros. They were to relieve the Indians, who had been enslaved and branded by the Spaniards, a practice Zumárraga opposed.

To the familiar burdens the pack burro had carried in Spain—wheat, barley, buckwheat, cotton, fruits, dairy products, mohair, wool, wood, pottery, and steel products—he added in the New World such products as cassava, corn, pineapples, coffee beans, yerba maté, squash, sweet potatoes, white potatoes, buffalo hides, turkeys, and ores.

For the people of northeastern Brazil, one of the first regions settled by Europeans, the burro was and is their most valuable domestic animal. He performs manifold duties, pulls two-wheeled carts laden with sugar cane and construction materials, and along country roads may be seen packing innumerable items, including the traditional cargo everywhere—water, firewood, and human beings. Recent statistics indicate a burro population of 1,192,000 in Brazil.[12]

Santana do Ipanema, in the Brazilian district of Alagoas, is a municipality of eight thousand residents. In 1969 it acquired a water system—a pipeline bringing water from nearby São Francisco River. Until completion of the pipeline burros had packed kegs of water to the city. The mayor, Adeildo Nepomuceno Marques, and other thoughtful citizens did not forget the burros' contribution. They erected a statue in their honor.[13]

Upon reading the account of this memorial, I wrote a letter to the mayor, congratulating him on the project. He replied in part:

> The donkey has given inestimable services to the progress of northeastern Brazil and to Santana, today a progressive city.

Today we use the services of this animal to carry water to our
outlying residential areas and also to carry earth, sand, cement,
wood, stones, and even man himself.

It was the great resistance of this animal to the vigorous northeastern climate that helped immensely in firmly establishing man
in this land. Without him I do not believe that our region would
be as well developed as it actually is today.[14]

The letter was accompanied by a photograph of the statue.

Burros were imported into Venezuela at a very early date. The
director of the National Library in Caracas told me of a book in
the library containing records for the years 1535 to 1607. Included
are transportation permits for livestock, including burros, and other
items entering Caracas from Margarita, an island off the coast of
Venezuela.[15] Margarita, 450 square miles of fertile land, was discovered by Columbus in 1498, and the first Spanish colonists moved
there in 1525. Most likely they brought burros with them from other
islands of the West Indies. There they established cattle ranches
and developed coastal fisheries. Burros packed the heavy salt for
both industries. Thus Margarita was a stepping stone for the burro
on his way into South America.

The director of the Caracas library provided me with further
information about the burro's culture in Venezuela:

The topographical references to the burro in Venezuela are
numerous. In the *Nomenclador General de Areas de Lugares
Habitados en Venezuela,* 1944 edition, we find a place named
Burritas; one named Burrito; three named El Burrero; sixteen
named El Burro; one El Burrito, and another El Burroxi; three
named La Burra, and six, La Burrera.[16]

Such place names indicate the early presence of burros in various
remote parts of Venezuela. Similar names are common not only in
the countries of South America but also in Mexico and in the
western regions of the United States once held by Spain.

As elsewhere, the burro is a part of folklore in Venezuela:

Statue honoring the burro in Santana do Ipanema, Alagoas, Brazil. Courtesy of Mayor Adeildo Nepomuceno Marques.

. . . in our own folklore there exists a curious or strange custom or disguise of a man with a skirt like those of the Crinolina. In front along the waistline is placed a burro head and in back is placed a tail of the same, made of "trapos." . . . The man in disguise goes up and down the streets of the town dancing a peculiar dance to the tune of a guitar and maracas. From the name Burriquita de la Crinolina we believe that the custom dates from the beginning of the nineteenth century.[17]

The mountains and plains of Peru also became the home of the burro. José de Acosta traveled the continent of South America for seventeen years, spreading the Catholic faith. Very likely he used burros for riding and for packing supplies during his years as a missionary. In 1571 he was in Peru. In his reports to his superiors in Spain he "dwelt at length upon the condition of the domestic animals, sheep, kine, goats, horses, asses, dogs, and cats, which the Spaniards had introduced into the New World and which were already thoroughly acclimated."[18] Cattle ranching quickly became productive; in 1587 thousands of cowhides were shipped to Seville.[19] The burro, for thousands of years a chief transporter of hides, undoubtedly carried many of them from the interior to coastal ports.

Fifty years after Columbus arrived in the Indies, the burro was well known in Mexico. An early manuscript on the conquest, edited by Henri Ternaux-Compans in the 1830's, quotes a letter to Antonio de Mendoza, vicèroy of Mexico in 1550, in which it is stated that "a well-behaved jenny has to be groomed in order to bring fifteen to twenty pesos." Thus burros were not only plentiful but also an element of colonial economy in some parts of Mexico at least by the middle of the sixteenth century.

During pre-Columbian times the only animal bearing burdens for man in South America was the llama. The llama was and is as

Burros in Mexico. Oil by Ambrose Patterson, 1934. Courtesy of West Seattle (Washington) Art Club.

useful to the Indians of the Andes as the camel (to which it is related) is to the Bedouins of the Middle Eastern deserts. He provides transportation, meat, and wool for clothing. The burro was reluctantly introduced into the llama's domain. He did not like the high, cold, mountains. Until he became acclimated to the rough terrain of the lofty Andes, he was at a disadvantage. Garcilosa de la Vega, writing in 1557, described a burro that he saw in Peru. The animal was small, emaciated, apparently worn out by the rugged demands made upon him. Burros were still scarce in the area for Garcilosa said that more animals were needed for breeding purposes.[20]

Well, the Peruvian burro survived, and today he may be seen doing his work, carrying articles of trade, handicrafts, and passengers and pulling crude plows in the high-terraced fields of the Andes.

Beginning about 1525 ships began rounding the southern tip of South America and sailing north along the west coast. Before long ships were stationed at Acapulco. Cargo from Spain and from West Indies ports docked at Veracruz or at Portobello on the eastern coast of Mexico. Part of the cargo was sold there, and the remainder was loaded on burros and mules and packed across Mexico to Acapulco. There the waiting ships loaded the cargo and then sailed south to Peru. Later the ships ventured across the broad Pacific to the Philippines, which Magellan had claimed for the Spanish crown in 1521.

The road laid out by Cortés in 1522 from Veracruz to Mexico City did an enormous business in transporting articles of commerce. The transport was chiefly pack trains of mules and burros. The cost of transporting goods on muleback varied, but twenty-five dollars a mule was not uncommon. Less was charged for the burro's service, for he carried a smaller load. Pack trains moved as much as fifty thousand tons a year over this famous road. Inns and blacksmith shops were established along it, and mule and burro shoeing was a lucrative business for three centuries, until the arrival of the railroad in 1873. Amozoc became the most important blacksmithing town on the road—and perhaps in all of the Americas. It had the advantage of an early start. In 1527, Pedro Jaime set up his anvil and bellows in the village. His shop made bridle bits, spurs, machetes, and shoes and shoe nails for mules, burros, and horses. During the period thousands of hoofs were trimmed and shod in the blacksmith shops, while in the inns and cantinas *los arrieros* (the drivers) waited, eating and drinking pulque and mescal.

Burros, mules, and llamas bore on their backs thousands of tons of rich ore from the almost inaccessible mines hidden in the rugged mountains of Central and South America. The animals were sometimes shod with shoes of gold or silver because those metals were cheaper, more abundant, and more readily available than iron or steel.[21] The pack animals, struggling over the winding, rock-strewn, tortuous trails with their heavy loads, wore down their bodies and legs. When they were no longer fit for transport duties, their emaciated and toil-consumed bodies became the prey of hungry wolves, buzzards, and condors. Sometimes dogs would be allowed to gnaw on their bones after their hides were removed for leather—their last contribution to man.

The llama is part of the mining lore of South America, as is the burro in Mexico and in the western United States. It is said that in Bolivia in 1544 a llama tied to a bush pulled back on its rope and uprooted the plant, exposing rock that later became the location of the rich Cerro de Potosí silver mine. The llama discovered nature's rich cache—but the burro helped pack the ore down the trail.

Potosí, once the largest and richest city of the New World, is a little over thirteen thousand feet in elevation, high and remote. In the 1600's it was a booming mining center with a privileged class that indulged in a gay social life. But inside the mountain numberless enslaved Indians worked, sickened, died, and were buried. "Records show that caravans of as many as 2,500 conscripts, with 5,000 members of their families and 30,000 animals, were sent yearly to Potosí from Peruvian towns as far away as four hundred miles."[22]

The rich mine at Cerro de Pasco, Peru, another of the great bonanzas of history, also depended upon the llama and the imported burro and mule to take from the mountain its rich silver ore. It too has a tragic history of inhumane treatment of man and animal.

In 1535 the bishop of Panama boarded a ship bound for Peru. As the ship was nearing its destination it was becalmed and drifted off course. It finally found sanctuary in a group of uninhabited islands off present-day Ecuador. Thus were discovered the fascinating Galápagos, the home of the giant tortoise and other exotic creatures. The bishop's ship had animals on board—horses, cats, dogs, cows, goats, and burros—originally destined for Spanish settlements in Peru. When the ship landed, the animals either escaped or were put ashore. Those that were not recaptured were left to roam wild in the Enchanted Isles.

Who said the burro was slower than the horse? Courtesy of U.S. Information Service, Bogotá, Colombia.

The sailors found the meat of the Galápagos turtles delicious, and later crewmen of ships that called at the islands put live turtles, some weighing several hundred pounds, into the holds to serve as fresh meat. Sometimes the turtles remained alive in the holds for a year.

The burros of the Galápagos were not the only feral burros in the New World. Many burros introduced into Mexico escaped from bondage and became wild. Then they were hunted as game.

Pack burros in a northern Chilean village, 1970. Courtesy of U.S. Information Service, Santiago, Chile.

Along the coast of Sonora and across the gulf in Lower California the Seri Indians added the flesh of the burro to their long-established diet of turtle.

Explorers and colonizers, both Spaniards and, later, other Europeans, took burros with them to virtually every part of South America. Charles Darwin, visiting in Chile during the voyage of the *Beagle* in the 1830's, commented on the presence of burros in that country. The burro's traditional role had unfolded there, for Darwin wrote, ". . . firewood, or rather sticks, are brought on donkeys from a distance of two and three days' journey within the Cordillera."[23]

East of Chile and across the Andes Mountains lies Argentina, with its broad and fertile pampas, a six-hundred-square-mile paradise for sheepmen and cattlemen. And livestock growers were not long in coming. As early as 1537 sheep, along with horses and burros, were brought into the Argentine. Today the burro, the mule, and the horse are still indispensable in the pampas, where the colorful gauchos, the South American counterparts of the western cowboy, carry on their work.

The burro accompanied the conquistadors to the New World, but he is most closely identified with the settlers—those who came to stay, to build homes, to till the soil, to ranch, and to engage in commerce and trade. He packed the gold and silver ores from the bonanzas, for a time. But his most useful work was on the farms, in the hills, along the trails, and in the marketplaces.

North of Argentina lies Bolivia, a land rich in mineral resources and forests. A letter from an acquaintance in Bolivia describes the present-day life of the Bolivian burro:

> The burro is used in Bolivia quite extensively for almost any job you can possibly imagine. It carries packs of potatoes, wheat, corn, flour, cornstalks, bread, vegetables, kegs of *chicha* (the national corn whiskey drink), firewood, water, and more. The animal is also used as a means of transporting people (by some

of the Indian population). Many times it carries the man on its back, while the woman walks alongside it!

The burro has many jobs aside from carrying packs. During the wheat harvest, it is used to trample the wheat on the harvest floor so that the grain will fall off the stalks. A rope is tied around the burro's neck and the farmer stands in the middle of the harvest floor while he directs the animal to go around in circles.

On Palm Sunday the burro has a very important role in the religious rites. A statue of Christ is placed on the animal's back and a large procession with palm-bearing people is held. The life-sized statue is made of heavy plaster, incidentally; therefore the burro has quite a load on its back.

The colors of the burros here in Bolivia range anywhere from an off-white to black. I would say that about forty-five percent are dark brown, forty percent are medium gray, and the other fifteen percent are other shades. There are not any green or blue ones, however. But there are pink ones! On June 24 is San Juan's Saint's Day, and, evidently he is the patron saint of reproduction or fertility, because the people paint *all* of their animals pink on that day so they will have many offspring during the year.

Pack burros, Bolivia, 1970. Courtesy of Wesley Brown.

One burro personality that I know best is the one belonging to my next-door neighbor, but he doesn't *do* anything! When I poke him, pull his tail, stick my tongue out at him, or shove him, all he does is look at me. I tried to see who could outstare whom, and he won. I have also played "chicken" along narrow trails with various donkeys, and I always lose. Just last week I was walking back home from a village, and I wasn't looking where I was going because of my preoccupation with a problem, and I ran head-on into a burro. We just stopped and looked at each other, and if he could have spoken, I'm absolutely certain that he would have called me a 'dumb burro'![24]

Sadly enough, in Bolivia as almost everywhere else in the world, the burro has been a symbol of scorn and humiliation. The following story, from Victorian days, is but one illustration:

Visitors to Bolivia are still told the tale of the British minister plenipotentiary who fell into the bad graces of a Bolivian president and was run out of the capital unclothed, undignified, and seated on an ass; whereupon Queen Victoria ordered a ship of war to La Paz to demonstrate her shocked displeasure off the Bolivian coast.[25]

America has given many plants to the world, and the burro has helped plant, cultivate, harvest, and transport them. Corn, or maize, cereal native to the Americas, is grown from Canada to Patagonia, at the southern tip of Argentina. The burro was early put to work helping raise this important food crop. Spaniards with Columbus found maize in Cuba. Among the very first foods Cortés and his soldiers ate upon entering Mexico were tortillas made from corn by the native women.

Beans, pumpkins, and potatoes, were other products the burro helped transport from fields to homes and markets. He carried bags of cacao beans in Brazil, and vanilla beans in Venezuela and Mexico. In Paraguay he may still be seen carrying baskets of leaves of a species of holly strapped to his sides. From the leaves is brewed a drink called yerba de maté, a tea popular in Paraguay and Brazil.

The burro carries many other products of the Americas. Cassava, or manioc, a plant of tropical America that greatly outyields wheat and is now a staple of every tropical country in the world, fills the burro's panniers. Indian farmers of Brazil and Uruguay gave the versatile peanut to the world, and the burro has been utilized in its harvesting and marketing. Cotton, indigenous to America and also to Arabia, India, and other countries, has long been a burden borne by the patient burro, as have sunflower seeds and the oil processed from them. Tobacco, also indigenous to South America, was grown by the Indians for smoking and chewing, as a medicine, as a disinfectant, as a food, and as a medium of exchange. The burro learned to eat the leaves of the tobacco plant, as well as to transport it.

The maguey plant, which grows on the rocky hillsides of Mexico, may be seen today on the way to markets on burros' backs. They may also be seen bearing kegs of pulque, the "poor man's beer," and bottles of tequila, made from the agave.

Mexican burros packing maguey. Courtesy of Ammex Asociados, Mexico City.

A Mexican burro at work. Photograph by author.

We have seen that the burro was an important part of the early settlement of the Americas. But of all the countries south of the border, in the popular mind he is most closely associated with Mexico and the Mexican people. With the miners, the ranchers, and the farmers, burros moved northward in Mexico, settling down in Guadalajara, Guanajuato, Queretaro, Durango, and Zacatecas. It was at the Casco silver mines, near Zacatecas, that Juan de Oñate organized his expedition to colonize New Mexico in 1598. Burros accompanied the expedition and were probably the first to arrive in what is now the United States.

Mexican burros helped make silver kings of the Spaniards and later the Mexicans, packing equipment, supplies, miners, and ores. They have long been part of the scene around the gold and silver mines of Taxco. In 1929 a burro brought a latecomer to Taxco, who also became a silver king, but of another sort. In that year William Spratling, an American teacher, decided to head south for his health. As he crossed the border into Mexico, he rode astride a burro. Once settled in Taxco, not only did he regain his health but also he founded Taxco's now-flourishing silver-jewelry trade and became known in his own right as one of the world's best silversmiths. His work in developing Taxco's silver trade so helped the artisans of the town that they hailed him as their favorite son.

Seldom does the humble carrier of rural Mexican freight enjoy the spotlight of fame. Yet about twenty-five years ago the burro was the subject of a song that became very popular in the cantinas of Mexico. The title of the song was "My Little Burro Doesn't Want to Go." It began:

> I've got to go to Chimuchu
> And my burro's very mad
> Because he didn't get alfalfa
> Because he didn't get corn.

The song continues, as the burro's owner rides along:

> He goes a few steps forward
> And takes a few steps back.

Then, after a hard day's work, the burro takes his owner to the corner cantina for some rounds of pulque. Later, the two head for home, the rider promising:

> Do not make me angry now,
> For soon we will arrive
> And I will give you corn.[26]

The Mexican burro, in common with his kin in the Old World, has served as a milk producer. Only thirty or forty years ago in the larger cities of Mexico jennies were driven from door to door by their owners and milked on the spot for customers. This practice can still be observed on the outskirts of Mexico City and in the larger towns. After the Indians obtained burros from the Spaniards, Navajo mothers made use of the milk for their children. And only a generation back, in isolated areas of New Mexico, jennies were milked for invalids.

The burro remains important in present-day Mexico. The burro population is ever increasing: in 1970 there were 3,295,000 burros in Mexico, as compared with 2,683,000 in 1952, an increase of 612,000 in about eighteen years.[27]

During a recent automobile journey to Mexico, I gave my wife an assignment. Upon crossing the border at Nogales, I handed her a pad and pencil and asked her to make a census of all the burros we saw during our three weeks' trip. I promised to give her help when the subjects of our census appeared on both sides of the highway.

The burro count went on as we continued our drive from Guaymas to Los Mochis. On earlier trips we had enjoyed the farming region around Cuidad Obregón and the Navojoa area. This time at Navojoa we reluctantly decided not to turn east to Alamos, an old silver-mining town nestling among the ore-drained hills. Burros loaded with firewood enter the town, hoofs clattering in rhythm on the hand-laid stone pavement. It was a custom that began in mining days. Today the miners are gone, and the customers are hotelkeepers and American and Canadian refugees from the rat race up north.

On this trip we continued on to Mazatlán. Between Mazatlán and Tepic we stopped alongside a rock-fenced maguey field. There two boys, leading burros with baskets roped to each side of their packsaddles, were gathering dried burro droppings. After crawling over the old rock fence, we visited with the boys and learned that they took the manure to the yard of their home, where they mixed it with water and soil to make adobe brick.

Our census included the colors of the burros we encountered. We saw gray burros, brown burros, burros of every shade. We drove slowly along the highway, dodging cows, goats, mules, trucks, and other tourists. We pulled off the pavement and waited for a boy riding along on his burro. The youngster was about twelve years old, a clean, handsome, friendly youth. We learned that he was going to a field for fodder. We inquired about his mount, and it was obvious that he loved his partner. When we asked the burro's name, the boy replied proudly, "Golondrina" (Swallow).

We traveled on to Guadalajara, Lake Chapala, and Morelia, and soon Mexico City loomed in the distance, a metropolis of seven million, not including burros. But they were there, chiefly in the suburbs and outlying districts.

After a week in the city we started northwest for Queretaro, then on toward Zacatecas. Twenty-five miles outside town we stopped to visit with a farmer in a field. He was plowing with four burros hitched to a light plow. While the implement was not heavy, the sod was very dry, and pulling the plow was hard work for the animals. I noticed that one of the burros was young—too young, it appeared to me, for work of any kind. When I asked the farmer whether he was not asking too much of the young burro, he had a ready reply: "Si, señor, pero el burro joven tiene ayuda" ("Yes, mister, but the young burro has help"). I could not win, and so I took my leave. Patting the young burro on the head, I said, "I'm sorry, burrito, your lot is surely a hard one."

As mentioned earlier, Zacatecas was once surrounded by silver mines that made millionaires of a few but old men worn out before their time of most. Nor did the burros and mules enjoy the riches. It was in this region that Juan de Oñate and his father before him skimmed off the millions.

At length we arrived in San Luis Potosí. In the downtown area we saw about thirty teenage boys riding burros and adding to the confusion of the busy market day. We noticed that many of the burros were "decorated" with spots and streaks of a reddish material and also that green ribbons were tied to their tails and to manes that

A Mexican burro (Acapulco) enjoying some refreshment. Courtesy of Ammex Associates, Mexico City.

were long enough. When we asked the boys about the festivities, which the boys (though not the burros) seemed to be enjoying, they reported that it was part of their initiation as freshmen in a local institute. It seemed to us that the burros were more mature than the freshmen.

In the early-morning heavy traffic of Torreón we were amazed by the expert manner in which one burro handled the confusion. The burro, a jenny with a young foal tied at her side, was pulling a large cart piled high with loose oranges. She wove the cart, her baby, and her owner through the traffic as easily as if she were leading her young through a pasture filled with cactus. We added an intelligent and brave jenny and her young to our census.

In Torreón we also learned an oddment of interest. In the United States carpenters' trestles are called, of course, sawhorses. We asked a carpenter what the Mexicans called them and asked if they were called *caballos*. His reply was "No, señor, en Mejico hay burros" ("No, mister, in Mexico they are burros").

On our journey we did not get to see two burros that have become well known to tourists. One is an attraction near the highway leading from Mexico City to Teotihuacán. The other is a familiar figure on La Roqueta Beach in Acapulco. The Mexicans call them *los burros borrachos* ("the drunken burros"). They have learned to drink soft drinks and beer. While the latter brew is much to their liking, too many swigs make them a little wobbly.

Following a night in Juaréz, we crossed the bridge over the Río Grande and entered El Paso. I asked the burro statistician how many we had seen. Her reply: "Un mil doscientos sesenta y ocho, señor" (1,268).

14. The Prospector's Friend

The first burros to sink their feet into the soil of what is now the United States were very likely those that accompanied the expedition of the Spanish colonizer Juan de Oñate. This band of settlers reached the Río Grande in April, 1598, at a point about twenty-five miles downriver from the present twin cities of Juárez and El Paso. There, on the banks of the meandering river, Oñate with much pomp, verbosity, and ceremony claimed for God, the king of Spain, and himself New Mexico and all adjoining lands.

At the Casco mines, near Zacatecas, the assembling place of the Oñate expedition, the first official inspection of the expedition's inventory was made, on December 9, 1596. This inspection and others that followed were made by a representative of the Spanish crown to determine whether Oñate was complying with his contractual agreement. The recorded inventories are comprehensive, revealing in detail the composition of the expedition as it moved toward the north. Men, women, children, servants, slaves—all were accounted for. The livestock was numerous and included cattle, sheep, goats, hogs, horses, mules, and burros. One inventory showed forty dozen pairs of shoes for burros. The various colonists had their own livestock; one inventory showed that thirty mules and burros bore Oñate's brand.

On their journey from the mines to the Río Grande the colonists experienced a number of irritating delays and consumed many of their supplies and livestock. Many animals strayed or were stolen. One official, Alonso Sánchez, according to an inspection made after a year of much delay, had remaining in his inventory "eleven carts, thirty-five oxen, thirty-five horses, two mules, two male burros, two female burros, fifteen cows, . . . two sidesaddles of ocelot skins with bridles of the same material, and one barrel of wine." Francisco de Sosa Peñalosa had thirty mares, some burros, three female Negro slaves, one mulatto slave, and one box containing a complete set of sacred vestments used in saying the Mass.[1] The burros may have packed the vestments, as they did later in New Mexico and in other southwestern areas for the missionary padres.

While the journey of the colonizers was marked by delays, hardships, sickness, scarcity of water, and travel over rough terrain, at least some of the burros crossed the Río Grande and later became permanent settlers at San Gabriel, near present-day Española, New Mexico.

Since his arrival in 1598 the burro has become established as an institution in the southwestern United States. One may speculate upon the astonishment, interest, and delight in the pueblos when the Indians, especially the children, were confronted by the little long-eared animal. His size and appearance were quite different

Prospector's Burro, ca. 1890. By Frederic Remington. Courtesy of Denver Public Library Western Collection.

Burro with Indian, going to market. Courtesy of Denver Public Library Western Collection.

from those of the horse, which had first visited the pueblos during Coronado's expedition. And his voice—how it must have entertained the children. The Indians took to the animal readily.

Burros in all probability labored at what was perhaps the oldest lead mine in the West, La Mina del Tiro, about twenty miles southwest of Santa Fe, in New Mexico, in the Cerrillos Hills. The Spaniards may have been working this mine when the Pueblo Rebellion broke out in 1680. They were certainly taking ore from it soon after the uprising was put down. Burros carried ore to the crude mill and then packed the "royal fifth" of the concentrate southward into Mexico on the first leg of its long journey to Spain. Much of the lead that was kept was used for bullets for hunting game and for "pacifying" the Indians.

From the Río Grande Basin the burro pushed into other regions of the West. He quickly became a favorite of the prospector, the miner, the wood and water hauler, and the sheep rancher. His hardiness and his surefootedness on the narrow and precipitous trails of the rugged mountains made him invaluable for packing not only ores but also all kinds of commercial merchandise between widely separated points. The burro's ability to survive on little water and limited forage brought him into service in severe environments.

Charles F. Lummis, a popular turn-of-the-century writer on western subjects, gave the burro full credit for his help in settling the West. Acknowledging that the Spaniards brought poultry, pigs, cattle, dogs, sheep, goats, and horses, Lummis maintained, however, that it was the burro that filled the greatest need: "Two-thirds of the New World would hardly have been civilized yet, without him. Also so far as Spanish America goes, . . . the burro has been the corner stone of history and the father of civilization. . . . he has developed more mines than all the railroads in the world."[2]

Lummis made his observations in 1896, during a prospecting and mining period that was still dependent upon the burro. His comparison of the work of the animal with that of the railroad may sound like a western tall tale. However, when it is realized that the iron horse was still a colt in the West of that time—and that the burro had been serving man's transportation needs for more than fifty centuries before James Watts invented the steam engine— Lummis' statement was accurate.

In the Southwest the burro is most closely associated with the prospectors and the miners. He carried tools, bedroll, and grub for the seeker-of-wealth. On his packsaddle were hung a water canteen, an empty lard bucket in which coffee was made, and a skillet for frying rabbit, bacon, or venison. If the prospector was a placer miner, the skillet also served an additional purpose: gravel was washed in it to separate it from the gold flakes or nuggets—the prospector hoped.

Burro in Boulder Canyon, ca. 1890. Courtesy of Denver Public Library Western Collection.

In his search for precious metals the prospector penetrated isolated and inhospitable regions, with only his burro as a companion. Frank Waters has given a vivid account of the life of Winfield Scott Stratton, one of Colorado's three great mining personalities (the other two being H. A. W. "Haw" Tabor and Thomas Walsh). Stratton worked as a carpenter and cabinetmaker during the winter months and prospected in the summer. He failed over and over again. For seventeen years he struggled in vain over a considerable portion of the Colorado Rockies, his clothes ragged and torn, his burro thin and footsore. Other prospectors were having little trouble finding ore, but Stratton's ill-luck was "as persistent as the burro at his heel." Yet every summer, year after year, a "strange, gaunt man" was seen "passing into the shadow of a dark mountain cabin, with a burro—patient, plodding, and silent as he."

Then at last this eccentric man, with the help of his burro, parted the waters of Cripple Creek. Stratton's Independence Mine, on the south slope of Pikes Peak, was a fabulous find, containing "gold so pure a man could carry out a fortune in his pants' pocket, . . . a mine that overnight made the Cripple Creek cow pasture the greatest gold camp on earth. A mere six square miles, 11,000 feet high, it supported 175 shipping mines, 11 gold reduction mills, . . . led the world in gold production, . . . $450,000,000 in gold."[3]

The burro contributed much to the discovery and development of such rich strikes. And occasionally he was allowed to share in the fruits of his labors. A case in point was a burro named Jack. Jack was owned by one O. O. Peck. One day (as one version of the tale goes), while he was untethered and foraging for himself, two prospectors, Noah Kellogg and Phillip O'Rourke, came upon him and took him in tow. Later, according to tradition, Jack was instrumental in helping the two men discover what became the rich Bunker Hill and Sullivan mines of Idaho. The legal owner of the burro, Peck, claimed that, because of his burro's part in the discovery of the rich strikes, a portion of the bounty should come his way. The Supreme Court of Idaho agreed. It rendered its decision: "This court is of the opinion that the Bunker Hill mine was discovered by Peck's burro, Phillip O'Rourke, and N. S. Kellogg, and, therefore, he [Peck] is entitled to one-third interest in the property." At the time of the court's decision the property was valued at fifteen million dollars.

Jack was given credit for his part in the discovery, and was rewarded with retirement. One version of the legend has it that Jack actually spotted the rich outcrop of silver ore. One day Kellogg, out looking for him, found Jack standing on one side of a canyon virtually mesmerized by the sun's reflection on an outcrop of rich silver ore on the opposite side of the canyon.

Jack, in his retirement, grazed, loafed, and occasionally brayed. Some miners, exasperated by Jack's voice—or most likely by his easy life—planned his demise. One day they caught unsuspecting Jack while he was leisurely grazing on the side of a hill and tied a stick of dynamite to his tail, lighted the fuse, and then started him downhill. An explosion ended Jack's days in this world.[4]

Many of the burro's more startling deeds on the western mining frontier are largely folklore. A number of them center around the legend of the prospector who strikes it rich while looking for a straying burro. Typical is the story of an old Nevada prospector who spent one morning looking for his burro. When he finally found the elusive animal, he was so exasperated that he picked up a rock to throw at him and suddenly realized that the rock was unusually heavy. Upon examining it carefully, he found that it contained heavy concentrations of native silver—a specimen from a rich ore outcrop nearby.[5]

Still other burros paid with their lives for their help in efforts to unearth nature's riches. In the early 1880's two prospectors, Allen Grosh and Richard Burke, left Gold Canyon, Utah, for California to try to obtain financial backing to develop some likely claims. It was winter, and the tall, rugged Sierras were filled with deep snow. It was futile to try to follow the trail in the snow, whose depth was too great for the burro's short legs. "Their provisions were exhausted. To turn back appeared as difficult and dangerous as to press on. After fruitless attempts to follow the trail, they killed the donkey . . . [and] took as much of his flesh as they could carry." With careful rationing the burro meat lasted until the men reached shelter. The remainder was left to freeze and to be gnawed on by wolves.[6]

Wherever prospectors and other fortune seekers traveled and congregated in the West, pack burros were very much a part of the scene. The silver strike at Gold Hill, Nevada, was typical: "Prospectors began to flank the new camp as soon as the news of the discovery of silver was announced. . . . The little Johnston colony was soon merged in this stream of fortune hunters. Rough-haired mustangs, gaunt mules, and sure-footed little burros climbed the Sierras loaded with stacks of blankets, bacon, flour, kettles, pans, picks, shovels, and other articles of a miner's outfit."[7]

The prospector and his shaggy-haired burro became institutions in the mining districts of the West. In one famous court case the lawyer for the defense in his effort to qualify his witness as an expert asked how long he had been a prospector. The prospector replied, "For thirty years."

When the attorney for the prosecution questioned the witness, the prospector replied that he had prospected for five years. The prosecutor, believing that he had trapped the witness, pointed out the discrepancy. But the prospector countered that he had prospected for five years and had spent the other twenty-five looking for his burros. The judge accepted him as a witness.[8]

The burro carried not only the prospector's gear, bedding, and grub but at times the prospector himself on short excursions from camp. One folk tale emphasizes how important it was to train a burro well. One warm day Old Tom of Colorado was carrying his prospector along the bluffs above some mountain gulches. The rider, as was his habit, fell asleep. Normally, the burro remained awake, but this time Old Tom too dozed off into slumber. He drowsed along to the edge of a cliff and walked right out into thin air. The downward plunge brought the pair out of their slumber. The prospector realized that if they landed at their present rate of speed both would be killed. "One hundred, two hundred, three hundred feet!" the rider counted off as they fell. When they were about fifty feet from the ground, the prospector called out, "Whoa!" Old Tom put on the brakes and eased gently to the ground. Safely on earth again, the two proceeded up the canyon.[9]

The burro was an important help in mining operations from the time of the Spaniards. He carried the crude equipment that was used to extract the ore from the host rock. The ore taken from the mines was placed in bags made of animal hides, hung over a forked-branch packsaddle, and then carried by burros to the arrastra, or drag mill. Such a mill was simple in design and operation:

> The device consisted of a circular floor of andesite blocks, laid tightly upon a subflooring of well-puddled clay, with the whole laid level or at a slight angle to the horizontal. A low stone coping, pierced by an outlet scupper at the low end, ran around the floor. In the center was set a substantial wooden post on a stone pillar-pivot. One or two beams were set horizontally on the pivot, and from the beams were loosely hung pairs or even quads of 150- to 200-pound drag stones of the same andesitic material. The drag stones were beveled slightly on the lower leading edge and were suspended thereby so as to "nip" the ore. The end of one beam extended over the coping and was provided with a harness for horse or mule. When used as a simple grinder, the arrastra was shallowly filled with crushed, dressed ore, the animal, blindfolded, was harnessed to the beam end, and a trickle of water was set going into the ore. As the animal promenaded about the arrastra, the drag stones ground the ore to a thin pulp or slime, which dribbled out the screen (in early times a pierced oxhide) in the scupper, whence it was led away for further treatment....[10]

From the eighteenth century to the early years of the twentieth the burro steadily played a diversified role in the mining economy that spread from New Mexico throughout the western domain. The burro played his part well, accompanying the prospector and then, after the strike, working in the mine tunnels, carrying baskets and buckets of rocks and ore, and later transporting the load to the mills. The Spaniards truly did a service by bringing this tough, patient, surefooted burden bearer with them from Mexico.

Mining is an old industry in the Southwest, predating the arrival of the Spaniards. There is evidence that as early as A.D. 800 turquoise was mined by the Indians in the hills near present-day Cerillos, New Mexico. This beautiful gem was highly valued by the Indians of the New World and has long been an important item of commerce in the Americas. The early-day Indians did not have burros or other work animals in the turquoise mines, and they had to develop burrolike patience in extraction of the stone. They heated the host rock and then poured cold water on it, causing fractures and bringing the encased turquoise to or near the surface. The Indian miner, using his stone mining tools, then chipped the stone free.

As early as 1609, only eleven years after Oñate's arrival in New Mexico, pack trains of burros and/or mules were moving between Chihuahua, Mexico, and the Río Grande Valley in New Mexico. On their northward journey the pack trains brought supplies and equipment, including religious vestments, clothing, hardware, pieces of furniture, and other necessities from headquarters in Mexico to the Catholic missions that were being established in the Río Grande Valley and other areas.[11] On the return journey the animal trains returned to Chihuahua loaded with salt from Quemado or Estancia. Turquoise and copper were also sometimes part of the return loads.

The Mexican muleteers, who soon became indispensable on the dusty, rugged trails between Mexico and the border provinces, excelled in trail craft—managing the animals and their packs. They endured all the hardships inherent on the trail—mostly nature's whims of weather. They camped along the trail, unpacking the freight. Later in the evening after their meal they sat on their bedrolls near the campfire, strumming their guitars and perhaps singing of loved ones far away.

Long trails and tall tales helped develop the prospector's culture. Perhaps, as he rode or strolled along behind his burro, his dreams of big strikes had some influence on his imagination. The following story is a case in point. John Allen, a prospector, with his two burros, Priscilla and Miles, was returning one day down Hanover Creek toward Santa Rita, New Mexico, to stock up on grub. Recent rains had turned the trail to sticky mud, and the going was slow. The burros repeatedly kept stopping, and the prospector had to push them along. At one place Miles, the lead burro, stopped, look-ing back at his master for help. As John later told the story, he swore at the burro but cleaned the mud from around Miles's feet. But the burro was still unable to lift them. John then discovered that Miles's shoes were fastened securely to an outcrop of magnetic iron ore. John removed the shoes from the burro's feet and prepared to continue down the muddy trail. However, new troubles arose. A pound of mineral-rich raisins in a bag on the side of the burro's packsaddle was attracted by the ore and tilted the load sideways. John's belt buckle rooted him to the spot. The problem was re-solved when the raisins and the buckle were discarded.[12]

For three centuries, from 1600 to 1900, the burro was a miner. In the early 1870's ore from the Little Gold Lode in the Las Animas district of Colorado was carried on burros to a smelter in Pueblo. The distance was long, but the ore, which yielded four hundred to nine hundred ounces a ton, made the journey profitable for the owners. A few years later a smelter was erected at Silverton, Colo-rado, so that processing could be carried out nearer the mines.

A burro pack train hauling joists to the mines. Courtesy of Denver Public Library Western Collection.

Nevertheless, burros remained important on the trail from Pueblo to Las Animas. On this strenuous route various supplies and equipment were packed on strings of burros. The route lay from Pueblo to La Veta Pass in the Sangre de Cristo Range, to Fort Garland, thence through the San Luis Valley to Del Norte, and through Cunningham Gulch.

The burro's work did not always end when the sun slipped behind the mountains. The social life of the people in the mining districts picked up tempo during the evenings, and the activity frequently made its demands on the little animal. The social life often centered around dances. Participants sometimes transported themselves and even musical instruments, such as melodions and fiddles, to the scene of the dance on burros.[13]

Burros also participated in the gold rushes of the Far Northwest. Soon after the purchase of Alaska from Russia in 1867, burros and their prospectors made their way across the border of that remote new territory. When gold was discovered in Alaska in 1880, the burro was probably looking on. In 1886 burros were helping the

Burros loaded for the mines, Ouray, Colorado. Courtesy of Denver Public Library Western Collection.

Photograph taken in 1886 in the Silver Bow Basin, Alaska, where gold was discovered in 1880. Silver Bow was the site of the first major gold discovery in Alaska, and consisted of both placer and lode deposits. Courtesy of *Alaska Journal.*

gold miners in Silver Bow Basin. It was a bleak, rough, snowy region, an environment hostile to burros' nature. But they were compelled to participate in man's mad rush for the "muck called gold."

The burro was also an important feature of the mining regions of western Canada. Soon after gold was discovered in the Yukon in 1896, pack trains of burros were carrying provisions from Edmonton, in Alberta Province, to the prospecting and mining regions along the Klondike River.

One famed prospector, Nicholas C. Creede, searched for gold for nearly twenty years, accompanied by his companion, a burro.

Together they trod the domain between the Mexican and Canadian borders. Finally, in 1890, Creede made his strike in Colorado and cashed in, leaving his faithful burro behind and settling on the California coast. There, wealthy at last, he spent the rest of his life in luxurious ease.[14] Creede, Colorado, bears his name, and in its mining heyday it was a prosperous, boisterous town. Famous lines from a little poem by Cy Warman, founder of the *Creede Chronicle*, evokes the atmosphere of the town:

> Here the meek and mild-eyed burros
> On mineral mountain feed
> It's day all day in the daytime
> And there is no night in Creede.[15]

Not many prospectors were as fortunate as Creede—and maybe few of them really wanted to be. For some prospectors, simply looking for wealth was the way of life they enjoyed most, not developing their finds or even spending the proceeds, which would have changed their pattern of living. Such men rejected the goal of riches when it was within their grasp. Instead, they sold their mining claims at a nominal price and used the money to purchase clothes, supplies, and grub and to pay their debts. Then, the hills and deserts beckoning, they once again loaded their burros and departed. Perhaps Sancho Panza, Don Quixote's servant, expressed the true sentiment of these ever-searching prospectors: ". . . let me now with my donkey tread again upon plain ground, . . . let everyone stick to the calling he was born to."

There are countless stories of the strong bond of friendship that developed between the prospector and his burro as they searched for nature's riches. Such stories have many themes in common. The burro was loyal to his master and would not leave the campsite except to play hide-and-seek at times, and even then he would never wander great distances as a horse would do. He was adept and surefooted on the narrow, dangerous trails through the mountains. He was well suited to sun-scorched deserts, for he could travel many miles on little water. Yet he seemed to possess an uncanny ability for finding water and was never fooled by the mirages that so often tantalized thirst-crazed man. Such a burro was the companion of William Witt, the Mojave Desert prospector, who in 1898 found the ore-rich rocks hidden in Providence Mountain.[16]

While the prospector's burro has often been maligned, he has had his supporters. On January 20, 1925, he was memorialized by William C. Russel at the Miner's Annual Sowbelly Dinner, held in Denver, Colorado. Russel had had a long association with the burro in various regions of the West, and he had led strings of pack burros across the hot deserts of California. He was convinced that "brains, brawn, burros, and beans (with some luck thrown in) constitute the four cardinal essentials to the success of the American Prospector." In his speech Russel gave a brief summary of the animal's history and praised his stalwart characteristics and the contributions of his breed to civilization. In closing, Russel urged that

A burro packed for the Klondike, 1898. Note the lifesaver. The all-Canadian overland route to the Klondike gold area was approximately 1,500 miles from Edmonton, Alberta, Canada. Courtesy of Provincial Museum and Archives of Alberta, Ernest Brown Collection.

a bronze statue of a prospector and his burro be placed in Denver's Civic Center or at some other appropriate site in the city.[17]

The *Denver Post* seized on Russel's suggestion and appointed a committee, with Russel as chairman, to carry out the project. The *Post* also sponsored a contest in which suggestions were to be submitted by readers and opened a subscription fund encouraging children to "send in the money for the cost of the statue and become inscribed in the *Post* Honor Roll." Somehow the project died, and today there is still no monument in Denver to honor the prospector and his burro, who did so much for the beginnings of Colorado and the West.

Many burros became famous in the prospecting and mining regions of the West, some by name, some merely as "burro." One such hero was Jack Bell's burro. One day Bell, a prospector in New Mexico, was bitten by a rattlesnake as he scrambled over the heat-baked rocks. He managed to climb on his burro, who carried him many miles across the desert to the camp of an Indian sheepherder. The sheepherder's wife applied a poultice that checked the spread of the poison and saved his life.[18]

Many stories about burros have their origin in the mountains of western New Mexico. James A. McKenna, a prospector who collected tales of the Black Range, made much of the burro's inquisitiveness: "All burros have a regular human lump of curiosity. They like to hang around the new mining camps. I have seen as many as twenty burros standing in front of a dance hall, or watching a big faro game, just as close to the door as they could get and as silent as ghosts."[19]

McKenna also told the story of a burro named Ladrone (Spanish for "thief"). Somehow Ladrone got into the Black Range country. Two brothers, Joe and Jim Hyatt, "adopted" him. One day while the Hyatts were in the hills prospecting, they were attacked by a mother bear who had cubs with her. Ladrone came to the rescue, chasing the cubs and diverting the mother's attention from the young men. The wise burro knew how to handle the critical situation. Sometime later the Hyatt brothers took a lease on an old mine and struck pay dirt. While they were working the property, Ladrone died. Joe and Jim selected a grassy flat area under a lone juniper tree for his final resting place. They dug the grave deep so that wolves or wild dogs could not dig up his bones.[20]

McKenna himself owned a Black Range burro named Old Hog. The two wandered together in the 1880's. Old Hog carried the grub, the bedroll, McKenna's tools, and at times McKenna himself. Old Hog served not only as McKenna's friend and helper but also as an Indian scout. For some reason he did not trust Indians and was always on the alert for them. McKenna tells of one day's adventures. The Apaches had been restless and had been giving the settlers trouble. McKenna and Old Hog headed for Kingston, about one hundred miles southeast in the Black Range.

> I struck up Noonday Creek . . . . Coming into a little park, I met an old turkey hen with a brood of young ones. She took no notice of me and went on scratching. . . . I headed for a shady nook under a cliff, . . . opened [a] package of food and turned Old Hog loose to graze. I was chewing away on a venison sandwich when I saw the burro stop feeding. Lifting his ears, he gazed for a minute up the creek then trotted over beside me. I slipped out of the cove and looked in the same direction. . . . What a sight! Crossing the creek . . . were six Indian bucks each wearing a stovepipe hat. . . . It did not take me long to get back to my hiding place. Old Hog kept close to my side as quiet as a mouse, watching me with big eyes. . . . Old Hog and me then lit out for Iron Creek in the Black Range. . . . In short time I reached a cabin. . . . No one was there, . . . but a pot of beans hung on a hook over the fire. Taking a tin plate, I helped myself. . . . In came two miners from Kingston who had been hunting. . . . I told them about seeing the Indians. But when I said the bucks were wearing plug hats, . . . I could see the two men look at each other. . . . "Well, fellows," I said, "I am going to pull out. . . . My old burro is still acting strange. He wants to get away. He sure has had his troubles with the Indians and can

scent one a mile away. So I am going on his judgment." Away we
went. Old Hog needed no punching to get out of Iron Creek
Canyon.[21]

McKenna's tale about Apaches in plug hats was not a tall one as
the two men suspected. It was later learned that some Indians had
raided a store and among the items they took were some plug hats.

Peter, an old prospector, whose range was the Burro Mountains
of southwestern New Mexico, had a burro with a strange taste in
food. Peter, in need of a set of teeth, made a trip to El Paso to get
them. He asked his partner, Tom, to meet him at the railway station on his return. Tom, thinking that Pete would bring groceries
and other items, took their burro, Butcher, to pack them.

Pete arrived without supplies but with his violin, a jug of corn
whisky, and a bag of molasses-covered popcorn. He and Tom
headed for their mountain claim. On the way Pete complained
about the bad fit of his new dentures, saying that "the El Paso
dentist must have been specializing in beaver molars."

"Let's hit the corn," Pete said, as they came to a bend in the trail
where there was a ledge of rocks to sit on. After a round of whisky
Pete opened the bag of candied popcorn. The popcorn and the
denture plates did not cooperate very well, and Pete removed the
plates to pull them apart. Then he laid the teeth to one side and
continued to munch on the popcorn with his gums. At last he put his
teeth back in his mouth, and the trio continued their journey.

This stop-and-go travel continued, as Butcher ate the spilled
kernels of popcorn. The jug was about empty and the big bag of
popcorn was almost gone when the sourdoughs made a last stop, a
quarter of a mile from the cabin. A big flat rock provided a resting
place. Pete again had trouble with his teeth—some popcorn had
stuck to one side. He took them out, laid them down, and got the
violin from the burro's packsaddle. Butcher followed Pete back to
the rock ledge. Pete, now somewhat overly tuned himself, played
for Tom the newest songs that he had heard in El Paso. At one

point, while Pete was tuning his fiddle, Butcher extended his neck and picked up the stuck-together denture plates and swallowed them, popcorn and all. Pete was sawing away on the violin.

Later, when he turned to pick up his plates and discovered they were gone, he exclaimed, "Well, I be jiggered, if that long eared jack ain't up and swallowed my store teeth!"[22]

No mining burro of the Rocky Mountains or of the West as a whole has received as much newspaper publicity as Prunes, of Fairplay, Colorado. Prunes spent a long life at work in the mines of the Alma and Fairplay areas. He was a good friend of Rupe Sherwood. Rupe, a versatile frontiersman, was born in Missouri in 1848 and rode a wagon train westward while still a youth. He was at various times a trapper, a hunter with Buffalo Bill, and a prospector and miner. His friendship with Prunes lasted for forty years.

When Prunes became a "senior citizen," he made daily rounds to the kitchen doors of Alma to beg for handouts. Sympathetic housewives soon learned that his favorite food was pancakes. Prunes survived a severe winter storm in which he got trapped in an old shed because the door blew shut on him. But when he was rescued, he was gaunt and weak and had begun to fail, for reportedly he had seen sixty-three winters. His teeth were gone, and he had trouble chewing his food. A group of miners held a meeting and decided that it was only humane to do away with old Prunes. Some time later a Fairplay businessman and others rescued Prunes's skeleton from the trash dump at Alma. His bones now lie alongside Fairplay's famous old Front Street. On the concrete monument marking the grave is inscribed:

> Prunes, a Burro—1867–1930
> Fairplay, Alma, All Mines
> in This District.

It is in front of this monument that the popular annual pack burro races between Fairplay and Leadville were begun.

Burros packed and ready to go from Edmonton, Canada, to the Klondike, 1898. From the Ernest Brown Collection, Provincial Museum and Archives of Alberta.

Shortly after Prunes's death, Rupe composed a long poem in honor of his old friend, "Me and Prunes." One version reads in part:

> So poor old Prunes has cashed in.
>   too bad, still in a way
> I'm glad the old boy's eased off
>   and calling it a day.
> I'm going to miss him scand'lous!
>   The world won't seem the same—
> Not having him a-standin' here
>   hee-hawing in the game.
>
> We've sure drawed cards together
>   a-plenty, Prunes and me.
> We've bucked the play in every way
>   the cards was dealt to we.

> Sometimes we filled our hands and won—
> so seldom, 'twas a joke—
> Most often we just bob-tail flushed
> and wound up stony broke.
>
> . . . .
> The trails were all alike to him;
> it was all in the game.
>
> . . . .
> He took all things just as they came.
> Old Prunes was a good sport!
>
> . . . .
> But I'm a'gamblin' if there be
> another life after this one
> It won't be just restricted to the
> things called man alone,
> But everything now living will
> surely live again. . . .[23]

Rupe Sherwood died, aged eighty-two, a year after Prunes. He had requested that his body be cremated and the ashes buried alongside Prunes's bones.

A prospector's friend, yes, but also a miner's helper. Mine operators large and small put burros to work. Tom Walsh, born in Ireland in 1851, came to America at the age of eighteen and was working as a bridge builder at Golden, Colorado, in 1872. Later he hunted for gold in the Black Hills of South Dakota and in the Colorado Rockies. He was a miner in Central City, but it was in Cripple Creek that he bloomed as a mine operator—his Elkhorn prospect paid off. In another location, Imogene Gulch, his mine, Camp Bird, produced fabulous pay dirt. Three feet of quartz vein permeated with specks of black mineral—telluride form—became the richest single producing mine of the mighty Rockies, yielding three thousand dollars in gold per ton of ore. The town of Ouray prospered. As Walsh often said, "It was so rich . . . a man could have knocked off a comfortable living for a family from it with an ice pick." This virtually free-milling gold was carried down the mountainside on strings of burros, each with a double packsaddle.[24] Walsh became a multimillionaire. It is to his credit that throughout his career this highly successful mining man strongly advocated kindness to animals. He would have thoroughly approved of the kindly prospector of the San Juan region, who hand-crafted snowshoes for his burro and taught him to walk in them.[25]

By and large the prospector and his burro have long since passed over the western horizon. Pickup trucks with four-wheel drive, planes, helicopters, and electronic devices have taken their place in the mountains, deserts, and solitudes that were once their domain. Very rarely one hears of men who still pick at the hills for ore. One such man was Inez López, of south-central Arizona. Not long before his death I paid López a visit.

López told me that he was born in the state of Aguascalientes, Mexico, on April 23, 1877. In 1900 he crossed the border as a migrant worker. López lived and prospected in one of the many rugged portions of the Tortolita Mountains. He lived alone—or almost alone—a dog, five cats, and three burros kept him company. The prospector had nothing but praise for his transportation. John, a light-colored gray burro with a pot belly, was his favorite. The other two were dark gray, younger, and similar in appearance and size with identical nearly white muzzles. López called them by the same name, Cambujo ("Mestizo"). When he called one, both responded. Characteristically, López, like western prospectors before him, spent much of his time looking through the hills and ravines for his burros. Even though he hobbled them, they strayed, sometimes breaking their soft rope hobbles and going quite a distance, inspiring López to feats of affectionate but exasperated prospector cussin'.

The animals served López well, packing provisions from Sonora, Ray, and Kearny, all in the Kennicott copper country. Kearny is about nine miles from López' comfortable eight-by-twelve-foot abode, perched in the hills on one of his prospects.

López told me that he began working with burros in 1886. He was nine years old—old enough to herd sheep on a large ranch in Aguascalientes. Burros carried his kegs of water, bedroll, firewood, and provisions. But it was in Arizona that he learned to appreciate the animal fully. He mentioned some of his experiences while we were resting after climbing almost to the top of a high ridge above his mountain home. He pointed out a place where he was attacked by a jenny in 1963. Three days before, the pregnant animal had disappeared from her normal grazing area near the shed and had gone to the very top of the mountain ridge. When López found her, she had foaled, but the burrito was weak. He decided to place the baby across his shoulders and take it down the steep mountainside to the house, where he could look after both the baby and its mother. However, after making his way about one hundred yards, the jenny, not understanding what he was doing, tried to prevent López from taking her baby away. She kicked at him and then charged, biting. López hit her across the face with his staff, but he stumbled over a large rock, falling and breaking four teeth and

Prunes, aged forty years. Courtesy of Denver Public Library Western Collection.

three ribs. The burrito's head hit a rock in the fall and was killed. López said that it was the only time a burro ever attacked him.

López, who was in his nineties when I met him, was still climbing his steep hills like a mountain goat. He died in May, 1972. Did he make his strike? It matters not. He and his burros, dog, and cats were contented. López was running the prospector's race.

Perhaps the prospector Tappan, the hero of one of Zane Grey's works, best illustrates the philosophical makeup of the old-time prospector and his feelings toward his burro companion. Tappan knew that he got much more out of prospecting than the pursuit of gold and thought of himself more as a naturalist or even a dreamer

López and his burros, 1970. Photograph by the author.

A modern-day Tappan. Courtesy of Capitol Lithocraft, Phoenix, Arizona.

than as a seeker of mineral wealth. He would talk to his burro at the end of a long, hard day on the desert: "Jenet, you're worthy of a happier life. . . . Here we are, with grub an' water, a hundred miles from any camp. . . . But for you and your kind, Jenet, there'd be no prospectors, and few gold mines." On the beginning of a new day, when Jenet was all packed and ready to depart: "Go along with you, Jenet, . . . look at the mountains yonder callin' us. . . . It's the life for us, my burro, an' Tappan's as rich as if all these sands were pearls." At sunset, after a day of travel in the heat over rough ground, Tappan would say: "Another day gone, Jenet, . . . an' Tappan is only older, wearier, sicker. There's no reward for your faithfulness. I'm only a desert rat. . . . Some sunset, Jenet, we'll reach the end of the trail. An' Tappan's bones will bleach in the sands. An' no one will know or care!"[26]

It may have been the mountains of the Grand Canyon drainage basin that tempted Tappan. Frank Waters caught the flavor of the unrivaled immensity of the region: "Out of this vast network of rivers emerges the Colorado itself. Dominating land and man, it is the greatest single fact, . . . bigger than its statistics." The region was an irresistible magnet, drawing prospectors into its limitless folds: "Nothing could have been livelier, more entrancing, and more pregnant with anticipation. Hills and gulches swarmed with men, burros and machinery."[27] Many of the prospectors and burros remained; their bones are hidden in the recesses of that enchanting land. Few realized their dreams of gold and silver; yet they won, even though they lost, for they ran the race in a rugged and soul-stirring land.

Prospectors who died, quit, or took other jobs turned their burros loose. Like the horse, the burro reverts to his feral traits and habits when he is free for any length of time. Wild herds of abandoned burros began to appear in the Grand Canyon country in the last quarter of the nineteenth century. Cowboys and "government men," responding to complaints of ranchowners and lessees of state and federal lands, declared war on the little animals. They were shot and poisoned, and their numbers were otherwise decimated. One source says that in 1920 four hundred burros were rounded up and sold for $1.50 each. Most of them were butchered, and the meat was processed and sold as dog food. In one instance a wild herd of burros was driven over a rim concealed by low bushes to crash to death below.[28] Herds of wild horses were similarly marked and became food for dogs and cats. In the 1920's about 375 wild burros were removed from Sitgreaves National Forest in Arizona and sold to butchers, ostensibly for the pet-food market. However, old-timers became suspicious; hot tamales seemed to have a different taste after the roundups.[29] The latter-day fortunes of the feral burros will be discussed in the next chapter.

15. Other Trails

Among the first animals to travel eastward over what became the famous Santa Fe Trail to Missouri were burros and mules. In his journal and diaries George Champlin Sibley, an early-day United States road commissioner, told about the first trade mission from Missouri to Santa Fe in 1825–27. He noted that burros moved along this trail from its inception.

According to Sibley, William Becknell and his party, all on horses, were the first traders on the trail. Upon disposing of their merchandise in Santa Fe, they secured mules, burros, and Spanish blankets to take back to Missouri.[1] These burros and mules were probably the first to cross the plains between New Mexico and Missouri.

Becknell also led the first wagon train westward across the plains. Mules, who quickly established a reputation for pulling strength and endurance, became favorites on the long Santa Fe Trail. The first pioneers to follow the trail encountered extreme hardships, including lack of water, especially between the Arkansas and the Cimarron rivers. At one critical point, to quench the agony of thirst, they cut off the ears of the mules and sucked the blood from them.[2]

Early accounts of observers on the Santa Fe Trail include mention of the burro, his work, and his fare. One of General Stephen Watts Kearny's army officers, Colonel W. H. Emory, writing in 1846, left us his view of the town of Santa Fe. He commented that the exteriors of the people's dwellings were poor but that, in contrast, the interiors were excellently appointed. The distant hills provided firewood for the inhabitants of the town. Strings of burros arrived throughout the day loaded with neatly arranged sticks of

A timeless scene: burros hauling firewood near Santa Fe. Courtesy of Denver Public Library Western Collection.

wood. It took a full day for a man and his burro to go to the hills and return with a load, which brought twenty-five cents—one day's labor for man and animal (the old days are good provided one does not have to relive them). The colonel commented on the denuded condition of the grazing areas around Santa Fe, pointing out that "the burro is the only animal that can subsist in this barren neighborhood without great expense." He also observed that, "generally, the burros when ridden were mounted from behind, after the fashion of leap-frog."[3] It is a custom that still prevails today.

Firewood was not the only load burros carried through the

streets of Santa Fe. By 1846 they could be seen carrying kegs of Taos lightning, which Ramon Adams has described as a "vile whiskey made near Taos, New Mexico, in the early days."[4] Vile or not, it was popular among those caught with their spirits down, and it had a wide sales distribution. It helped Denver and other struggling young settlements hold on and keep their courage in the mid-nineteenth century. One source reports a freight wagon that was heartily welcomed in Denver: "Uncle Dick Wootten and his wife . . . arrived on Christmas Eve from New Mexico with a blessed wagon load of groceries and Taos Lightning."[5] It was said that those who indulged in the "vile whisky" did not have to worry about becoming alcoholics, for those who drank it would not live long enough anyhow.

In 1906 a correspondent for the *Los Angeles Times* provided his readers with a colorful description of Santa Fe. To him the most fascinating part of Santa Fe was Burro Alley, a one-block street running from San Francisco Avenue to Palace Avenue. The alley bounded a famous house of chance containing gambling rooms, "dance studios," and provisions for other entertainments for the mountain men. La Tules, the beautiful Spanish hostess, ran the liveliest place in town. In the alley the pack burros gathered as their owners and drivers talked shop about their burros, problems of wood gathering and customers, and the low price of firewood. The correspondent was convinced that the Mexican-American could manage the burro more effectively than the gringo could. He also believed that no one ever fed a burro—he had to rustle for himself.[6]

The treatment of the burro in Santa Fe during the 1920's and early 1930's was indicative of the fading burro culture there and elsewhere in the United States. Many of the animals ran loose; they had no homes and no one to feed, water, or care for them. After their duties had ended for the day, they were turned loose to find what fare they could. The homeless little animals grazed on lawns, sought out vacant lots where they nibbled weeds, and were known to sample flowers in the gardens. They were hauled off to the city pound and charged with vagrancy. Come Saturday a public auction was held, and the offenders were sold—usually not bringing over twenty-five cents each. They were then worked for a day or two and turned loose again, to be picked up and auctioned off the next Saturday.[7] Many burros went through this pattern of existence for years. Today they have virtually disappeared from Santa Fe, but during their "golden age" they were as familiar a sight on the city streets as the mountain men.

The Spanish mule, offspring of the mustang mare and the burro jack, was also an important part of western culture. Many cowboys working cattle in the rough country, preferred the hybrid to the horse. His agility, surefootedness, and easy gait, inherited from his sire, gave him an advantage over the horse. Samuel Bowles lived in the mountains and traveled on muleback. He has left us his impression of his mount:

Firewood-packing burros resting in Burro Alley, Santa Fe, New Mexico. Courtesy of New Mexico State Library.

My mule, did you ever ride a mule? . . . he is pretty sensible, and so obstinate! But it takes a long while to beat a new idea into his head, and when it dawns on him, the effect is so overpowering that he just stops in amazed bewilderment and won't move on again until he is relieved of the foreign consciousness, and gets back to his own original possession. The whole process is startling human; it inspires you with faith in the idea of the transmigration of souls. I know so many people who must have been mules once or will be—else there is no virtue in the fitness of things.[8]

Another western mule did not fare as well. Buffalo Bill Cody relates in his autobiography that one night, while serving as a government dispatch bearer, he dismounted from his army mule to drink at a creek. The animal jerked loose and started down the creek and then to the wagon road leading to Fort Larned, their destination, thirty-two miles away. The mule kept up a jogtrot that was just a little too fast for his rider to overtake him. Finally at sunrise, only half a mile from the post, Buffalo Bill, thoroughly exasperated, pulled his rifle to his shoulder and shot the mule dead.[9]

In a more settled and tranquil environment the mule may break even or get ahead of its master. Witness this anonymous monologue:

Over the hill trailed a man behind a mule drawing a plow; said the man to the mule, "Bill, you are a mule, the son of a jackass, and I am a man made in the image of God. Yet, here we work, hitched up together year in and year out. I often wonder if you work for me or if I work for you. Verily I think it a partnership between a mule and a fool, for surely I work as hard as you, if not harder. Plowing or cultivating we cover the same distance, but you do it on four legs, and I, on two. I, therefore, do twice as much work per leg as you do.

"Soon we will be preparing for a corn crop; when the corn is harvested I give one third to the landlord for being so kind to let me use this small speck of God's universe. One third goes to you, and the balance is mine. You consume all of your portion with the exception of the cobs, while I divide mine among seven children, six hens, two ducks, and a banker. If we both need shoes, you get them. Bill, you are getting the best of it, and I ask you, is it fair for a mule, the son of a jackass, to swindle a man, a lord of creation, out of his substance?

"Why, you only plow and help to cultivate the ground and I alone must cut, shuck the husk from the corn, while you look over the pasture fence and say hee-haw at me.

"Fall and most of the winter the whole family, from Granny to the baby, pick cotton to help raise the money to pay the taxes, buy new harness and pay the interest on the mortgage on you. And what do you care about the mortgage? Not a damn. You onery cuss, I even have to do the worrying about the mortgage on your tough ungrateful hide.

"About the only time I'm your better is on election day, for I can vote and you can't. And after election I realize that I was fully as great a jackass as your papa. . . . And that ain't all, Bill. When you're dead that is supposed to be the end of you. But me? The parson tells me that when I die I gotta go to hell forever. That is, Bill, if I don't do just as he says. . . . Tell me, William, considering these truths, who has the better of things?"

As mentioned earlier, the Grand Canyon has known burros since the days of the conquistadors. Perhaps no burro personality of the area has received more fame than Brighty, a long-time citizen of the canyon. Brighty cherished his freedom, but he was ready and willing to help people, provided he was treated with consideration. He merely wanted to set his own limits on his work. Brighty became known as the "hermit of Bright Angel Creek," a favorite haunt of his in the life he loved. He first appeared in 1892, grown and grazing quietly near an abandoned tent in a canyon on the Kaibab Plateau. Two cowboys found him there. The fate of his owner was never determined. But Brighty went on to make history.

During the thirty years he is known to have lived in the Grand Canyon country, Brighty fought for his freedom. He was skilled in escaping the cowboy's rope by holding his head low and running into the brush. Brighty loved to be petted and willingly carried children on his back. But when adults had designs on him and succeeded in capturing him, eventually he found a way to regain his freedom.

He was at first an interested spectator and later a cooperative worker when engineers were constructing the suspension bridge across the Colorado River. He carried materials, equipment, and

The only known photograph of Brighty of Grand Canyon. Photograph taken about 1922. Courtesy of *Sunset Magazine* (reproduced August, 1922).

supplies for the crew. The engineers were appreciative and did not forget his interest in their project. When the bridge was completed, they chose Brighty for the honor of being the first citizen to cross it.[10]

The hermit of Bright Angel Creek spent the winters in the lower part of the canyon. Then, as spring approached, he slowly worked his way up to the North Rim and onto the Kaibab Plateau for the summer, unless he had pleasant and what he considered worthwhile work to do. One of the projects he enjoyed was serving as official water boy for the National Park Service on the North Rim. Each spring for six years Brighty would appear at the camp, after crossing the bridge he had helped build. One spring he did not show up. One member of the crew wrote, "Camp has not been the same, nor will it ever be while memory of the faithful burro lives."[11]

Brighty was a solitary creature, but at times even he grew lonesome and welcomed human company. His craving for companionship proved his undoing. One December a fugitive from the law came across Brighty near the bottom of the canyon. The man was trying to escape to the winter-isolated North Rim. Brighty helped the stranger up the tortuous trail through a severe snowstorm. Finally the fugitive came to an empty ranch house, broke in, and, finding some provisions, decided to spend the winter there. However, only a few hours later a second man arrived, this one coming from the north. There was not enough food for both, and so Brighty was sacrificed to provide meat.[12]

Fame sometimes comes only after death. In 1958, more than three decades after Brighty's tragic end, Marguerite Henry, in her book *Brighty of the Grand Canyon*, made him famous. The book was later made into a movie. What burro played Brighty's role? Not a Grand Canyon burro, but one named Jiggs, from Illinois.

While Brighty was living and working in the Grand Canyon, Fly, another burro personality, was contributing to the plains culture along the Texas–New Mexico border. Sheep ranching or cattle ranching—it made no difference to the western burro. Some of the best old-time cowboys learned to ride astride a burro as youngsters. Sometimes the tolerant burro carried a whole family of children, boys and girls, accommodating as many as could hold on between his long ears and paintbrush tail. Fly, of West Texas, was such a burro.

Fly showed up as a burrito on the Holt Ranch, near Midland, Texas, at the beginning of the twentieth century. There the Stephen Crosby family adopted young Fly and reared him on bread and milk. Bob Beverly, a pioneer of Lovington, New Mexico, described Fly's rather unique appearance. The burro had a

> sad countenance, something like a boy looks after he is whipped for misbehaving in church. . . . Around the nose, Fly looked as though his nose had been stuck in the flour barrel, and generally had. . . . Along the underside of Fly, it looked like a mirage of an early morning in springtime on the plains, . . . and on top of his back, Fly had the color of a half dried cow chip. . . .
>
> Fly fattened on the feed bestowed by the Crosby children . . . and soon learned while others toiled for a living, to be ready at all times to be at the right place, and at the right time, to appreciate a lot of the eatables for his benefit.

This Texas burro grew up, well fed and well treated, and in return allowing four or five of the Crosby boys to learn to ride on him. About 1905, Fly followed the Crosby family, chuck wagon, and cattle from Texas to a place on the old LFD Range, near what is now Lovington, New Mexico. He became a celebrity in the region from his exploits in stealing feed from the horses and his antics around the chuck wagon on the range. Fly carried the Crosby boys to the first school in Lovington—that is, when he could be persuaded to make the effort.[13]

The burro was as useful to the sheepherder as he was to the cattleman. The tender of sheep and his burros often led lonely lives in remote areas. The herder took cues from his pack animals, becoming tough and resilient, learning to live extremely simply and

Primitive Beauty. Navajo artist Charles Lee preparing a mural depicting the burro at work with sheep. Courtesy of *Albuquerque Journal*, June 21, 1970.

to roll with nature's inevitable punches. Herman W. Albert, an early-day prospector, described the sheepherders he and his four burros visited during their high-country prospecting: They were "above timberline all summer long with neither the opportunity nor the inclination to wash themselves, much less bathe. Their whole outfit is packed on one lone burro, and often I have seen them turn their dishes over to their hungry dogs for washing."[14]

The sheepherder in the big country of the West had to be inventive. Above all, he had to make use of what he found in his environment for facilities, food, and medicine. According to Solomon Bernal, a retired sheep-rancher acquaintance of mine, old-time herders drank a tea brewed from sheep droppings. The brew was considered especially effective to "bring out the measles."

A pioneer merchant, Carl Floersheim, Sr., formerly of Springer, New Mexico, told me of an incident of his earlier years pertaining to sheep and a burro. A rancher had loaded sheep on a train bound for the Chicago market. The sun was sinking when the last sheep was put into the end car, and some space remained. As a joke one of several burros standing nearby was put aboard the last car. The door was closed, and the long train pulled out for Chicago. Floersheim said that he often wondered about that lone burro's arrival with the sheep at the stockyards and the looks of surprise and the laughter of the stockyard men when they found him among the consignment of woollies.

The sheepherder's burro was often part of the bitter controversy that arose on the open range between the cattlemen and the sheepmen. Competition between the two groups for grass and water holes was keen. The cowboys, who almost to a man hated sheep, would ride up on their mustangs and yell, "Get your damn sheep and burros away from this water hole!" Sometimes the sheepmen moved; sometimes they didn't.

One burro that worked on a sheep ranch in Arizona got into trouble—but in this case not with cowboys but with a woman. And he landed in court. Blue Boy worked on a sheep ranch owned by the Colin Campbell Livestock Company, near Ash Fork, Arizona. In 1930 the Arizona Livestock Company acquired all of the capital stock of the Campbell company. The purchase included some burros. Though no proof exists that Blue Boy was among the animals sold, in 1933 and for some time thereafter he was performing duties for the Grand Canyon Sheep Company, also owned by the Arizona Livestock Company.

It seems that a lady tried to help a small boy put a rope on Blue Boy, but in the attempt she was allegedly injured by the burro. She brought a damage suit of $12,500 against the Arizona Livestock Company, which was supposedly the owner of the animal. In 1938 the representatives of the livestock company protested in both the superior court and the state supreme court that there was no proof that it owned the burro. The court exonerated Blue Boy, saying: "A burro is to the common knowledge of all residents of the West, ordinarily one of the most gentle and inoffensive of animals, . . . also . . . harmless so long as it is not molested. . . . [It is common practice] in cow towns of the Southwest for children to rope and ride burros indiscriminately of ownership."[15] The burro has a pretty good batting average when he has the opportunity to bring his case before the bar.

Black Jack is a modern burro-in-the-flesh sheepherder. He was brought to my attention by Mrs. L. R. Crosthwaite, of Mosquero, New Mexico. This four-legged, long-eared herder was trained by

Black Jack working with sheep, 1970. Here he is shown taking care of a herd alone on the ranch of R. E. Trujillo, Mosquero, New Mexico. Courtesy of Cecile Crosthwaite.

Burros have always been a part of frontier life. A photograph of the J. D. Semler family before their sod house, pictured in Nebraska in 1886. Courtesy of Solomon D. Butcher Collection, Nebraska State Historical Society.

R. E. Trujillo on his ranch several miles northeast of Mosquero. Trujillo says that Black Jack, although young, is doing an acceptable job and that, furthermore, his labor saves the wages of a two-legged herder. Black Jack tends more than one hundred sheep. He grazes with them, takes them to water, lies down with them for a siesta at noon, and even sleeps with them in the open pasture at night. Of course, Black Jack also protects them from menacing dogs and any other enemies that might venture near. Trujillo says that he has trained dogs and goats to do herding jobs for thirty years or more but that is his first burro pupil. He adds that Black Jack is a precocious student, for it took him only a few weeks to learn his responsibilities.

Many are the tales of burros that have come down to us from the early days of the western pioneers. Louis C. DeBaca, a descendant of an old family of western ranchers, tells this true story of a pregnant woman and a pregnant jenny.

A young pioneer ranch couple started for a neighbor's home some distance away for the service of a midwife. The wife was placed on the jenny and the journey got underway. The husband did not expect the female burro to give birth so soon. However, nature is not to be stopped in its processes, and en route the jenny dropped her foal. The couple waited, and it was not long before the burrito was up on his wobbly legs. Soon after he had begun to nurse, the husband helped his wife remount the jenny, and they continued their journey, the newborn colt clinging close to its mother's side. All arrived at the friend's home in time for the next borning.

Some Arizona tales are less appealing. During World War II meat was at a premium. Two Rotarians of Tucson, Arizona, did something about the matter, as revealed in a letter from the late J. F. McKale, of the University of Arizona:

> On Wednesday, December 1, 1943, I served the Rotary Club with burro at the Pioneer Hotel. Present were twenty visitors from different parts of the United States and about 125 Tucson Rotarians.
>
> We plotted as follows: Three weeks before the meal was to be served, we let it be known that we were going mule-deer hunting.
>
> After this build-up, Ronstadt got a cowpuncher to kill and dress an old burro. [Two] veterinarians inspected the carcass so we wouldn't run afoul of the law.
>
> Shortly before the meal the chef told us that this was the toughest venison he had ever tried to cook, and I remember his words, "It is as tough as a mule."

I had the burro ears wrapped up in a newspaper, and after the meal, standing next to the nearest exit, I announced what they had been eating, and threw in the two ears.

When I finally returned to Rotary meetings, they held a big trial and fined me $10.00. I never spent $10.00 and enjoyed it more.[16]

To be truthful, the reader who has eaten at border towns in the 1930's and 1940's has probably eaten burro, if he ordered the venison listed on the menu. Burros were more plentiful and easier to obtain than mule deer, and the gringos didn't know the difference anyway—both animals have long ears. A case in point is the story of two hunters who recently drove their pickup truck to a check station on the Colorado border. They pointed out their kill to the game warden. The dead animal sprawled out in the back of the pickup was a burro. The novice hunters thought they had killed a mule deer.

History shows that the burro has packed or pulled nearly every item moved by man. However, as a mail carrier he has not been prominent—his rate of speed has disqualified him. Yet Pinta, a burro owned by Ramón Quintero, of Tubac, Arizona, carried mailbags for Uncle Sam for over two decades, from the 1920's well into the 1940's.

Ramón Quintero was responsible for getting the mail from the Tubac postoffice to the Southern Pacific Railway and returning with the incoming mail. He met the train twice daily, upon its arrival from Tucson and later when it came in from Nogales. The Nogales train was frequently late because of the tardy arrival of the connecting train from Hermosillo and towns farther south in Mexico. Ramón and Pinta would patiently wait alongside the railroad tracks for its arrival. When it finally chugged to a stop, Ramón would load the mailbags on the obliging Pinta, and the two would cross Santa Cruz Creek and amble about a mile to the general store and postoffice, operated by Tubac's long-time merchant and postmaster William Lowe.

The only time Pinta presented a problem to Ramón was when the Santa Cruz Creek, swollen by rains, reached river proportions. Then the burro, not sure where the bottom of the creek was, resisted crossing it. Sometimes Ramón had to carry the bags high on his shoulders and even on his head while fording the waters. Meantime, Pinta watched safely from the bank. Doubtless such unorthodox deliveries appall the mail carriers of modern times, but as one writer commented: "In our modern age of grim efficiency and mechanical dispach . . . it is exhilarating to meet old Ramón Quintero and his faithful burro." Reminding his readers that these two were traversing ground once traveled by Apaches, conquistadors, padres, prospectors, and miners, he concluded that "no letter ever inscribed had a nicer journey; no more faithful hands could carry it. It's grand to know that in our modern 20th century America there is a whisper some place of a more leisurely life of less hurried times."[17]

It should be obvious from the foregoing stories that burros are versatile, intelligent animals. Those who accuse them of stupidity simply do not know them. Burros can be trained to perform not only special tasks but also feats of entertainment. True, training requires patience on the part of the trainer—and also on the part of the trainee. Burros have performed in circuses, usually in skits featuring the antics of clowns. But burros—and mules—have also been taught uncommon acts. The sixteenth-century Arab traveler, Leo Africanus, witnessed burros performing for Egyptian crowds in Cairo. At least as late as 1967 a burro in the Hagenbeck Zoo in Hamburg was delighting spectators with his special act. In Moscow a burro performs in an entertaining and educational program designed to instruct and to promote an appreciation of animal life. A girl brings before a group of children a burro who beats a drum by hitting a pedal with a front foot. When the girl asks the animal to stop playing, he pounds the drum even more rapidly and loudly, his technique for asking for additional sugar. After the girl provides the goodie, the animal drummer stops his pounding.[18]

Rodeos and horse shows have trick-performing burros and mules.

A white burro, billed as originating in Scotland, regularly performs in a solo act with the famed white Lipizzan royal stallions from Vienna, Austria.

Not only has the burro been successful as a student in a special learning process but also he has served admirably as an instructor in teaching colts, cows, and bulls proper behavior. No trainer excels the burro in gentling and training young colts and fillies to lead. Wayne Dinsmore tells of the usefulness of the burro in teaching the young colt:

> The weanling is haltered with a strong leather halter which fits perfectly, then tied to the neck strap of a female burro, the rope being only about a foot long, then left in a circular corral. Weanling can pull, haul, and fight all he wants to without injury. He is tied to the burro for half an hour the first day. While still fast to the burro he is brushed lightly and handled enough to convince

A burro gentling a young quarter horse and teaching it to lead. Courtesy of American Quarter Horse Association.

him that the man will not hurt him. On the second day the procedure is repeated for half an hour. The weanling by this time has learned to lead with the burro and does not fear the man who works with him. The manager [of the King Ranch, Texas] says the burro is much safer than a man to teach youngsters the first lessons in leading.[19]

At one time cowboys in the brush country of southwestern Texas made use of the burro to bring in a wild steer that could not be caught and brought to the corral or shipping pen. Even when the cowboys managed to rope these contrary ones, they were a long way from the corral. Ray Cowart, of Henderson, Texas, related how the burro was employed to bring in the stock, and about his other contributions on the cattle range. The cowboys

used both lead steers and burros for this task. They usually hog-tied these wild steers when they roped them and went back to the ranch or wherever they were keeping the burros or lead steers and brought them out to where the wild steer was tied down. They would then neck the burro with the wild steer, untie his feet and let him up and turn the two loose. It was sometimes two or three days, but the non-cussin' long-eared cowboy, using his built-in attributes—patience, toughness, and time —brought the wild steer to headquarters. Since the burro was fed regularly here, he would return, bringing his guest, the wild bovine, with him.

Burros were also employed prior to the advent of trailers, to neck together with the wild horses that were roped on the range and couldn't be led. The burro, in due course, would appear at the home corral delivering the now more gentle horse.[20]

The use of the burro with wild steers and wild horses was also common in Cowart's ranching operation at Henderson when yearling bulls were gentled and taught to lead. He wrote, "One of the biggest jobs of the whole thing was getting the burro beside the squeeze chute (where the bull was being held) and to stand still long enough to crack the door of the chute and get him hooked up." However, after a couple of bulls had been tied to him—with a special harness with a breast strap and breeching—the burro knew what to expect and therefore cooperated with the scheme, "just about as well as you would expect a burro to" (from this comment I know that Cowart is well acquainted with and tolerant of the traits of the burro). Some of the bulls weigh about a thousand pounds—far more than the burro—and are young and strong. Obviously the smaller burro often has a difficult time disciplining his aggressive pupil. Mr. Bull pulls and pushes the burro and wins the first few rounds. But when the yearling lags behind, Señor Burro lets fly with both his hard hind feet. A few rounds of this and the bull changes his mind—he elects to walk alongside his teacher and behave.[21]

> The red bull riles
> And the burro smiles
> And he weareth the red bull down.

A bull is usually trained to lead in a corral. Then, after a few lessons, the sessions may continue in a nearby pasture the size of a football field. There the young bull may have an opportunity to

A Texas burro gentling and teaching a young Santa Gertrudis bull to lead, Henderson, Texas. Courtesy of Ray Cowart.

graze with his teacher. The situation is somewhat comparable to the football squad of the late coach, Alonzo Stagg, of the University of Chicago. Stagg was noted for working his squad hard (his most explosive expletive was "*Jackass!*") Bob Zuppke once commented, "It's true that Stagg doesn't swear, but when practice is over, there are no human beings left on the field. The whole squad is grazing."[22]

In the 1930's the western burro entered a new field—and thereby split politics wide open. Those forces which supported him and those which opposed him had confrontations over his destiny. The antiburro crowd proposed legislation that would exterminate the feral burro. However, the animal's friends were many and would be heard. Newspaper correspondents from the Rocky Mountains to the Pacific Coast wrote in his defense. They urged and at last achieved a renewed appreciation of the burro and his role in the history of the West. But his existence remained precarious. Ranchers objected to burros eating grass and drinking water in competition with their cattle. Big-game conservationists preferred the bighorn sheep for the rough and difficult terrain in which the burro had found a home.

Perhaps California has done more than any other state to meet the problem of the wild burro. In 1960 the California Department of Agriculture reported that more than four thousand wild burros were inhabiting the southeastern part of the state, the hills surrounding Death Valley, Saline Valley, and Panamint Valley in Inyo County. There is no doubt that the burro, with his undiscriminating appetite, is a tough competitor for other wild animals.

In 1952 a press release issued in southern California let it be known that the wild burros of the desert mountain ranges would make good hunting, particularly inasmuch as there was no closed season on them. Shortly thereafter hundreds of dead burros were found by people exploring the desert. "Sportsmen" with high-powered rifles were in their own peculiar form of heaven. However, humane organizations objected, as did citizens interested in the

Feral burros in Arizona, 1968. Courtesy of Arizona Highway Department.

historical importance of the little animal and convinced that he should be preserved.

Among the many citizens of California in sympathy with the plight of the wild burro was the well-known personality Death Valley Scotty, long-time resident of the region. Until his death in 1954, Scotty allowed feral burros to scrounge for food on the hillsides and in the canyons surrounding his luxurious Death Valley home. At times Scotty would even hold open house for the burros, allowing them to saunter through the halls of his mansion.

The agitation by friends of the feral burros had results. A law had been passed in California in 1939 making it unlawful to capture or kill burros for the purpose of using carcasses for animal food, but the law did not prevent "hamburger" being made from burro flesh for human consumption, nor did it prevent shooting burros for "sport." In 1953 an amendment was passed declaring it illegal to kill undomesticated burros for any reason. Later, in 1957, the California legislature declared that undomesticated burros were state property. In the same year the state legislature also created a burro sanctuary in southeastern Inyo County. California is unique in this action; no other state has recognized the burro by law or has set up a sanctuary for him. Today permits are issued by the California Department of Agriculture to those persons who wish to capture a burro for a pet or for some other peaceful purpose, such as packing (the United States Park Service is to be consulted for a special permit by a person desiring to capture burros in Death Valley National Monument).[23]

Elsewhere the feral burro has not fared so well. And it is not yet known what the future portends for him. Patricia des Roses Moehlman, a student of ecology, is studying wild burros in Death Valley. She is collecting information about the several thousand burros roaming the desert and hills of the West. When her studies are complete, Miss Moehlman, who has published a preliminary report of her work,[24] undoubtedly will be able to record for the first time the behavioral patterns of the wild burro.

Water is scarce in Death Valley, as it is in other deserts of the world. To obtain water, burros of the Sahara nibble on acacias and eat wild watermelons, but the feral burros of the dry canyons of Death Valley have used their ingenuity in different ways. Neil M. Clark has reported some techniques used by Death Valley burros when they encounter water pipelines. In one instance a two-inch pipeline about two miles long, whose upper end originated in a covered spring, had been abandoned by a prospector when his claim proved disappointing. The pipeline, which lay on top of the ground, was old and rusty. Smart burros learned to kick it in weak spots, thereby getting enough water for a little drink. In another area traversed by a line, two clever old burros cooperated to obtain a drink. One would clamp his strong teeth around the pipe close to a coupling while his partner would do likewise. Each would work in the opposite direction, like animated pipe wrenches, until the coupling was unscrewed and a supply of water gushed out. Then, so the story goes, these conservation-minded burros screwed the pipe together again.[25]

Despite his ingenuity in finding water and food, the feral burro is often a tragic figure, and one whose plight is no credit to the indifferent descendants of those he once helped settle the land. A letter from G. E. Beal, a mining engineer in Yucca, Arizona, gives a vivid description of the life to which the abandoned burros are reduced:

> In this area there are six roaming burros—a couple of them have been used by prospectors for packing supplies and then turned out to forage for themselves. [They] are colored rusty brown and black—all have white noses, . . . noticeable at a distance. Their slant eyes are deeply set and it is hard to tell in which direction they see. The burros of the desert are very cagey, cautious, extremely alert at all times, and they always spot the invader of their area long before you do. They fear only man. They can handle themselves admirably among coyotes and will attack a dog by just heading right for him and knocking him out with a swipe of their forefeet. They travel from canyon to canyon and usually reach a spring every second or third day. They will not drink water every time they find it—just partake of it on the regular schedule. When from a distance they see a man, the leader lets out a snort. All perk their heels and head the other way. Whenever the group rests, one always stands guard. . . . The jenny, or female, usually leads. They roam from camp to camp eating everything thrown out in waste. . . . If one "feels" you may be a friend, and you feed it something, it will keep making visits like a beggar. If a camp becomes abandoned, the burros push in through doors and really rummage around. When they need to be scratched, they just rub against the house even to the extent of destroying the flimsy ones.

They cannot be caught except by cowboy style. . . . Frequently
the prospector has his whole pack dumped when they [the
burros] feel ornery.

When tamed they make good pets and are very bold. Most
often they will poke their heads inside a tent or shack, and their
persistency at times becomes annoying.

They are not killers, . . . but experience makes them aggressive . . . when a dog or coyote approaches. . . . They are far more
intelligent than bovines, horses, and the like, and no animal is
superior for alertness. . . . They feed on sagebrush, prickly-pear
cactus, and eat the vegetation popular with cows. Those that I
have fed here are wild about Quaker Oats. . . . they will sacrifice
their independence for good oats, hay, and barley, rather than
forage.

Like a horse when age creeps upon them, their heads are held
lower, and gray hair grows about their chin, forehead, ears, and
spinal column. . . .

I am a lover of all wild life, and in the mining business I can
observe closely. The only other area where I have seen burros
was near Goodspring, Nevada, near the California state line.
There, the burros were gray and white and blended well into
the limestone country. They stand motionless when they spot
someone, and often you can't pick them out until you get within
about 500 feet. A lot depends whether they stand in a skyline or
outline—usually they stand just below the brow of any hill.

Reddish brown and white and coal black are also some of their
markings. Of the dozens I've seen, only one was coal black and
she traveled with a broken-down old mule. . . . All have small
feet . . . but make the imprint of a small horse. When they are
nervous, they snap their tails and move on. They know the
canyons and springs like a book and make the rounds of their
area like clockwork. Camps they usually hit at night, and if the
camps are inhabited, it means they arrive about 2 A.M. If uninhabited, they spend the night. At times when I was alone here
they spent several days because of the handouts.[26]

Beal is sympathetic toward the feral burro, but others take a dim view of his presence. Not only do some ranchers object to the wild burro because of his superb competitive ability in pre-empting forage and water, but also civil engineers of the Arizona State Highway Department look with a critical eye on the burros' night raids on the stakes driven along the course of planned highways (perhaps the wild burros are in rebellion against the engineers' invasion of their habitat).

Mela Meisner Lindsay believes that a "battle of the burros" is taking place in Arizona. The lines are drawn between the proburros and the antiburros. Some groups favor eliminating wild burros from the scene or greatly reducing their numbers. Sportsmen and their organizations are seeking to persuade the legislature to repeal the old law protecting livestock—including burros—from being shot.

In all fairness it must be admitted that, in pulling up newly planted highway stakes, the burro poses but a temporary problem. He likes to chew on the pitch-permeated stakes, and he finds the pretty colored plastic ribbons attached to them appetizing, for they are made of soybeans. At least one senior project supervisor, Ford McKee, is not hostile toward the burros. He recognizes their historical prominence and rightly says: "Their ancestors helped make this country what it is today. Their faithful, plodding hooves helped make some of our first highways when they were only narrow footpaths hand-cut by prospectors wandering off in search of some dreamed-of gold strike."[27]

The problems posed by feral burros are not confined to the western regions of the United States but may also be found in northwestern Australia. According to the office of the Australian consulate general in San Francisco:

> There are fairly large numbers [of burros] in the northwest of western Australia where before the days of the motor truck they were used in big teams to haul wool from the outback station properties to the port of shipment. The animals went wild from station properties with the introduction of the motor truck, and they have increased to pest proportions in many places. Profes-

sional shooters are often engaged to reduce their numbers. One such shooter is said to have destroyed 1,200 near Wyndham in the far north of western Australia in a five month period in 1955.[28]

The opposing forces continue their feuds, but somehow the burro endures. Fortunately the American public, through the federal government and its various agencies, helps protect him and his kin, the wild horse.

In 1967 a statement by Boyd L. Rasmussen, director of the United States Bureau of Land Management, encouraged the proburro contingent. He assured the American people that herds would receive protection, that efforts would continue for the preservation of wild burros and wild horses on the 170,000,000 acres under the control of the bureau. In that year it was estimated that about seventeen thousand wild horses and eight thousand burros roamed over those lands. It was the bureau's policy to keep the numbers manageable. The director, along with many other concerned citizens, looked upon the animals as representatives of a colorful chapter in the history of the West. "They belong," he said simply.[29]

The Yellowstone National Park has its panhandling bears; Yosemite, its chiseling deer. Tourists crossing the Navajo Indian Reservation of Arizona sometimes see burro hobos along the highway awaiting free-handed travelers. Feral burros also graze along the highways near Tuba City, Arizona, in the northeastern section of the state. Among them are some that are adept at spotting softhearted vacationers.

Tourists, receptive to the quiet approach and the soft touch of these beggars—and anyone who isn't is surely without feeling— will soon learn that they are not at all fussy about what they eat. They have adjusted their stomachs to the foodstuffs the average tourist carries in his car or camper. Crackers, cookies, corn chips, sandwiches, fruits, nuts offer no dietary problems to the shaggy-haired highwaymen.

The Navajo reservation is not the only region where the sleepy-eyed but mentally alert burros supplement their natural grazing habits along the highways. Many of the national parks, forests, monuments, and other lands now shelter some of these little outcasts. Things are looking up for them. They are no longer the prey of "shooters" and indiscriminate hunters. In December, 1971, President Richard M. Nixon signed a bill designed to protect the 11,000 undomesticated wild burros and the 9,500 wild horses that roam free on the public lands of the West. The bill was the direct outgrowth of a "young people's lobby," a letter-writing campaign organized by grade-school children to save an irreplaceable remnant of America's history.[30]

Not all of the burro's history is, as they say, "respectable." Wetbacks, Mexican laborers who cross the Río Grande illegally to work in the United States, often do so on the backs of burros. Illicit trade, including international smuggling, has been part of the burro's experience. During Prohibition days pack burros smuggled tequila and other bracing drinks north across the Río Grande to alleviate the dehydrating effects of those trying times. Smugglers have been known to use strings of pack burros under cover of darkness to bring another valuable product from the Mexican side of the river. The candelilla, a desert plant, clothes itself in wax to conserve its precious moisture. The plants are pulled and boiled in water to which sulfuric acid has been added. Then the wax is skimmed off and used in the manufacture of shoe polish, floor wax, and chewing gum. The Mexican government sets the price of the valuable wax, but the gatherers (called "waxers") who have gone to much trouble to process the product, want more money. The wax is duty-free in the United States, and so they sell to gringo smugglers who come with burros from the north side of the Río Grande.[31]

During the fall and winter the water in the Río Grande often runs low, and as a diversion adventuresome tourists can drive from Big Bend National Park across the rocky bed of the river and proceed to Boquillas, Coahuila. On the east one can see the Serrania del

Burro, a popular name for the range. But the depth of the water can be deceptive: a drowned-out car motor is not uncommon. In that event Mexican boys charge a nominal fee to lead the tourist across the river on a burro. Later, of course, the river has to be recrossed.[32]

Across the international boundary line that separates New Mexico and Chihuahua live the Tarahumaras. These Indians have long resisted external cultural assimilation, but they did welcome the arrival of the burro. Today the animal is employed in the Tarahumaras' austere economy, and they have even put to use a byproduct of his tail. The craftsmen of this mountain tribe string violin bows with durable burro hair. The young women weave hair from the burro's tail into a ball somewhat larger than a baseball. The barefoot women kick the ball in a popular game that sometimes covers many miles. The men? They play the game the hard way, with a wooden ball.

West of the land of the Tarahumaras and over the rugged Sierra Madre Occidental is the coastal resort town of Puerto Vallarta. Burros were a part of a celebration held there one day in August, 1970. The scene was a meeting of two presidents, Richard M. Nixon of the United States, and Gustavo Díaz Ordáz of Mexico, who exchanged greetings at the airport. Security agents had not planned their strategy to cope with the Mexican burro. At one point during the motorcade's journey, while confetti from cheering crowds along the route showered down on the two chiefs of state, a lone burro, obviously unimpressed though decked out in flowers, strolled into the path of the black limousine. The security agents had a tug of war with the burro before he consented to give way to the visiting dignitaries. The presidents? They laughed, thoroughly enjoying the proceedings.

16. Other Burros

Burros have a way of getting involved in the private lives of their human masters. Once I heard an elderly couple telling about their elopement many years before. It seemed that the girl's father disapproved of her beau. As the woman told it:

> It was 1883. Pa didn't like him, asked him to leave the ranch house. One morning after Pa had gone on a trip, we borrowed two burros. Ma helped us. She was the romantic kind and practical too. The housekeeping things were tied up in a feather bed —such as a skillet, tin cups, plates, and clothes—and away we went.

Elopement and weddings are all in a day's work for a burro. As a Bulgarian proverb states, "When a burro is invited to a wedding, it is because there is either no wood or no water." And, according to the story above, there is no transportation.

Burros participate in celebrations of all kinds, and sometimes they are the featured performers. For example, there is the burro race. Such races take place in many countries, but they achieved their greatest fame in the American West. One burro race of particular importance was the contest held on the last Sunday in July each year between Fairplay and Leadville, Colorado. The two towns sponsored what was billed as the World's Championship Pack Burro Race. The two towns alternated as hosts for the event; that is, in the even-numbered years the race started in Leadville and ended in Fairplay, while the reverse was true in the odd-numbered years.

In 1968, Harold Bristol, of Frisco, Colorado, and his lanky paint burro, Jack-of-Spades, won the twentieth annual Leadville-to-Fair-

Early-day burro contest, near Cimmaron, New Mexico, 1900. Courtesy of Fred Lambert.

play World's Championship in a field of eighteen starters. The time was 3 hours, 25 minutes, 2.3 seconds for the 22.9-mile course, which included traversing the 13,180-foot Mosquito Pass. Bristol received one thousand dollars for his efforts. Jack-of-Spades got his picture taken and was returned to his pasture. For the fourth consecutive year Jan Lucas, of Penrose, Colorado, with her jenny, Rocket, won the women's race in 5 hours, 40 minutes, 5.9 seconds. Her prize was three hundred dollars. Her total winnings to that time were twelve hundred dollars. Rocket had cost her twenty-five dollars.

The rules of the contest are strict. The human participants are not allowed to ride their burros or to inflict any physical punishment on them. They may, however, pull, push, or carry them.

The odds are that the race is harder on the owners than on the burros. In the 1968 race the most interesting moment came when a small, reddish-colored burro approached within four blocks of the finish line in Fairplay. There he stopped. His almost exhausted human counterpart tried to coax him on, but the burro took a good look at the crowds of spectators lining the streets and brayed. He repeated this comment several times before being persuaded to cross the white line on the pavement in front of the judges. Even so, he took third place.

The night preceding the 1968 race a "burro ball" was held. Guests dined at a Leadville restaurant appropriately named the Golden Burro. After the race they spent the night in Fairplay at the Brown Burro Motel.

Beginning in 1969 the Leadville–Fairplay burro races were changed. Leadville now sponsors its own event, called the Bur-

Joe Gavinick, of Leadville, Colorado, and Ringo winning the 1970 Leadville race. A few days after the event Joe and Ringo also won first prize in the Fairplay burro race. Courtesy of *Herald Democrat*, Leadville, Colorado.

Readying burros for the world championship wild-burro races, Beatty, Nevada, 1970. Courtesy of Beatty Lions Club.

Rodeo. The race is labeled the world's highest, for the course goes from Leadville to the top of Mosquito Pass and back, a distance of twenty-one miles. The first-place winner among the participants in the 1970 races was Joe Glavinick, of Leadville, and his burro, Ringo, with a time of 2 hours, 32 minutes, 20.3 seconds.

Fairplay and Breckenridge now cooperate in sponsoring a burro race that goes over rugged 11,541-foot Hoosier Pass between the two towns, a distance of twenty-six miles. In 1970 the race was held only a few days after the Leadville festivities, but Joe Glavinick and Ringo again won the first prize, covering the distance in 3 hours, 37 minutes. May Wicker, of Denver, walked off with the first prize in the women's division. The women's race was from Breckenridge to Fairplay.

The Lions Club of Beatty, Nevada, also sponsors an annual

burro-racing contest, held in September of each year. Beatty, situated near the Nevada-California line, borders Death Valley. The
festivities at Beatty last for three days and nights with a lot of
"Baubles, Beer, and Bar-B-Q" as fringe benefits. The 1970 event
was the tenth annual contest. The burros at Beatty are owned and
provided to the contestants by the Lions Club. The animals are
gathered from the desert and the hills surrounding the town. The
region is one of sparse vegetation. Local stockmen describe it as
"10-30 country," meaning that a steer must have a mouth 10 yards
wide and be able to run 30 miles an hour to get enough to eat.

The burros are "branded" (numbered with paint), and the contestants draw their animals by lot. The race covers about twenty
miles on each of the two days. The participants, or "wranglers," as
they are called, draw a fresh burro for the second day's race. However, the routes for the two races are different, though both start
and end at the same line in Beatty.

The officials of the Beatty races also insist that the burros are
humanely treated, and no abuse of the animals is tolerated. It is,
however, legal for the burro to kick or bite the human contestant.
The contestant is not permitted to ride—he must hoof it just as his
companion does. A twelve-foot rope separates the two. There would
seem to be, however, considerable spread between their I.Q.'s. What
burro would voluntarily choose to run twenty miles for fun or
money? And when he wins, the best he can hope for is to be turned
loose on the desert again.

"Don't look now, but here they come!" might well be the excla-
mation of a Philmont, New Mexico, burro, as he watches the arrival of the first group of boys, heralding a new season at the Philmont Scout Ranch. Perhaps the little animals view the invasion
with mixed emotions. It indicates that their winter leisure is ended
and that under the pack they must accompany the scouts and their
leaders up the mountain trails for an experience in hiking and
camping. But to these "pack jacks," as they are referred to on the
ranch, it also means new friends and the return of old ones. In most

instances it is a mutual friendship; the boys grow fond of their four-legged trail companions. A burro loves affection, attention, and tidbits—candy, peanuts, bread scraps, crackers, cookies, colas, and what-have-you-to-offer.

The Philmont scout headquarters are four miles south of the historic town of Cimarron. This area lies along the eastern base of the mountains and streams that bank the snow-capped Sangre de Cristo Range. Cimarron was once the headquarters of Lucian B. Maxwell, a feudal lord of an immense domain that totaled 1,750,715 acres. The Philmont property, carved from this large tract, is a beautiful spread covering 137,000 acres of forested lands and *vegas.* It was donated to the Boy Scouts of America by Waite Phillips, an Oklahoma oilman. The terrain is alive with activity during the summer season, when thousands of teen-age boys participate. It is likely that the two hundred burros at Philmont represent the largest

Mike Henson, a native of Illinois, instructing Boy Scouts and their leaders in the proper way to pack a burro for a trail trip. Courtesy of Public Relations Service, Philmont Boy Scout Ranch, Cimarron, New Mexico, July, 1970.

domesticated herd in North America maintained for a specific purpose.

While he owned the ranch, Phillips stocked it with cattle, buffalo, and even a camel. The camel's only companion was a gray burro, and the two were always together in the pasture. One day in the middle 1930's a bolt of lightning hit the camel and the burro. The camel was killed, but the little gray burro, though injured, got up and wobbled away, doubtless grieving for his friend.

Most people are surprised to learn that burros have great sensitivity and form close attachments to other animals. It has been recorded that when a burro dies in the presence of a long-time companion and friend, the survivor will often pine away and die. Cotton and Satan were two burros of Seven Falls, a popular tourist attraction near Colorado Springs, Colorado. The little animals were popular with the natives and the many visitors to the region. They

Learning to load a burro. Photograph by Ian Bentley. Courtesy of Public Relations Service, Philmont Boy Scout Ranch, Cimarron, New Mexico.

willingly posed for photographs together, sometimes with tourists astride them. One day as the inseparable burros were walking along the base of a steep hill, a heavy log rolled down, striking and killing Cotton, who was reported to be close to the half-century mark. Satan did not leave the spot where his friend had fallen, and within a day he too died. Who can say that he did not die of sorrow? This trait of burros has been noted for many years. In 1864, Thackeray observed that no donkey "ever witnessed the death of another without himself soon pining away and dying."[1]

The National Forest Service has long employed burros to pack supplies and equipment into remote areas. The animals in the service are well cared for. They are fed a plentiful supply of grain and hay and are shod as needed. They are trained to get into pickup trucks and trailers for transport. In the 1930's strings of burros were used during the summers in the Selway National Forest in Montana. J. N. Hessel wrote an article about the animals, telling of their wariness and their hesitancy in crossing a suspension bridge. He told how the burros liked to hang around the rangers' camp to beg for handouts of grub. He also described their fondness for hiding in the bushes when it came time for the day's work.[2]

A burro named Henry was a forest ranger par excellence. He spent most of his working life in New Mexico and Arizona. Henry, a paint, or piebald, was a pack burro for Forest Ranger Henry Woodrow, for whom he was named. When Woodrow retired in 1941, Henry was transferred from the Mimbres Ranger Station of the Gila National Forest in New Mexico to the Clifton District in Arizona. There Henry was assigned to Forest Ranger Crawford Riggs. Henry became a favorite of the ranger both as a pack animal and as a means of transportation when the going got too rough for a horse. But fate again twisted Henry's tail. When he was about twenty years old, he and two other burros were assigned to the Apache National Forest in Arizona. When they are not needed for work, Forest Service animals are sometimes turned loose to graze. Henry and his two burro companions were granted this privilege one day

Henry, the New Mexico Forest Service burro, 1969. Photograph by author.

in 1955. A few days later the rangers were unable to find them. A rancher near the forest reported that he had found the remains of a burro beside a campfire at a spot used by Mescalero Apache woodcutters. When no trace of Henry or the other burros was found after a diligent hunt, the rangers concluded that all of them had been served up by the woodcutters.

Eight years later, in 1963, a ranger of the Gila Division stopped his truck and trailer near Fort Bayard, New Mexico. He heard the sound of a burro trotting toward the pickup. The burro was a paint, and he brayed as he approached the trailer. The ranger noticed two "U.S." brands on the animal's left hip. He let the burro get into the trailer and took him to the main corrals. The burro's unusual coloring plus the two government brands enabled the rangers to identify him as the long-lost Henry. He was back with the Forest Service and in his native New Mexico.

No one knew where or how Henry had spent his eight-year interlude. He was now nearly thirty years old, but he was in good condition. It is only about a hundred miles as the crow flies between the Arizona forest where Henry disappeared and the point where he asked for a ride near Bayard. But a burro doesn't fly. Henry had to cover many difficult miles over mountains, deep gorges, high cliffs, streams, and fifty or sixty fences. Only one fence remained between him and his home pasture when he was spotted by the ranger.

Henry's odyssey would be most interesting if it could be retraced. His trail was cut in only one place: it was learned that he was delayed for two years at a ranch, where two boys adopted him. But his homing instinct was not to be denied. He pushed off into the mountains toward home. Today he is still with the Forest Service rangers, living serenely in semiretirement in the Mimbres Ranger District, Gila National Forest, New Mexico.[3]

Another burro, also known as Henry, serves on a football field at the University of Texas at El Paso. El Paso Henry is the mascot for the Miners. During the spring and summer months he takes it easy, relaxes, and grazes on the Yerby Farm in the Upper Valley, not far from the Río Grande. But when fall comes, Henry's activities pick up. He attends all the football games, watching from the sidelines. He is an impressive sight, decked out in his rich-looking orange blanket. The members of the Kappa Sigma fraternity have pledged Henry and provide care and food for him during his working season.

Jeannette Smith recently described El Paso Henry, his work, his personality, his contribution to the football team, and his life as a country gentleman between seasons. She quoted an evaluation of Henry's service given by the president of the student association: "Henry symbolizes the school spirit of the student body, and reflects the stubbornness and determination characteristic of the athletic teams at U.T. El Paso. Students notice that when Henry kicks up on the football field so does the team."[4] Miss Smith captured the easy spirit and the mañana philosophy of the southwestern burro as represented by this gray-colored shoulder striped mascot: "Henry's career as a celebrity is seasonal, but that's the way he likes it. His yearly schedule gives him ample time to relax, to enjoy the bountiful beauties of nature, and to ponder the complexities of the hustle and bustle of the world around him. Of his two roles, Henry undoubtedly prefers the remote, unassuming one. To him the atmosphere of quiet and serenity must truly be *la dolce vita*."[5]

Henry is a handsome, streamlined, photogenic animal. He replaced a burro named Clyde, who apparently was not very prepossessing. Clyde's center of gravity was exceedingly low, his wheelbase short, his backbone bent, his belly large and swaying. He was not the most inspiring of animals, and Henry was chosen in his stead. I wonder what became of poor old rejected Clyde.

Other burros have served as mascots or good-luck symbols for various clubs, organizations, and conventions. El Paso Henry is more fortunate than some mascots, for there are some men who stretch the meaning and intent of symbolism. One night several years ago a group of conventiongoers, somewhat phased in the liquid mist of the Las Vegas, Nevada, cocktail lounges, boarded a plane home for Chicago, with a burro for a mascot. The pilots and hostesses on the plane were also apparently having a ball. The flight engineer, who had a camera along, took pictures of the scene. The burro had been turned loose in the aisle. The passengers, by now at the playful stage, started throwing things at each other. The burro, frightened, backed into the partly open cockpit door. Someone on board with a little sense held his foot against the door to keep the burro from landing in the cockpit and crashing against the controls. It is not known what happened to the mascot after the high, wild ride to Chicago (though the odds are that if he is free, he is on his way back to his home in Nevada—hoofing it). At any rate, the incident was instrumental in establishing stricter rules of conduct for personnel and passengers aboard airplanes.[6]

Rollicking conventioneers often pull innocents into their celebrations. The 1968 convention of the Hoo Hoo Club, a lumbermen's organization, was held in Albuquerque. One night the group was holding a barbecue outside a hotel near the foot of Sandia Mountain. The weather turned cold, and the members adjourned to the hotel lobby, taking with them a burro that had been donated to the local club to be raffled off. The proceeds were to help defray the expense of bringing the convention to Albuquerque. The raffle brought in $540. The animal was subsequently given back to the local club, and there in the hotel lobby the burro was auctioned off for $450. The buyer turned out to be the Hoo Hoo Club of Anchorage, Alaska. Let James M. Doolittle, a Hoo Hoo of the Albuquerque Lumber Company, finish the story:

> It is my understanding that the buyers of the burro had no place to keep it and until they could find a place, prior to its being shipped to Anchorage, it was left at a hotel. During this time, it reportedly kicked in two sliding glass doors and fell into the swimming pool. The pool had to be drained to recover this esteemed animal. The last I heard, it was about to be shipped to Anchorage, and the rumors of the incident are that it had started to kick the shipping crate apart and was making the airlines uncomfortable. . . . I understand that the shipping costs will be approximately $2,000. . . . The dollar figure now totals somewhere in the neighborhood of $3,500.00.[7]

Burros have served as mascots for branches of the armed forces. During World War II the Canadian Royal Air Force wanted a burro for a mascot. The state of Colorado provided one of its "Rocky Mountain canaries" (reportedly the son of Prunes, of Fairplay), and the young burro was flown to Canada. Rosie, a gray burro with a transverse stripe over the shoulders, served as a mascot for the United States Air Force at Hicks Air Field, near Fort Worth, Texas.[8]

Provided they are well treated, mascots have relatively easy lives. Such was not the case with Shorty, another famous burro of Fairplay. Shorty, so called because of his stubby legs, worked at many mines in the surrounding hills and was owned by various miners. But the time came when the profitable ore from the mines played out. Too, the years were stacking up heavily on Shorty's low-slung back. He was turned loose, as was the fate of many prospectors' and miners' burros. Poor old Shorty had to rustle for himself, and during severe winters, when deep snows covered his grazing region, the aged burro suffered. In time he grew blind. Then a bit of help came Shorty's way. A homeless mongrel dog appeared in Fairplay and became the constant companion of the blind and homeless burro. A family who had befriended the dog named him Bum. Bum would take the lead along the streets of Fairplay and to the outskirts of town where grass was available. There, while his blind friend grazed, Bum had fun chasing chipmunks.

Shorty and Bum, Fairplay, Colorado. Courtesy of Denver Public Library Western Collection.

In the winter the two resorted to begging. Bum led his blind companion from one friendly kitchen door to another for handouts. Bum came to know which of the residents were generous and which were not. He would lead Shorty to a likely door, and Shorty would announce their arrival with a bray. The housewife would respond with food, and Bum would take the pancakes or other leftovers to Shorty and lay them before him. Only after that would he eat his share.

Then one day an automobile, the animal's deadly enemy, hit Shorty and killed him. Bum later met his death the same way. A small monument was erected in Fairplay to honor the two devoted friends.[9]

In the little village of Placitas de los Ranchitas, just south of Santa Fe, New Mexico, lived old Juan and his burro, Miguelito. Miguelito was also very old and had a habit of falling down. One night Miguelito did just that—and fell into an abandoned well. Fortunately the well was dry.

Juan, unusual for him, got up late the next morning. He noticed that Miguelito was not at the door to greet him when he stepped out. Berating himself for having slept too long, doing Miguelito an injustice, Juan went to look for him, searching among the nearby hills and arroyos and around houses. The neighbors learned of Juan's concern. Later some boys found Miguelito and ran to tell Juan. He picked up a bottle of tequila and hurried to the site. Looking down from the rim of the well, he saw his old friend and exclaimed, "Pobrecito compadre!" Upon hearing his master's voice, Miguelito raised his head and brayed in delight.

Juan lowered himself into the well and drank in celebration of their reunion. He also gave Miguelito a portion of the contents of the bottle. Then sleep overcame them both. Later some of Juan's neighbors found the two celebrants asleep, awakened them, and hoisted them from the well.[10]

Charles D. Willard, of Cottonwood, Arizona, told me the story of Old Ned, who over the years became a fixture in that town. A faithful and gentle burro, for many years he carried children to school. During the summer he could be seen standing in the middle of a street asleep. Understanding people would walk or drive around him. Old Ned was given much freedom in the town, for he was trusted and loved. He would, however, call regularly at his master's front gate for his breakfast of barley. Sorrow came to the town when disaster overtook Old Ned one stormy night. The bank gave way on the edge of a pit, and the old burro fell in and was covered with dirt. He died of suffocation a short while after he was pulled out of the pit. He was forty-four years old.

Jess Matthews, a long-time resident of Maxwell, New Mexico, tells about a burro that one day appeared in the village out of nowhere. Some local boys assumed ownership and caretaker duties and christened the burro Lucky. As subsequent events proved, the name was not well chosen. The youngsters got some pieces of harness, threw them over Lucky, and hitched him to a two-wheeled cart. They drove him around in the community. One day while the boys and some of their friends were riding in the cart, Matthews, something of a practical joker, picked up a corncob and placed it under the burro's short tail. Lucky took off down the street, running wild, bouncing the cart over chuckholes, and scattering boys along the way.

On another day, Jess says, the youngsters were driving along in front of Menapace's Saloon, down east of the Santa Fe Railway tracks. Some cowboys who were at the bar having a few came out and led the burro, cart, and boys, into the saloon. The revelers bought the burro a drink and encouraged him to swallow it. However, the boys objected and told the tormentors that they were going to get their big brothers to deal with them. The cowboys, wisely deciding that it was time to leave for the ranch, headed out of town.

One night the boys staked Lucky in a swale, or low spot, just north of the village to graze. During the night a storm arose, water rushed into the swale in a torrent. Poor burro! He wasn't tall enough. Early the next morning the boys went to see how their burro had fared. There he was, swimming round and round, still tethered to the stake. One of the boys quickly dived into the water and released him.

About the same time a small circus came to town. The boys, believing that Lucky would become a performer in the circus, sold him to the manager for a dollar. Jess learned, however, that the little burro was to provide fresh meat for the circus lion. Jess quietly made his way to the burro, who was tied near the circus tent. With his pocket knife he cut the rope holding Lucky. He reports that no race horse could have equaled the frightened burro's speed as he made his getaway. He had scented his Nubian ancestor's dreaded enemy, the lion. But, though Lucky was spared that time, the machine age finally overtook him. One day on a road west of the village an automobile crashed into him. Lucky's luck had run out.

Many are the tales of friendships between human beings and burros. The following story is an example:

The New Jersey Turnpike toll-booth attendant said to his companion: "Did you see what I saw?"

"I think so, but I don't believe it."

Shaken as they were, the toll-booth men really knew they weren't seeing things.

There was a girl who passed their way in a VW convertible one recent night with a donkey sitting beside her.

She was 22-year-old Jane McMillan, of Los Olivos, California. Her passenger—she prefers to call him a burro—was from Greece.

Jane, a student at the Parsons School of Design, New York City, had been in Europe several months, touring with a group of Parsons students. She bought a new VW in Munich and began touring on her own after the rest of the students went home.

She wound up in Greece, where she befriended the burro and named him Nonda.

"He was only four months old and no one wanted him," she said. "Somebody at the American Farm School at Thessalonika gave him to me and somebody else dared me to take him home.

"When it was time to come home we drove to Athens. Some

Jane McMillan and her adopted Greek donkey. From *Small World*. Courtesy
of Volkswagen of America.

people were surprised to see a burro riding in style. We did fine, though. He spent ten nights sleeping in the car while we were waiting to sail, but he had lunch on the Acropolis every day. I ate sandwiches and he ate grass."

Jane had some trouble getting the burro's passage. The steamship line manager said it was impossible.

But Jane, who has wit, charm and intelligence, said it was very important. The manager said it had never been done before.

Jane, who also has blonde hair and expressive eyes, pleaded. The manager demurred.

"I love him," Jane said fervently. That did it.

They installed Nonda in a shower room aboard the cargo ship *Hollandia*. The voyage took 23 days to New York.

"He was a good sailor," Jane said. "But he was not housebroken. I had to clean the shower room daily.

"When we got to New York, they said he had to go through quarantine. It was just before Christmas and I said he was going to be in the Nativity scene at Radio City. That didn't work. . . . He *had* to go to quarantine."

When Jane set off for the West Coast, she had a bale of hay in the back seat, straw on the floor and two paper sacks of grain. People did double-takes all the way.[11]

Burros, like other animals, have served as pets since the time of their domestication. Breeders specializing in pet burros are scattered around the nation (suggestions on selecting and caring for pet burros are provided in the following chapter). An especially popular breed is the Miniature Mediterranean Donkey, as he is called by the breeders. Perhaps the first American breeder of the miniature donkey was Robert W. Green, of Trenton, New Jersey. In May, 1929, he purchased, sight unseen, six females and a male from their native island of Sardinia in the Mediterranean. Green, a retired Wall Street broker, had never seen a miniature donkey, but he found immediate enjoyment in the companionship of the little animals. He described them as having "the affectionate nature of a Newfoundland dog, the resignation of a cow, the durability of a

Only twenty-eight hours old, a registered Miniature Mediterranean Donkey, Danby Farm, Millard, Nebraska. Courtesy of Danby Farm, Millard, Nebraska.

mule, the courage of a tiger, and an intellectual capacity only slightly inferior to man's." (Some of Mr. Green's customers agreed, for one of them wrote, "You might talk to me about disposing of one of my children, but not the donkey.")

By 1935, Green's breeding herd had increased to fifty-two. The burros had been given such colorful names as Christopher Columbus (who was born on Columbus Day), Nanette, Jillette, Crackerjack, Miranda, Impheus, and Palermo. Green especially admired Palermo, a jenny:

> I remember one time Palermo came running up to the barn from the far end of the pasture. She was whimpering and doing everything but talk. Mr. George Groff, the farmer I had then, knew

something was wrong. He let her lead him down the field, and there was her new colt with its little head caught in the wire fence and ready to strangle to death. You've just got to admire an animal as smart as that.

While he and his wife hated to part with any of the little animals, it became a practical necessity. They inserted a small advertisement in the April issues of *Town and Country* and *House Beautiful.* A photograph of one of the animals was included in the advertisement. The ad was captioned "Diminutive Donkeys" and said: "The ideal pet for children. Attaining height of from 30 to 35 inches when fully grown, they are absolutely safe to ride and drive. Prices range from $50 to $100." Green was swamped with orders. He could not fill nearly all of them.[12]

Today there are many American breeders of the Mediterranean donkey. Stock from the original herd, and from later importations from Sardinia, Sicily, and other European areas provide pets and service animals for a growing clientele.

Dr. Claus Strumpf, of Bissendorf, Germany, is a breeder of the small animal as a household and yard pet. He reports that his Zwergesel, or dwarf burro, weighs up to 150 pounds, attains a height of about thirty-six inches, and lives about twenty-five years. Strumpf says that the little animals are ideal children's pets, can be raised in an apartment since they require little exercise, are lovable and intelligent, and can be house-trained.

One of the Zwergesel burros, Sonja, lives in Northville, Michigan, at the home of Mr. and Mrs. Jay Zayte. The Zaytes are enthusiastic about her good health and her obedience. She will come when her name is called. Sonja loves to mow the lawn and will even trim the rose bushes. Nor has she any objection to taking a ride with the family in the car.[13]

The social status of burros is rising, and it is about time. However, in the Mediterranean area where these small burros originated, they do not receive the care or consideration given them in this country. The Miniature Mediterranean is small because over the centuries he was abused, overworked, underfed, and subjected to too close inbreeding. Yet, although the mature donkeys average only thirty-two to thirty-seven inches tall at the withers, they are strong and durable. Centuries of conditioning have produced an animal that can pull carts with loads much larger and heavier than he (of course, that is true of the standard-sized animal as well; no other animal carries or pulls as much in proportion to his weight as the donkey does).

Dwarf burros are not confined to the southern European countries. The donkeys of Ireland are also dwindling not only in size but also in numbers. In 1960 there were eighty thousand donkeys in Ireland. Eleven hundred were sent to other lands in 1961, but the number exported in 1968 totaled thirty-five hundred. The drain on the supply is obvious. Some of the Irish are concerned about the problem. The secretary of the Society for the Prevention of Cruelty to Animals has written: "There is much more appreciation for the Irish donkey abroad than at home. Unless some steps are taken to encourage breeding or to control exports, we may soon lose him entirely."

Such trends have prompted people in this country to take steps to preserve the little animal. Hence the establishment in 1958 of the Miniature Donkey Registry of the United States, whose headquarters are in Omaha, Nebraska. Mr. and Mrs. Daniel Langfield, of Omaha, were instrumental in founding the registry. They are the owners of Danby Farms, of Millard, Nebraska, where some of the miniature animals are kept. The registry stipulates, among other criteria, that the animal must have the characteristic transverse stripe across the withers before it can be registered. The registration number is tattooed inside the animal's upper lip.

Miniature donkeys are especially appealing to children. They have had a beneficial effect upon disturbed and homeless children. "Animal therapy" is an important part of the treatment program at the famed Glenn Cunningham Youth Ranch, near Augusta, Kansas.

The ranch has been in operation for about twenty-five years. Each child at the ranch is given an animal of its own to care for and to love. Among its eighty-four hundred alumni, there has never been a boy or girl who was not fond of animals, according to Cunningham, the famed track star of the 1930's.

The burro has borne or pulled just about every kind of load that is movable. His cargo has even included outlaws. During the last half of the nineteenth century outlaw Coal Oil Jimmy's gang made the Turkey Mountains, west of Fort Union, New Mexico, their hangout. One day two members of this horrendous bunch of stagecoach robbers and cattle thieves learned of a two-thousand-dollar reward offered for two of the gang's leaders. That night they made their way to where the two men were sleeping and killed them. They loaded the lifeless bodies on burros, tied them on with ropes, and took them to Cimarron. A wooden shutter was removed from a window of the St. James Hotel, and the dead outlaws were passed through the window and deposited on a pool table. The assassins collected the reward, together with a bonus—one-way tickets to the East, with the compliments of the Land Grant Administration.

Burros also bore the victims of feuds. A mid-nineteenth-century sheepherder named Cecillio Lucero, who lived near Las Vegas, New Mexico, decided to do away with a cousin and another sheepherder. After he killed them, he tied the bodies behind two harnessed burros and let them remove the evidence from the scene.[14]

Sometimes the burro is himself the victim of malfeasance. An Associated Press release of October 6, 1968, gave an account of modern-day livestock rustling in Kenya, East Africa. The report read, "Rustlers' tactics this year have caused the loss of 20 lives, 17,000 head of cattle, 4,700 goats, many donkeys." The lowly burros were not worth the effort to count them. Yet Kenya's horse-mounted police patrol enlisted the burro and the mule to pack food supplies, submachine guns, and other equipment in their efforts to track down the rustlers.[15] The police use them but don't trouble to enumerate them.

It must be noted that the burro has not always gone unappreciated. A nineteenth-century visitor to New Mexico recorded this note in his diary: "When New Mexico has become a state, the faithful burro should be engraven on the coat of arms as an emblem of all the cardinal virtues."[16] Of course, when it came time to choose a seal for New Mexico, no one paid any attention to this sound advice. It was thought more fitting to choose two eagles and a snake for the design. With 314 years of service and sacrifice to the people of the new state to his credit, the burro would have been my choice.

Another early traveler in the West noted the part played by the burro in its settlement. Reuben Gold Thwaites gave a vivid account of his extensive western journeys. He noted: "I must not forget paying a passing tribute to that meek and unostentatious member of the brute family, . . . *el burro,* . . . poor man's friend, . . . carries all grain, hay, wood, etc., even the whole family, . . . no bridle, saddle, etc., rider sits back on haunches and uses stick to guide."[17]

Burros in front of the Palace of the Governors, Santa Fe, New Mexico, date unknown (ca. late 1800's). Courtesy of New Mexico State Library.

While the prospector, the miner, the sheepherder, the wood hauler, the trapper, the freighter may not have had the means or influence to honor the loyal little burro, they did what they could to see that he was remembered: they named places for him. In Montezuma County, high in the Colorado Rockies, is Burro Peak. There is Burro Mountain in Río Blanco and Burro Canyon in Las Animas. In Ouray County runs Burro Creek. Back in the 1870's in present-day Monterrey County, California, burros helped in the prospecting and later in the development of a rich ore find. In their honor the region was named Los Burros Mining District. The Hopi Indians of Arizona have a Burro Springs on their reservation. Farther north, in the Grand Canyon area, one of the many small canyons bears the name of the animal. And Burro Creek rises in Yavapai County.

According to T. M. Pearce, an authority on New Mexico place names: "A place name map of New Mexico would not portray faithfully the story of the land if the picture of a patient wood-hauling burro did not appear. The services of this faithful beast of burden are recorded in a number of place names."[18] It is appropriate for New Mexico to have many burro place names, for the animal has lived in this state longer than in any of the other forty-nine. Not far southwest of Silver City rise the Little Burro Mountains. Fifteen miles north of Silver City we find Burro Springs. This watering place was frequented first by the Indians, then by the explorers, and later by the settlers. In Harding County is Burro Arroyo. There is a mountain pass just northeast of Raton where a crippled burro once grazed. The Spanish name for the pass is Paseo Manco de Burro (Crippled Burro Pass).

Thus, though there are few formal monuments to the burro, humble men have seen to it that places where his hoofs have trod are stamped with his name, evoking an era when his long ears and his loud bray signaled that he was present and accounted for.

Occasionally we learn of people whose dedication and devotion

Above: The proprietors of the Lockwood Home of Rest for Old and Sick Donkeys, Whitley, Surrey, England. Top: Mr. and Mrs. John Lockwood. Below: One of the Lockwoods' patients. Both photographs by author.

renew our faith in humankind. Mr. and Mrs. John Lockwood, of Surrey, England, are two such people. This compassionate couple have dedicated their lives to providing a home, medical attention, food, and loving care for homeless burros. They are especially concerned for old, crippled, or sick animals who need help most.

The Lockwoods operate a thirty-five-acre farm that includes pasture, barns, and other facilities. Their sanctuary is known as the Lockwood Home of Rest for Old and Sick Donkeys. The fortunate burros that come under the ownership of these good people live out the remainder of their lives happy and contented. For most of them it is an existence they have never known before.

The Lockwoods never sell or allow a single burro to leave the farm once it arrives there. When an animal dies, he is buried on the farm, and a marker is placed on his grave bearing his name.

How did this burro sanctuary begin? One day in 1955, Lockwood was attending a market and saw a man mistreating two burros. John, deeply angered, gave the offender some of his own medicine, knocking him down. The altercation resulted in a fine for John, but, he says, "It was all well worth it." He also purchased the two old burros and took them home. Those two refugees from man's inhumanity were the first members of the Lockwood Home of Rest for Old and Sick Donkeys.

Today there are about 225 burros at the home. We wrote to the Lockwoods about their venture and received the following information from Mrs. Lockwood:

> We purchase only the sick and disabled animals or those about to be destroyed because they are no longer required. We give them whatever treatment is necessary to recover their health and a little happiness for the first time in their lives. . . . Some unfortunately, die before we have a chance to help them. . . .
>
> We have a local veterinarian in attendance almost every day to give the poor animals injections or whatever treatment is required and this is very costly indeed. . . .
>
> It is a very sad thing that so many donkeys work hard all their

Top: An aging mother and her baby at the Lockwood Home. Below: One of the oldest donkeys at the home. Both photographs by author.

Top: Old Poncho, fifty-four years old when this photograph was taken in 1971, now a resident of the Lockwood Home. Photograph by author. Below: John Lockwood, benefactor of old and sick donkeys, 1970.

lives, often carrying loads far too heavy for their size and strength, only to end up in the Knockers' Yard (place of killing and processing) when they are no longer required by their owners. That is one of the reasons why we started the Farm. We would attend markets where these poor creatures were put up for sale, and having bought them, would bring them triumphantly home to love and care for until the end of their days.

My husband lives only for his animals and this Home of Rest now costs 14,000 pounds [$33,600] a year to run. . . . We are planning ways and means of meeting these higher costs. . . . Also one can adopt a donkey, in name, for one pound [$2.40] per year. . . . Our only reward is our pleasure in seeing how wonderfully these animals respond to kindness and affection that they have never known before.

Do come to see for yourselves our very dear and Happy Family.

In March, 1971, my wife and I did just that and found it a richly rewarding experience. In the meantime each of us had adopted a burro, and the certificates of adoption are on the wall in our study.

Portions of Lockwood's letter accompanying the certificates follow:

We are delighted to send you the two certificates. I have chosen for you two very dear members of our "family." Both are a little over middle age and in good health. Flossie was a cripple when she came, but after much careful nursing and much love, she is now better, but of course will never be cured. Both are delighted at being chosen and feel *very important*. . . .

Every donkey in the herd has a blanket; some have their names embroidered in the corners. Some blankets have been knitted by old ladies over 90, others by school children in very bright colours, which strike a very cheerful note on a cold and freezing morning. Every day come birthday cards for the "darlings," and at Christmas hundreds of greeting cards arrive at the door. One donkey received a tin of peppermints from New York, and another very old one who sadly left us, received some beautiful artificial flowers, also from New York. So you see they have friends all over the world. To date 35 countries in all.[19]

The following lines by an unknown author assuredly apply to the John Lockwoods, of Surrey, England:

> When I have given animals their care
> Let everyone know I've said my prayers.

17. The Burro as a Pet

Today many Americans are discovering the charms of the burro as a backyard pet. He has long since proved his worth as a companion, especially for children. As an animal upon which a child can learn to ride, he has no peer. He responds to children even more than to adults (perhaps another indication of his intelligence). The sociable burro likes people, wants to be in the center of things, and enjoys being talked to. He is cooperative and willing to serve, especially when he is treated as a partner. Under such conditions he gives his owner much pleasure and happiness. After all, the best way to treat a pet burro is in the fashion that Joanna treated Ulysses, as narrated in a children's book by May Sarton. Warmhearted Joanna rescued overworked little Ulysses from a cruel donkey driver on the island of Santorini, in the Aegean Sea. She applied salve and gauze to his fly-infested belly wound, fed him a little hay, and shared with him her daily lunch of tomatoes, cheese, and bread. She also bought him a hat (which he ate) and a string of large blue beads. But most important of all, she gave him love, which he heartily returned.[1]

In England also the burro is becoming increasingly popular as a pet. R. S. Summerhays, in a delightful book entitled *The Donkey Owner's Guide*, describes the recent interest in pet burros among the staid English.[2] Robin Borwick, another Englishman, has also described the unique appeal of burros:

If a horse gets loose in High Street all the men wave their umbrellas and the women hold their children tight. If a cow gets loose, the men dial 999 to report a mad bull and the women push their children into the supermarket or china shop and shut the

Certificate of Adoption

This is to Certify that.............................
........Mr. Frank. Brookshier...............
has adopted a donkey named "Flossie".........
for a period of one year from October 30th 1970...
and has donated the sum of One Pound towards its upkeep.

Date..30.10.'70....... Signed John Lockwood

The Lockwood Home of Rest
for Old and Sick Donkeys.

Certificates of adoption by author and wife, 1970.

door. Pigs and sheep cause less chaos and dogs and cats are completely ignored, but a loose donkey causes a traffic jam because everybody wants to pet it.[3]

Burros are practical little fellows and do not expect anything beyond the simple necessities of life—though they are not averse to a few comforts. To these animals luxury is the love and attention of their owners, and their responses are beguiling. Like any other

Certificate of Adoption

This is to Certify that......................................
.......Mrs. Florence Brockshier.........
has adopted a donkey named "Old toncho,"..........
for a period of one year from October 30th 1970.....
and has donated the sum of One Pound towards its upkeep.

Date 30.10.'70....... Signed John Lockwood

The Lockwood Home of Rest
for Old and Sick Donkeys.

pet a burro will become lonely and bored when he is left alone too long. But given reasonable care and affection, he will reward his owner with a lifetime of love and trust.

The ideal pet burro is a newly weaned foal—usually six to eight months old. I would venture that there is no cuter or more appealing animal in the world. By selecting a young animal, the owner will have the pleasure of seeing him grow up and, if he wishes, have the opportunity to learn how good an instructor he is in training the youngster to do whatever chores may be expected of him. If

A burro at work in Las Vegas, New Mexico. Courtesy of Denver Public Library Western Collection.

a foal is not available, the prospective burro buyer may safely purchase an older animal, provided he has been well and gently cared for.

At the outset anyone contemplating buying a burro who intends to keep him within city limits or other incorporated community should first determine whether there are any regulatory or restrictive ordinances. Even though there may be no prohibition against burros, some neighbor may object to the new resident, principally

Burro riders at the turn of the century, in Manitou Springs, Colorado. Photographs below by W. H. Walker. Courtesy of Denver Public Library Western Collection.

A newborn burro, not yet dry. Courtesy of Danby Farm, Millard, Nebraska.

because of his voice. Therefore, it is courteous first to inform any neighbors of the project. It is likely that, after the burro arrives, the neighbors, and especially their children, will welcome the newcomer.

If "noise" is a factor, it is advisable to secure either a jenny or a gelding, because their brays are generally more moderate than those of the jack (too, the jack may, as he matures, become restless and less attractive as a pet). Some burros, like some people, just naturally bray more than others. But luck may be on the purchaser's side, for some burros, especially those who have care and company, bray very seldom. A lonely burro may raise his voice in protest. My burro, Catrino, seldom brays, but he has Pal, my horse, as a constant companion, as well as my almost daily attention. When my wife and I are away from home, our neighbors across the road care for them. Pal and Catrino both, I believe, look upon this attention as a kind of bonus. Sometimes Elaine, the neighbors' pretty young daughter, comes over, climbs a wooden section of the fence, and calls them by their names, talks to them as they approach, and pats them on their heads.

Burros come in many colors, sizes, weights, and shapes, and the selection depends upon the buyer's preferences. There are two main physical types suitable for pets and for riding and working in harness. One, the standard burro, has an average height of about forty-four inches. The smaller animal, descendant of the Mediterranean miniature described in the preceding chapter, averages

Luis, with an eight-year-old friend. Courtesy of Danby Farm, Millard, Nebraska.

Luis resisting introduction to the outdoor feeding area. Courtesy of Danby Farm, Millard, Nebraska.

about thirty-four inches high. Both make good pets. Because of his small size the miniature is particularly valued as a pet for a handicapped child. One of these little animals, properly trained—either by the breeder or by the owner—to pull a cart, can be of inestimable joy to such a child. Some breeders specialize in animals trained for these easy chores.

In some of the federal and state-owned lands of the West where bands of feral burros—"cimarrones"—range, burros may be had free of charge. Generally it is necessary to get a permit to obtain one—and then the problem is to catch him! People with the time and patience to do so, however, can take credit for saving one little animal from the guns of hunters or ranchers. For, despite laws pro-

Deborah Kay Ault, Age 7 with PEPI, Registry No. 34. Picture taken at DANBY FARM, Millard, Nebraska.

Top: Pepi, a Miniature Mediterranean Donkey, with rider. Below: a day-old Miniature, Ro-Salia. Both photographs Courtesy of Danby Farm, Millard, Nebraska.

tecting them, burros still die at the hands of gun-happy hunters and ranchers, who resent the grass and water the burros consume.

There are other avenues open to a prospective burro buyer. He can purchase one from an individual owner. In such cases it is advisable to make a personal inspection of the animal to observe his temperament, responses, and general health. If the buyer plans to show the animal in competition someday, then he should make a close examination of the burro from his ears to his hoofs. Guides for this purpose are available.

The American Donkey and Mule Society, Inc., a nonprofit corporation with publication and correspondence offices in Denton, Texas, provides services for people interested in burros. For a nominal charge the society will provide a list of literature regarding all aspects of long-eared animal husbandry, among which is a mimeographed sheet entitled "Judging Small Donkey Conformation." Not long ago I obtained a copy of this sheet and took it to Catrino's corral, where I compared its standards with Catrino, who cocked his ear and looked.at me with a quizzical expression that seemed to say, "I know I measure up!" Catrino was right. Though he may not possess show-ring possibilities, it is safe to remark that he comes much closer to qualifying now than he would have at the time I bought him a few years ago.

Catrino was a lonely young burro when I first met him on the edge of the village where I live. The lady to whom he belonged had received him as a gift. She did not have any facilities to care for him, however, and her only recourse was to tether him in a small area of native grass near her house. His tether rope was too short and was frayed. Even though Catrino was short and weak himself, he would sometimes manage to break loose. He would seek better forage, which included neighbors' lawns, shrubbery, and flower beds. One man threatened to shoot Catrino unless something was done about the matter. So it was at this crucial stage that the harassed lady, knowing of my sympathy with and fondness for burros, asked if I would buy him. The price was fifteen dollars, and the deal was closed without any haggling. Soon afterward a friend of mine, seeing Catrino and learning of the transaction, said to me, "Man, you got took!" He was wrong, as it turned out, but I tell the story to illustrate one way to become a burro owner.

Another way is to place an advertisement in the want-ad columns of the local newspaper or to make a regular check of the columns. Local veterinarians or county agricultural agents may also put one on the trail of a burro in need of a home. In a large city the pound or zoo may have one available. But the best way to obtain just what you want is to visit or write a breeder specializing in burros. The American Donkey and Mule Society will provide the names and addresses of reliable breeders.

After you have found your burro, the next consideration is appropriate shelter and care for him. In much of the western and southern United States the burro can get along without manmade shelter. But an unprotected animal suffers in severe winters in the mountains and high altitudes, and even in the southern states cold winter rains are bad for him. While he is endowed with long, thick hair with water-repellant qualities, a hard rain soaks through it, causing colds and other ailments. Wherever you live, it is a good general rule to provide some sort of shelter.

The shelter should be enclosed on three sides, with the fourth open, facing south. The structure may be an old building suitable for conversion into a stable. To house only one animal, it need be no more than eight or nine feet square and about six or seven feet high to allow headroom for a person to stand upright in it. The roof can be hip-style or a oneway sloping or shed roof. A prefabricated portable structure is satisfactory and readily available. For such a building a suitable concrete foundation is recommended, though other kinds of foundations are acceptable, including those made of treated timbers. The building itself may be constructed of any number of materials, depending on availability and cost.

Mother Earth serves well for a floor; wheat or oat straw is optional for bedding. The droppings should be regularly removed (no

Burros are popular as pets the world over. Above: French burro pet in northern France. Courtesy of Elizabeth Moreaux. Opposite: A burro in Western Australia, 1970. Courtesy of Kirwan Ward.

big job, for the burro will usually deposit them in the same place each time) and taken to the compost heap. A water container is necessary. It may be anything from a pail, which is filled and carried to the animal at regular intervals, to a small galvanized water tank with an automatic piped-in supply. A small box to hold loose salt or a fifty-pound commercial salt block is advisable. Such a supply will provide a salt lick for one burro for one or two years, or even longer. The salt discourages stomach worms and furnishes some trace elements.

A manger may be erected inside the shelter, or some portable container may be used for hay and a smaller container placed nearby for grain supplements. However, the feeding equipment may be placed outside the shelter if the climate is mild. Throughout much of the West, where rainfall is light and snows not excessive, outdoor feeding is satisfactory. If it is properly stacked, baled alfalfa, oat hay, or other baled forage can be kept outside with little damage from the weather. However, one burro consumes only about half a ton during the winter months, and that amount can be stacked in a corner of the garage, with enough room left for a bag of feed grain or pellets.

During the growing season good-quality grass is all that a burro needs; he will thrive on it, and should there be some coarse plants in the pasture, so much the better. A burro delights in munching on coarse forage, including hay, providing it is not musty or spoiled. An acre of grazing pasture, well watered, should be sufficient for a small burro.

For proper grazing management, a fence should surround the area, and it should be fenced in two equal parts, thus affording a simple rotation system. The fence may be any one or a combination of several kinds—rail, pole, board, or barbed or woven wire with appropriate posts. An over-all fence height of forty-eight inches will restrain most burros. Even though he may be able to get out of an old or deteriorated fence or a poorly constructed new one, a burro will rarely go far. Instead of kicking up his heels on gaining his freedom, as a horse will often do, the burro will amble along, sampling the grass and nibbling at weeds and bushes, going no farther from home base than his appetite and curiosity take him. He may, however, cross the road to take a look inside a neighbor's open gate. He may or may not enter, but if he does, he will likely do little or no harm, for his hoofs are small and his nibbles dainty. In fact, it may just be that the neighbor will welcome the intruder, provided he saunters to a spot where unwanted grass, bushes, or weeds are flourishing.

The owner who does not have an enclosed pasture or who wishes to supplement it can make use of the tether. The burro can then be led to grass or forage alongside a nearby road, in a vacant lot, on a lawn, or in an orchard. The tether is more appropriate for an old burro than for a young one. The latter needs more exercise than tethering permits. The burro should have either a buckled strap around his neck with a ring in the collar or a rope, nylon, or leather halter on his head. The rope, one-half or three-quarter inches in diameter and about thirty feet long, depending on the size of the area to be grazed, should have a swivel with a snap or clip attached at each end. One end is attached to the collar or halter and the other to a ring at the end of an eighteen-inch-long iron pin or wooden stake driven into the ground. A heavy weight can be used in place of the stake. The swivel will lessen the chances of the animal becoming entangled in the rope. However, unlike the horse, the burro who gets himself tangled up will generally patiently wait for help to come, thus avoiding rope burns and other injuries.

One word of warning: While tethering has its place in caring for a burro, it can be inconvenient for the owner and trouble for the animal, because the practice tends to lead to neglect. The burro may exhaust his grazing area and water long before the owner comes to move him.

The local feed dealer stocks supplementary feeds and will suggest the kinds and amounts for the burro. It is best not to provide too highly concentrated a feed, for it is not good for the animal. A mixture of two parts rolled maize, one part crushed oats, and one part bran makes a suitable ration fed once a day or halved and fed twice, morning and evening, depending upon the activity of the burro. Feed manufacturers process a pellet feed for horses which is also suitable for the burro, but care should be exercised to see that not too much is given—only one double handful a day. Rolled maize, together with hay, will serve the burro's needs. Maize has enough, but not too much, protein. It is wise to consult the feed dealer about rations and daily amounts required. The common tendency among pet owners is to feed them too much. The owner should observe his pet daily to determine how much food he needs.

In addition to hay and feed pellets, table scraps, stale bread, some fruits, and virtually all vegetables, cut into small pieces, are acceptable to burros. No meat should be offered; it is toxic to equines.

Most experienced trainers frown on allowing a burro to eat out of one's hand. It is a common and enjoyable method of feeding but is objected to, for some animals will pester or even snip at a person when goodies are not forthcoming. If the owner wishes to hand-

English burritos, 1971. Photographs by author.

The proper way to feed a burro. Photograph by Ian Bentley. Courtesy of
Public Relations Service, Philmont Scout Ranch, Cimarron, New Mexico.

feed his pet—and I confess that I plead guilty (though never sugar cubes, candies, or other sweets)—the following is the safest method: Place one or two commercial feed pellets in the palm of the hand with the fingers close together and with the thumb extended backward. Extending the pellets grasped between fingers and thumb may mean that upon withdrawing the hand one may find a finger missing, so strong are the teeth and jaws of the burro. Furthermore, the extra morsel may set up the toxic condition referred to above.

The care of a burro includes attention to his hoofs. They should be trimmed when the need arises. Depending upon the individual burro, the hoofs may require trimming as often as twice a year. Others may seldom require trimming. Climate, weather, and terrain also determine the frequency of trimming. Shoes are seldom required unless the animal is expected to do much walking over stony trails or to serve as a pack animal in the mountains. Unless you have a real knack with animals or some experience with hoof trimming, it is best to let your veterinarian or some other skilled person do the trimming.

The anatomy of the burro's hoof is no different from that of the horse. However, the various parts differ in proportions and texture. Unlike the hoofs of the horse, the burro's hoofs are not brittle but elastic. This is an advantage, for they are less likely to become sore. However, they will grow long. Perhaps nothing about the burro is more neglected than his feet. I have seen some hoofs that have grown out as much as eighteen inches. This needless condition causes deformities and makes it extremely difficult for the animal to move. The wild ass in his native habitat never has this problem, nor do the feral burros of the West. They travel terrain that keeps their hoofs well trimmed.

Instructional books are available for the inexperienced person who wants to learn how to trim hoofs and shoe a burro. The art of shoeing is far from lost. Some universities and colleges are now offering courses in it.

An owner should early begin familiarizing the animal with having his feet elevated. The burro will thus be prepared for the trimming and, when necessary, the shoeing process when the time arises. The soles of the feet should be examined frequently anyway. A horseshoer's knife—or a screwdriver—will serve to remove dirt, dried mud, manure, and any small stones that may have become wedged in the sole and in the crevices around the frog.

The burro is subject to the same ailments that afflict horses. However, the burro is more resistant to diseases. When he does show indications of sickness—which will be rare—it is well to call the veterinarian, who will doctor him much as he would a horse. But one should not be misled by a long period of immobility. If your burro is standing, chances are he is not sick but merely taking a rest. The burro can and does sleep while standing, though more often he lies down for his rest.

On those mornings when I decide to take a six- or eight-mile ride on Pal, I curry him before we depart. This ritual is repeatedly interrupted by Catrino, who slowly and quietly but determinedly pushes between me and Pal so that I must curry him too. Then I walk to the other side of Pal to renew my chore. But here comes Catrino, and again he has to have his turn at the currycomb.

In due course Pal is bridled and saddled, and we are on our way, Catrino following. Catrino usually lags behind a hundred yards or so, nibbling at greenery alongside the country road, inspecting unusual objects and open gates and visiting with animals across fences. Then, realizing that he has fallen behind, he plays "catch up," racing toward us. Upon arriving, he thrusts his muzzle alongside my leg, seeking a feed pellet or two that he knows I have in my pocket. He considers that he is entitled to this reward by virtue of closing ranks.

Catrino and Pal enjoy these outings. We usually travel roads into the 3,240-acre Maxwell National Wild Life Refuge. Catrino stops to look at a bright-colored pheasant cock that darts across a field or trail, watches a cottontail rabbit as it scampers to its burrow, observes the wild ducks rising in flight from Lake 13. In the late fall, with his antenna-like ears, he listens to the honking of the Canadian geese, views at a distance their graceful landing on the lake, where they pause for rest, protection, and feeding in the fields of green wheat and rye provided in the refuge. During fishing season, meandering along on the ample wide, long dike of the lake, Catrino may visit with fishermen—but not if they are holding poles or rods in their hands. Apparently as a burrito Catrino was struck or even beaten with a pole of some sort, and I have noticed that when I have a shovel, a pitchfork, or some other such tool, he shies and moves away from me. I have never used a whip on him or struck him with a stick or pole, but surely he remembers a past sad experience.

Catrino's fearful actions re-enact those of a young burro in a Mexican folktale—a burro who was being trained for his duties. His owner gave him a hard beating for some reason and then turned him loose in the corral.

There the youngster met an old burro, who said, "What's the matter, son?"

"Oh," the young burro replied, "my owner just gave me a bad beating."

Then he asked the old burro, "How old does one have to be before man stops beating you?"

The old burro replied, "Listen, my son, in a burro's life, there is nothing but beatings, from the day you are born to the day you die, and just hope you're lucky that man doesn't make a bass drum out of your hide when you die, for then someone will keep beating on you on Saturdays and Sundays, even after you are dead."[4]

Fortunately for Catrino, he never has to fear such a fate.

Catrino never stops observing or amusing himself in his own fashion. As we start our journey homeward, he may decide to wallow or take a few enjoyable rolls in the green grass. First he selects a likely spot, circling it with head lowered, making a visual olfactory inspection accompanied by low, muffled snorts, which become more audible, signifying his pleasure as he rolls his body from one side to the other on the ground. He then stands up and shakes the loose

Riccardo, a registered Miniature Donkey, who has been adopted by the Robert Mairs family of Pasadena, California. Courtesy of Danby Farm, Millard, Nebraska.

dirt from his body. Once more invigorated, he is ready to play catch up again—unless his attention is distracted by a jackrabbit—his namesake—hurriedly bobbing away from a shallow scratched-out bed under a dry tumbleweed near a bunch of grass or yucca. Magpies may momentarily capture Catrino's interest, their black-and-white feathered wings spreading as they chatter noisily.

Not far from the corral—and by now Catrino is close behind, I give the command to Pal: "Let's go!" And he does just that—off in a gallup, which he thoroughly enjoys. Catrino accepts the challenge, responding with a dash that brings him even with Pal and me. Then, as I loosen the reins a bit, Pal edges into the lead—but only for a short distance, because if it's one of his speedier days, Catrino will tilt his ears back and pass us, kicking up his heels at us as he goes by. All three of us love these rides. In fact, on days I cannot join them, Pal and Catrino will race each other around their pasture in a playful manner entrancing to watch.

A burro is a good pet. He is affectionate by nature and rarely bites or kicks. However, I have known burros with a peculiar sense of humor. In their quiet and subtle manner they think that they can be boss. Occasionally Catrino seems to believe that he is master of all he surveys. On such occasions I have found it best to adopt the schoolteacher's policy: "Be gentle, but firm."

The pet burro needs little training. However, a few behavioral patterns are desirable. It may be that the new owner wants his pet to do a few simple chores, such as pulling a cart, packing a reasonable load on a camping trip, or even performing in the show ring. It is likely that your pet will enjoy doing these tasks, provided he has been trained properly. If you want your pet to perform in such exotic tasks, your local library or bookstore can give you guidance. A few fundamentals are listed below as a preliminary to further study.

Training a burro generally presents few problems. The first step is to gain the animal's confidence. You must prove that you are his friend and that you can be trusted. Trust is established by talking to the burro, repeatedly calling his name, walking up to him slowly, and gradually touching and rubbing the top of his neck and across his withers. Every burro loves to be petted, curried, and brushed, and performing these little favors convinces him that you are a friend. And, of course, feeding him is the most persuasive gentling act.

When you place a halter or a bridle on his head for the first time, it is a good idea to ask an experienced friend to help you do so. He can also suggest the proper size and appropriate tack—halter, rope, bridle, blanket, saddle, and harness. There are books aplenty to advise in detail, step by step, how to catch, bridle, saddle, and harness the burro and the tack to use. Tack used for the pony is generally adaptable to the burro, especially the bridle and bit. Since the burro does not have pronounced withers, for riding purposes a crupper or britching should be attached to the saddle or riding blanket to keep them from slipping forward on his back.

It is very important to make sure that the burro understands what he is to do. This part of the training will require patience, for the animal may have his own idea about the matter. Firmness, tempered with patience, is essential. The regular use of the same expressions in training will be effective—"Whoa," for "Stop," "Get up," for "Go," and other short, simple, clear commands. The burro has a good memory, and, once he learns his commands, he will not forget them. Be sure that he understands what is required of him. It is well to keep in mind that a burro will remember bad habits as well as good ones. Always encourage and reward acceptable behavior. The burro is somewhat like a child: he was not born with unacceptable traits, but he can acquire them.

So much for the basics of training. The sensitive owner will quickly learn what to expect of his pet—and what to concede to the animal's own self-esteem.

The burro owner can become so fond of his pet that he begins to think of him as a member of the family. There are limits beyond which it is unwise to go, however. A man in Camden, New Jersey, recently included his two burros as dependents on his income-tax return. An alert Internal Revenue Service auditor got suspicious when he read the dependents' names—Happyjack and Sassafras.

That warning noted, a burro is a rewarding pet, and if this book has encouraged the reader to acquire one of his own, I can only say welcome to the club.

Notes

CHAPTER 1

1. Food and Agriculture Organization, *Production Yearbook* (Rome, 1971), XXIV, 303, table 104A.

2. *Much Ado About Nothing*, act 4, scene 1.

3. Juan Ramón Jiménez, *Platero and I* (tr. by Eloïse Roach, Austin, University of Texas Press, 1957), 92.

4. Sir J. Gardner Wilkinson, *The Manners and Customs of the Ancient Egyptians* (rev. ed., Boston, S. E. Cassino and Company, 1883), III, 300.

5. Cecil G. Trew, *From "Dawn" to "Eclipse": The Story of the Horse* (London, Methuen and Company, 1939), 67.

6. Joseph Nathan Kane, *Famous First Facts: A Record of First Happenings and Discoveries and Inventions in the United States* (New York, H. W. Wilson Company, 1950), 509; Douglas Southall Freeman, *George Washington: A Biography* (New York, Charles Scribner's Sons, 1954), VI, 58.

7. In James W. Freeman (ed.), *Prose and Poetry of the Live Stock Industry of the United States* (Denver and Kansas City, National Live Stock Historical Association, 1905), 147.

8. *Raton Comet*, July 21, 1882, quoted in *Albuquerque Journal*.

9. Robin Borwick, *People with Long Ears: A Practical Guide to Donkey Keeping* (London, Cassel, 1965), 10.

10. *Ibid.*, 170.

11. C. B. Glasscock, *Gold in Them Hills* (Indianapolis, Bobbs-Merrill Company, 1932), 186–89.

12. *The World Book Encyclopedia* (Chicago, Field Enterprises Educational Corporation), I, 474*b*.

13. Carleton Mitchell, "Our Virgin Islands," *National Geographic Magazine*, January, 1968, pp. 68, 80.

14. Pliny, *National History* (Cambridge, Harvard University Press, 1940), Vol. III, Book 8, 119.

CHAPTER 2

1. Wilkinson, *Manners and Customs of the Ancient Egyptians*, III, 301.

2. Act 1, scene 3.

3. *The History of Herodotus* (tr. by George Rawlingson, New York, Tudor Publishing Company, 1928), 243–62.

4. Wang Shih-chên, *A Collection of Minor Historical Incidents from the Later Han to the Chin Dynasty Inclusive from the Second to the Fifth Century, A.D.*

5. See *The Bestiary, a Book of Beasts: Being a Translation from A Latin Bestiary of the 12th Century, Made and Edited by T. H. White* (New York, G. P. Putnam's Sons, 1954), 82–83.

6. William Walsh, *Curiosities of Popular Customs and of Rites, Ceremonies, Observances, and Miscellaneous Antiquities* (Philadelphia, J. B. Lippincott and Company, 1897), 73.

7. William Makepiece Thackeray, "Respecting Asses," *Cornhill Magazine,* Vol. IX (January–June, 1864), 69.

8. John Lockwood Kipling, *Beast and Man in India* (New York, Macmillan and Company, 1891), 86.

9. William Jones, *Credulities, Past and Present* (London, Chatto and Windus, 1880), 37.

10. *Register,* quoting *Denver Tribune,* June 2, 1871.

11. George M. Darley, *Pioneering in the San Juan* (Chicago, Fleming H. Ravell Company, 1889), 184–85.

12. Henry Pickering Walker, *The Wagonmasters* (Norman, University of Oklahoma Press, 1966), 222.

13. *Report of Regular and Special Meeting of the Colorado Bar Association, Eleventh Annual Meeting at Fort Collins, Colorado, July 23, 1908, Special Meeting at Denver, Colorado, January 23, 1907,* II, 114.

14. *District Court of Appeals, California, 1919,* IV, 529.

15. *Albuquerque Journal,* August 5, 1972.

16. L. L. K., "Philosopher of the Desert," *Living Age,* June 14, 1924, pp. 1137–40.

17. Theodor Lessing, "Asses and Masses," *Daily Living Age,* November, 1931, pp. 260–62.

18. *Poetry of Our Times* (ed. by Sharon Brown, Chicago, Scott, Foresman and Company, 1928), 182.

19. William MacLeon Raine and Will C. Barnes, *Cattle* (Garden City, N.Y., Doran and Company, Inc., 1930), 319.

20. "To a Young Ass," in *Selected Poems of Samuel Taylor Coleridge* (ed. by James Reeves, London, William Heinemann, Ltd., 1966), 13.

CHAPTER 3

1. Pierre Teilhard de Chardin, *The Phenomenon of Man* (New York, Harper and Brothers, 1959), 120.

2. Herbert Wendt, *Out of Noah's Ark* (tr. by Michael Bullock, London, Weidenfeld and Nicolson, 1956), 364.

3. Hugo Obermater, *Fossil Man in Spain* (New Haven, Yale University Press, 1924), 254.

4. Henry Fairfield Osborn and H. E. Anthony, "Close of the Age of Mammals," *Journal of Mammalogy*, November, 1922, p. 219.

5. Robert Ardrey, *African Genesis* (New York, Atheneum, 1965), 194.

6. Ernest P. Walker et al., *Mammals of the World* (Baltimore, The Johns Hopkins Press, 1964), 1312.

7. Luis Salvano and Mateo Torrent, *Ganada Asnal y Ganado Mular* (Barcelona and Madrid, Spain, Salvat Editores, S.A., 1959), 20.

8. Letter to the author, September 4, 1966.

9. Frederick E. Zeuner, *A History of Domesticated Animals* (New York, Harper and Row, 1963), 367.

10. J. Frank Dobie, Mody C. Boatright, and Harry H. Ransom (eds.), *Mustangs and Cow Horses* (Austin, Texas Folk-Lore Society, 1940), 192–94.

11. Gilbert Chesterton, "The Donkey," *Home Book of Verse for Young People* (ed. by Burton Egbert Stevenson, New York, Henry Holt and Company, 1958), 352.

CHAPTER 4

1. C. A. Reed, "Animal Domestication in the Prehistoric Near East," *Science*, December 11, 1959, p. 1639.

2. Sylvester Sieber and Franz H. Mueller, *The Social Life of Primitive Man* (St. Louis, Herder Book Company, 1941), 269.

3. Robert Myron, *Prehistoric Art* (New York, Pitman Publishing Corporation, 1964), 46.

4. Phyllis Flanders Dorset, *The New Eldorado: The Story of Colorado's Gold and Silver Rushes* (New York, The Macmillan Company, 1970), 111.

5. *Ibid.*

CHAPTER 5

1. Harold J. Peake, *Early Steps in Human Progress* (Philadelphia, J. B. Lippincott and Company, 1933), 98–99.

2. Sir E. A. Wallis Budge (tr.), *Book of the Dead* (2d ed., New York, Barnes and Noble, Inc., 1909), 375n.

3. P. D. C. Davis and A. A. Dent, *Animals That Changed the World*, adapted from F. E. Zeuner, *A History of Domesticated Animals* (New York, The Macmillan Company, 1966), 19.

4. Arthur Treadwell Walden, *Harness and Pack* (New York, American Book Company, 1935), 107.

5. Lewis Spence, *An Encyclopedia of Occultism* (New Hyde Park, N.Y., University Books, 1960), 37.

6. Alan M. Bateman, *Economic Mineral Deposits* (New York, John Wiley & Sons, Inc., 1956), 6–7.

7. *The Jewish People, Past and Present*, Vol. I of *The Jewish Encyclopedia* (New York, Martin Press, Inc., 1946), 36.

8. Food and Agriculture Organization, *Production Yearbook* XXIV, 309, 310, table 106 (Mainland China, 11,620,000; Ethiopia, 3,900,000).

9. Letter to the author from the Zoological Society of London, September 4, 1966.

10. Henry Dufton, *Narrative of a Journey Through Abyssinia in 1862–63* (2d ed., London, Chapman and Hall, 1867), 4.

11. Helen Schreider and Frank Schreider, "In the Footsteps of Alexander the Great," *National Geographic*, January, 1968, p. 21.

12. *Time*, October 12, 1970, p. 20.

CHAPTER 6

1. Geoffrey Bibby, *Four Thousand Years Ago* (New York, Alfred A. Knopf, Inc., 1962), 82.

2. H. Frankfort, *Cylinder Seals* (New York, Macmillan and Company, 1935), 65.

3. H. R. Hall, *The Civilization of Greece in the Bronze Age* (London, Methuen and Company, Ltd., 1929), 84.

4. Alice Fleming, *Wheels* (Philadelphia, J. B. Lippincott and Company, 1960), 8.

5. Herman Dembeck, *Animals and Man* (tr. by Richard and Clara Winston, Garden City, N.Y., National History Press, 1965), 164.

6. H. W. Janson and Dora Jane Janson, *History of Art* (Englewood Cliffs, N.J., Prentice-Hall, Inc., 1964), 53–54.

7. Maxwell W. Read and Jeanette M. Lucas, *Animals on the March* (New York, Harcourt, Brace and Company, 1937), 100.

8. Ralph Linton, *The Tree of Culture* (New York, Alfred A. Knopf, Inc., 1956), 94–95.

9. Zeuner, *A History of Domesticated Animals*, 373.

10. C. J. Frazier, "The Language of Animals," *Archeological Review*, Vol. I (April–May, 1888), 81–91, 161–81.

11. Christen Phelps Grant, *The Syrian Desert* (New York, Macmillan and Company, 1938), 51.

12. J. A. R. Thompson, *The Greek Tradition* (New York, Longmans, Green and Company, 1931), 68–69.

CHAPTER 7

1. Robert Young, *Analytical Concordance to the Bible* (Grand Rapids, Mich., William B. Eerdman's Publishing Company, n.d.), 58.

2. *The Jewish Encyclopedia* (New York, Funk and Wagnalls Company, 1902), II, 221.

3. Spence, *An Encyclopedia of Occultism*, 37.

4. Ernest G. Wright, *Biblical Archaeology* (Philadelphia, Westminster Press, 1962).

5. Jones, *Credulities, Past and Present*, 334.

6. Louis Simond, *A Tour in Italy and Sicily* (London, Paternoster-Row, 1828), 281.

7. Margaret Mackay, *The Violent Friend: The Story of Mrs. Robert Louis Stevenson* (Garden City, N.Y., Doubleday and Company, Inc., 1968), 512.

8. Berriot M. Saint-Prix, *Memoires de la Société Antiquaries*, 1829.

9. Ernest H. Kantorowiez, "The King's Advent," *Art Bulletin*, December, 1944, pp. 207–31.

10. According to Davis and Dent (*Animals That Changed the World*, 103–104), some Semitic tribes of Arabia down to the time of Mohammed worshiped a god who took the form of a donkey. These influences may have entered ancient Judea, for there is evidence that some of its people worshiped a donkey totem.

11. *The Catholic Encyclopedia* (New York, Encyclopedia Press, Inc., 1934), 793.

12. Story told by a missionary named Jessop who served in Syria in *Leisure Hour Magazine*, January 16, 1875, p. 46.

13. *Encyclopedia of Islam* (London, Lujac and Company, 1927), 84.

14. Kipling, *Beast and Man in India*, 84.

15. Will Durant, *The Age of Faith* (New York, Simon and Schuster, 1950), 260.

16. Kipling, *Beast and Man in India*, 92.

17. James Hastings et al., *Encyclopedia of Religion and Ethics* (New York, Charles Scribner's Sons, 1908), I, 502.

18. "The Impossible Stairs," *Denver Post*, December 9, 1962, p. 6.

19. For this Mexican folk tale I am indebted to Mrs. Betsy Hutchins, of the American Donkey and Mule Society, Inc., Denton, Texas. Mrs. Hutchins learned of the story from Henry Schipman, Jr.

CHAPTER 8

1. Zeuner, *A History of Domesticated Animals*, 364.

2. *Ibid.*, 378.

CHAPTER 9

1. Irma Wassal, "Onager," *Commonweal*, Vol. XXXI (April 19, 1940), 547.

2. James C. Baum, "Hunting the Wild Ass," *Atlantic Monthly*, Vol. CXLVIII (August, 1931), 150.

3. Ernst Schwartz, "The Onager, Wild Ass of Persia," *Nature Magazine*, April, 1938, p. 236.

4. Quoted in Thackeray, "Respecting Asses," *Cornhill Magazine*, Vol. IX (January–June, 1864), 71.

5. Philip Robinson, *The Poets' Beasts* (London, Chatto and Windus, 1885), 121.

6. A few years ago during a visit to Budapest, it was my good fortune to meet Sándor Bókónye, of the Budapest National Museum. Bókónye is an authority on the history of the domestication of animals in eastern Europe. We discussed the place of the burro in this region, and he indicated that there was very little evidence for any early presence of the domesticated burro in that area.

7. Vera Gromora, *On the Possible Date of Appearance of the Domestic Ass in Central Asia, Report* of the Academy of Sciences of the USSR, Vol. LVI, No. 2 (1947).

8. Thomas Pennant, *History of Quadrupeds* (3d ed., London, Band J. White, 1793), 13.

9. *The Travels of Marco Polo* (ed. by Manuel Komroff, New York, Liveright Publishing Corp., 1930), 40.

10. *The Sacred Books of the East* (ed. by F. Max Muller, Oxford, Clarendon Press, 1894), XLI, 224–25.

11. *Ibid.*, V, 67–69.

12. *Ibid.*, XXIX, 366.

13. Kipling, *Beast and Man in India*, 3–4.

14. *Ibid.*, 93.

15. *Ibid.*

16. *Ibid.*, 94.

17. *Indian Tales: A Collection* (Madras, G. A. Natison and Company, 1920), 65.

18. *Ibid.*

CHAPTER 10

1. Arthur De Carle Sowerly, "The Domestic Animals of Ancient China," *China's Journal*, October, 1935, p. 234.

2. Quoted in Will Durant, *Our Oriental Heritage* (New York, Simon and Schuster, 1935), 655–56.

3. H. G. Creel, *Chinese Thought from Confucius to Mao Tse-tung* (Chicago, University of Chicago Press, 1960), 56.

4. Tr. by Yun Chio (Nanking, University of Nanking, 1947).

5. H. D'Ardenne de Tizoc, *Animals in Chinese Art* (London, Benn Brothers, Ltd., 1923), plates XVIII and XIX.

6. *Encyclopedia of World Art* (New York, McGraw-Hill Book Company, 1959), I, plate 489.

7. *The Travels of Marco Polo*, 107, 109.

8. P. L. Simmonds, *A Dictionary of Useful Animals and Their Products* (London, E. and F. M. Spon, 1883), 4–5.

9. Quoted in Glover M. Allen, *The Mammals of China and Mongolia*, Vol. XI, Part II of *Natural History of Asia* (New York, American Museum of Natural History, 1940), 1284.

10. Sven Hedin, *My Life as an Explorer* (tr. by Alfheld Heubsch, Garden City, N.Y., Garden City Publishing Company, 1925), 303–304.
11. Sir Charles Bell, *The People of Tibet* (Oxford, Clarendon Press, 1928), 23.
12. Chau Ju-Kua, *Chu-fan-Chi* (tr. by Friedrick Hirth and W. W. Rockhill, (St. Petersburg, Imperial Academy of Sciences, 1911), 171.

CHAPTER 11

1. *The History of Herodotus* (Chicago, Encyclopedia Britannica, Inc., 1952), 11.
2. Gisela Richter, *Animals in Greek Sculpture* (New York, Oxford University Press, 1930), 21.
3. *Encyclopedia of Superstitions, Folklore, and the Occult Sciences of the World* (Chicago, J. H. Yevdale and Sons Company, 1903), 573.
4. Spence, *An Encyclopedia of Occultism,* 37–38.
5. Will Durant, *The Life of Greece* (New York, Simon and Schuster, 1939), 453.
6. E. Cobham Brewer, *Dictionary of Phrase and Fable* (Philadelphia, J. B. Lippincott Company, 1930), 69.
7. Aristotle, *History of Animals* (tr. by Richard Criswell, London, George Burton and Sons, 1883), Book VI, Chap. XXIII, 171–72.
8. *Ibid.*
9. Victor Hehn, *The Wanderings of Plants and Animals from Their First Homes* (London, Swan Sonnerheim, 1885), 110.
10. *Athenaeum,* Vol. II (September 28, 1895), 421.
11. A Virginia Farmer (tr.), *Roman Farm Management* (New York, The Macmillan Company, 1913), 138.
12. *Ibid.,* 117.
13. *Ibid.,* 138.
14. Pliny, *Natural History,* quoted in Will Durant, *Caesar and Christ* (New York, Simon and Schuster, 1944), 310–11.
15. Thackeray, "Respecting Asses," *Cornhill Magazine,* Vol. IX (January–June, 1864), 71.
16. Zeuner, *The History of the Domestication of Animals,* 381.
17. Thackeray, "Respecting Asses," *Cornhill Magazine,* Vol. IX (January–June, 1864), 71.
18. Zeuner, *A History of Domesticated Animals,* 381.
19. Durant, *Caesar and Christ,* 384.
20. George Jennison, *Animals for Show and Pleasure in Ancient Rome* (Manchester, Manchester University Press, 1937), 127.
21. *Ibid.,* 145–46.
22. Will Durant, *The Age of Faith* (New York, Simon and Schuster, 1950), 539.
23. *Time,* January 17, 1969, p. 60.

CHAPTER 12

1. C. A. Pietrement, "Origin of the Donkey," *Popular Science Monthly*, April, 1883, p. 787.

2. Rossel I. Vilá, *Comparative Osteology of the Horse and the Ass*, (Barcelona, Editorial Catalonia, S.A., 1921), 11.

3. Hehn, *The Wanderings of Plants and Animals from Their First Homes*, 461.

4. Geoffrey, *Four Thousand Years Ago* (New York, Alfred A. Knopf, Inc., 1961), 62, 73.

5. Pennant, *History of Quadrupeds*, 11.

6. Brewer, *Dictionary of Phrase and Fable*, 69.

7. Honoré de Balzac, *The Wild Ass's Skin* (New York, Peter Fenelon and Son, 1900), 38-43.

8. Leo Rosten, "Erasmus," *Look*, June 1, 1965, p. 81.

9. *Encyclopaedia of Ethics and Religion* (New York, Charles Scribner's Sons, 1908), I, 502.

10. William S. Walsh, *Handbook of Literary Curiosities* (Philadelphia, J. B. Lippincott Company, 1911), 134.

11. *Ibid.*, 134.

12. William S. Walsh, *A Handbook of Curious Information* (Philadelphia, J. B. Lippincott Company, 1913), 305; C. P. Skrine, *Chinese Central Asia* (London, Methuen and Company, 1926), 105-23.

13. Thackeray, "Respecting Asses," *Cornhill Magazine*, Vol. IX (January–June, 1864), 71.

14. J. A. Hammerton (ed.), *Manners and Customs of Mankind* (New York, William H. Wise Company, 1936), IV, 1035.

15. Zoe Oldenbourg, *Catherine the Great* (tr. by Ann Carter, New York, Pantheon Books, Inc., 1965), 50.

16. "Asses' Milk for Infants," *Popular Science Monthly*, January, 1883, p. 426.

17. Philip Gilbert Hamerton, *Chapters on Animals* (Boston, Roberts Brothers, 1877), 116.

18. Thackeray, "Respecting Asses," *Cornhill Magazine*, Vol. IX (January–June, 1864), 72.

19. Pennant, *History of Quadrupeds*, 11.

20. Stevenson, *Travels with a Donkey in the Cévennes* (New York, Charles Scribner's Sons, 1908), 7.

21. *Ibid.*, 198.

22. *A Plea for Animals* (coll. and ed. by Frances E. Clarke, Boston, Lothrop, Lee, and Shepard Company, 1927), 137-38.

23. C. J. Cornish, *Animals of Today: Their Life and Conversations* (London, New Amsterdam Book Company, 1899), 37.

24. Edward G. Fairholme and Wellesley Paine, *A Century of Work for*

Animals: A History of the RSPCA, 1834–1934 (London, John Murray, 1934), 87.

25. "Thoughts upon Asses," *Edinburgh Magazine*, January, 1840, pp. 57–64.

26. Quoted in James Cole, "The Art of Simpling," *Cornhill Magazine*, Vol. IX (January–June, 1864), 70.

27. Bertha S. Dodge, *Plants That Changed the World* (Boston, Little, Brown and Company, 1959), 154.

28. "Asses, Dogs, Cats, Etc.," *Catholic World*, August, 1866, pp. 688–90.

29. *The Complete Poetical Works of William Wordsworth* (New York, Thomas Y. Crowell & Company, 1892), 127–29.

30. Robinson, *The Poet's Beasts*, 97.

31. "Donkey Derby," *Chamber's Journal*, August 26, 1865, pp. 540–42.

32. *Leisure Hour*, August 7, 1875, pp. 520–25.

33. Borwick, *People with Long Ears: A Practical Guide to Donkey Keeping*, 15–16.

34. "With Lord Byron at the Sandwich Islands in 1825" (extract from the MS diary of James McCrea, Scottish Botanist, Honolulu, 1922).

35. Henry L. Sheldon, "Reminiscences of Honolulu—No. 20," *Saturday Press*, Vol. II, No. 21 (Whole No. 73), (January 21, 1882), 1.

36. Mackay, *The Violent Friend: The Story of Mrs. Robert Louis Stevenson*, 471.

37. *Ibid.*, 475.

38. *Ibid.*, 477.

39. Sir Irving Benson, *The Man with the Donkey: John Simpson Kirkpatrick, the Good Samaritan of Gallipoli* (London, Hodder and Stoughton, 1965), 92–93.

40. *Ibid.*, 90.

41. *Ibid.*, 91.

CHAPTER 13

1. "The Oil Merchant's Donkey," *Adventures in World Literature* (ed. by Rewey Belle Inglis and William K. Stewart, New York, Harcourt, Brace and Company, 1948), 245–46.

2. Jiménez, *Platero and I*, 175.

3. *Ibid.*, 100, 169, 176.

4. *Ibid.*, 122–23.

5. By Edgar L. Ashley, quoted in Walter A. Dyer, "The Donkey That Wouldn't Budge, A Christmas Legend," *Country Life*, December, 1926, pp. 44–46.

6. Count de Buffon, *Natural History of Man, the Globe, and of Quadrupeds* (New York, World Publishing House, 1817), I, 184–85.

7. Charles F. Lummis, *Flowers of Our Lost Romance* (New York, Houghton Mifflin Company, 1929), 11.

8. Robert M. Denhardt, "The Southwestern Cowhorse," *Cattleman*, December, 1938, pp. 21–22.

9. John J. Johnson, "The Introduction of the Horse into the Western Hemisphere," *Hispanic American Historical Review*, November, 1943, pp. 587–610.

10. Samuel Eliot Morison, *Admiral of the Ocean Sea* (Boston, Little, Brown & Company, 1942), 399.

11. *Time*, June 28, 1948, p. 25.

12. *Mexico City News*, August 4, 1969.

13. *Ibid.*

14. Letter to the author, September 24, 1969.

15. Letter to the author from Enrique Planchart, director of the National Library, Caracas, Venezuela, February 23, 1945.

16. *Ibid.*

17. *Ibid.*

18. George Brown Goode, *The Beginnings of Natural History in America*, Annual Report of the Smithsonian Institution (Washington, D.C., 1897), 357–406.

19. *Ibid.*

20. Lummis, *Flowers of Our Lost Romance*, 10.

21. *Ibid.*

22. Loren McIntyre, "Flamboyant Is the Word for Bolivia," *National Geographic*, February, 1966, p. 184.

23. Charles Darwin, *The Voyage of the Beagle* (Boston, Harvard Classics, 1909), 375.

24. Letter to the author from Julia Pacheco, Cochabamba, Bolivia, 1968.

25. Harold Osborne, *Bolivia* (2d ed., London, Royal Institute of International Affairs, 1955), 1.

26. "My Little Burro," *Time*, June 28, 1948, p. 25.

27. Food and Agriculture Organization, *Production Yearbook*, XXIV, 307, table 106.

CHAPTER 14

1. George P. Hammond and Agapito Rey, *Don Juan de Oñate: Colonizer of New Mexico, 1595–1628* (Albuquerque, University of New Mexico Press, 1953), I, 247.

2. Charles F. Lummis, "Brother Burro," *Land of Sunshine*, Vol. IV, No. 3 (February, 1896), 107–108.

3. Frank Waters, *Midas of the Rockies* (Denver, University of Denver Press, 1949), 105, 15.

4. Mrs. James Rose Harvey, "Long Eared Express," *Denver Post*, October 12, 1947, p. 2.

5. B. A. Botkin, *A Treasury of Western Folklore* (New York, Crown Publishers, Inc., 1951), 438.

6. Eliot Lord, *Comstock Mining and Mines* (Washington, U.S. Geological Survey, 1883), IV, 30.

7. *Ibid.*, 57.

8. C. B. Glasscock, *Gold in Them Hills* (Indianapolis, Bobbs-Merrill Company, 1932), 19–20.

9. Botkin, *A Treasury of Western Folklore*, 656.

10. Otis E Young, Jr., *Western Mining: An Informal Account of Precious-Metals Prospecting, Placering, Lode Mining, and Milling on the American Frontier from Spanish Times to 1893* (Norman, University of Oklahoma Press, 1970).

11. Hobart Stocking, "The Mineral Wealth of New Mexico," *New Mexico Magazine*, April, 1946, p. 32.

12. *Ibid.*, 33.

13. Ray H. Cooper, "Early History of San Juan County," *Colorado Magazine*, September, 1945, p. 211.

14. Rufus Rockwell Wilson, *Out of the West* (New York, Press of the Pioneers, 1933), 361–62.

15. Quoted in *Denver Post*, January 4, 1935, p. 15*b*.

16. Wilson, *Out of the West*, 361–62.

17. William C. Russel, *A Tribute to the Burro* (Denver, Colorado Mining Association, 1925), 1–16.

18. Wilson, *Out of the West*, 365.

19. James A. McKenna, *Black Range Tales* (New York, Wilson-Erickson, Inc., 1936), 120.

20. *Ibid.*, 130.

21. *Ibid.*, 76–77.

22. *Ibid.*, 173.

23. Quoted in *Denver Post*, October 16, 1949.

24. Glenn Chesney Quiett, *Pay-Dirt* (New York, D. Appleton-Century Company, 1936), 314.

25. Darley, *Pioneering in the San Juan*, 184–85.

26. Zane Grey, *Tappan's Burro* (Roslyn, N.Y., Walter J. Black, Inc., 1923), 4–7.

27. Frank Waters, *The Colorado* (New York, Rinehart and Company, 1946), 13.

28. W. C. Barnes, "Wild Burros," *American Forests*, October, 1930, pp. 640–42.

29. Walter D. Wyman, *The Wild Horse of the West* (Caldwell, Idaho, Caxton Printers, Ltd., 1948), 261.

CHAPTER 15

1. George Champlin Sibley, *The Road to Santa Fe: The Journal & Diaries of George Champlin Sibley, 1825–27* (ed. by Kate L. Gregg, Albuquerque, University of New Mexico Press, 1952), 215.

2. Josiah Gregg, *The Commerce of the Prairies* (Chicago, Lakeside Press, 1926), 8.

3. Quoted in LeRoy R. Hafen and Ann W. Hafen, *Old Spanish Trails: Santa Fe to Los Angeles* (Glendale, Arthur H. Clark Company, 1954), I, 30.

4. Ramon Adams, *Western Words* (new ed., Norman, University of Oklahoma Press, 1968), 318.

5. Irving Stone, *Men to Match My Mountains: The Opening of the Far West, 1840–1900* (Garden City, N.Y., Doubleday and Company, Inc., 1956), 194, 197.

6. "The Versatile Burro," *Los Angeles Times*, April 1, 1906.

7. Frank Applegate, *Native Tales of New Mexico* (Philadelphia, J. B. Lippincott Company, 1932), 59–62.

8. Samuel Bowles, *Our New West: A Record of Travel* (New York, Hartford Publishing Company, 1869), 100–101.

9. William Frederick Cody, *An Autobiography of Buffalo Bill (Colonel W. F. Cody)* (New York, Rinehart Publishing Company, Inc., 1920), 141–42.

10. Thomas Heron McKee, "Brighty, Free Citizen," *Sunset Magazine*, August, 1922, pp. 42, 70–71.

11. A. E. Demarary, "The Passing of Brighty," *Outing*, February, 1923, p. 225.

12. *Ibid.*

13. Letter to the author from Bob Beverly, of Lovington, New Mexico, July 5, 1945.

14. Herman W. Albert, *Odyssey of a Desert Prospector* (Norman, University of Oklahoma Press, 1967), 42.

15. *Report of Cases Argued and Determined in the Supreme Court of the State of Arizona, April 25, 1938–to November 28, 1938* (Phoenix, 1938), LII, 596–99.

16. Letter to the author from J. F. McKale, professor emeritus of physical education, University of Arizona, December 10, 1965.

17. R. C., "Carrying the Mail to Tubac," *Arizona Highways*, May, 1941, pp. 36–37.

18. "Children Run Show at Moscow Circus," *Albuquerque Journal*, August 7, 1964.

19. Wayne Dinsmore, *Training Riding Horses* (Amarillo, American Quarter Horse Association).

20. Letter to the author from Ray Cowart, Henderson, Texas, November 24, 1970.

21. *Ibid.*

22. Herbert Crisler, "My Most Unforgettable Character, Alonzo Stagg," *Reader's Digest*, December, 1962, p. 123.

23. James W. Koehler, *The California Undomesticated Burro*, Bulletin of the California State Department of Agriculture, January–February, 1960, pp. 1–6.

24. Patricia des Roses Moehlman, "Getting to Know the Wild Burros of Death Valley," *National Geographic*, April, 1972, pp. 502–17.

25. Neil M. Clark, "The Tales They Tell About Burros!" *Saturday Evening Post*, December 13, 1952, pp. 1–2.

26. Letter to the author from G. E. Beal, Yucca, Arizona, n.d.

27. Mela Meisner Lindsay, "Rebellion of the Burros," *Denver Post*, March 2, 1969.

28. Letter to the author, January 21, 1969.

29. *Grit*, November 5, 1967.

30. *Albuquerque Journal*, December 19, 1971.

31. Nathaniel T. King, "Big Bend—Jewel in the Texas Desert," *National Geographic*, January, 1968, p. 120.

32. *Ibid.*, p. 128.

CHAPTER 16

1. Thackeray, "Respecting Asses," *Cornhill Magazine*, Vol. IX (January–June, 1864), 69.

2. J. N. Hessel, "Mountain Canaries Came North," *American Forests*, Vol. XXXIX (September, 1933), 390–91, 428.

3. Ray Davis, "Homesick Henry, the Boomerang Burro," *Western Horseman*, July, 1966, pp. 74, 143, 144.

4. Jeannette Smith, "The Importance of Being Henry," *Nova* (University of Texas at El Paso), Vol. IV, No. 1 (Fall, 1968), 3.

5. *Ibid.*

6. "Get the Jackasses Out of the Air," *Saturday Evening Post*, July 27–August 3, 1963.

7. Letter to the author from James M. Doolittle, Albuquerque, New Mexico, October 7, 1968.

8. Jane and Woodrow Wirsig, "Meet the Mascots," *Saturday Evening Post*, June 19, 1943, p. 20.

9. Caroline Bancroft, *Two Burros of Fairplay* (Boulder, Johnson Publishing Company, 1968), 18–32.

10. Frank Applegate, *Native Tales of New Mexico* (Philadelphia, J. B. Lippincott Company, 1932), 65–76.

11. Arthur F. Lenehan, "Overland Donkey Tale," *Small World: Magazine for Volkswagen Owners*, Spring, 1963, p. 19.

12. Berton Roueché, "The Cute Little Fellows," *New Yorker*, May 4, 1946, pp. 46–52.

13. "Pet News," *Ladies' Home Journal*, March, 1969, p. 26.

14. Andrew K. Gregg, *New Mexico in the Nineteenth Century: A Pictorial History* (Albuquerque, University of New Mexico Press, 1968), 21.

15. *Denver Post*, October 6, 1958.

16. W. W. H. Davis, *El Gringo: or, New Mexico and Her People* (Santa Fe, Rydal Press, 1938), 48.

17. Reuben Gold Thwaites, *Early Western Travels* (Cleveland, Arthur H. Clark Company, 1905), 321.

18. *New Mexico Place Names: A Geographical Dictionary* (ed. by T. M. Pearce, Albuquerque, University of New Mexico Press, 1965), 20.

19. Letter to the author from Mr. and Mrs. John Lockwood, Surrey, England, October 29, 1970.

CHAPTER 17

1. May Sarton, *Joanna and Ulysses* (New York, W. W. Norton and Company, Inc., 1963).

2. R. S. Summerhays, *The Donkey Owner's Guide* (London, Thomas Nelson and Sons, Ltd., 1970), 12.

3. Robin Borwick, *People with Long Ears: A Practical Guide to Donkey Keeping* (London, Cassell, 1965), 80–81.

4. *Folktales of Mexico* (tr. and ed. by Americo Paredes, Chicago, University of Chicago Press, 1970), 58–59.

Index